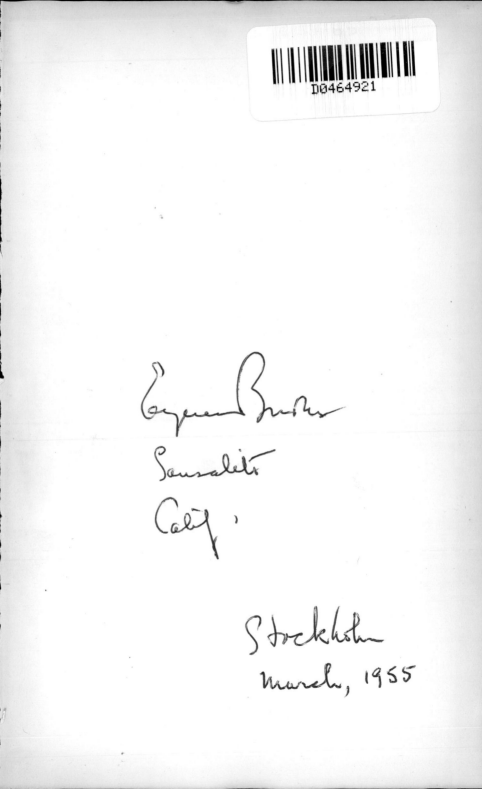

Eugene Burner
Sausalito
Calif.

Stockholm
March, 1955

FRANS G. BENGTSSON

A Walk
to
an Ant Hill

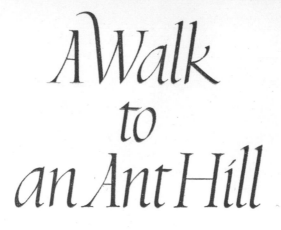

A Walk to an Ant Hill

AND OTHER
ESSAYS

by FRANS G. BENGTSSON

TRANSLATED BY
MICHAEL ROBERTS AND
ELSPETH SCHUBERT, NÉE HARLEY

———

P. A. Norstedt & Söners Förlag
STOCKHOLM

Printed in Sweden

Kungl. Boktryckeriet / P. A. Norstedt & Söner

Stockholm 1950

CONTENTS

A WALK TO AN ANT HILL

VERY DAY about three o'clock, if the weather is
tolerable, I free myself from books and desk in order to take a
walk round the lake. It is a lovely lake, at least for Scania,
surrounded by woods, with beeches on the north side and a
number of different kinds of trees around the south; there is
no trace of either fields or houses within sight, and the water
is as clear and clean as that of its westerly sister lake; like two
blue eyes, separated by a narrow isthmus, they lie below the
massive brow of the Halland Ridge. It takes about three hours
to go round the lake if one is in no special hurry. Walking on
the highroads can scarcely be called a pleasure nowadays; one
meets with too much intermittent din and disjointed bustle,
feeling oneself barely tolerated, without, as compensation, experiencing the least breath of adventure and excitement such
as can be accorded by walking in a city street. On woodland
paths, however, and along narrow country lanes, frequented at
most by an occasional horse and cart, or a creaking timber load
moving slowly on its way, the pedestrian may still appear at
his leisure, without necessarily feeling like an affected ar-
chaism.

All along the system of bays and headlands on the southern
and eastern shores of the lake, the path meanders capriciously
through different belts of trees, shadowed by long grass and
threaded by intertwining roots where leafy wood predominates;
descending here and there in some hollow, edged with bog
myrtle and alder, and sometimes serving, in different places
after rain, as a sort of lesser canal; then winding upwards under
the fir trees on the steep slopes of the headlands, covered softly

by the tender clear green moss which makes the light of late summer, streaming sidewise through the openings of arched branches in a pattern of arabesques and diamonds, seem as heavily lustrous and purely metallic as ever any rain of gold between the shutters of Princess Danae's bedchamber. It is a quiet pathway, suited to unreflecting absorption and vague dreaming, and upon which one can imagine oneself a hundred miles from the nearest human being. There is never a sign of anyone approaching; no disturbing sound is heard — at the most a squirrel's chatter, or the note of a tomtit or a sandpiper — while the terrain, and the changing aspects of scenery which gradually unfold themselves are, in their quietude and simplicity, just sufficiently varying to save the walk from monotony, and prevent it from taking on a semblance of dutiful, health-giving exercise. The path rounds a long headland, by name Flagpole Point — not for any reason of there being a flagpole there, but because its slender fir trees may fittingly be turned to such as time goes on and they are thinned out — and at the extreme end of which two particular trees, seen from the lake in a straight line behind each other, show the skilled fisherman the way to a wellknown perch shoal. Continuing for some way close beside a steep sandbank, along whose verge sway young samples of ash and maple — trees that it is always a pleasure to see for the reason that they are uncommon here — it brushes past a tiny bay, something the shape of a waterlily leaf, deeply shadowed and always still, where there is usually a family of mergensers, and where, on rare occasions, even a loon may be observed, engaged in giving an exhibition of trick diving.

Soon after this, I come to the headland beyond which the silver chest of Charles XI lies sunken, and where the prick of a guilty conscience invariably awaits me. There lie 17 000 dalers of silver, stolen by freebooters from the Swedish army, and I have not yet begun to write their story. Little peasant superstition worth mentioning is to be found in the district with regard to these men of the woods, but one or two authentic monuments still exist. On an island close to the shore, some distance to the left, can be seen the scanty ruins of a castle which they plundered and occupied, and where the Swedes discovered them and burned them alive; north of the lake, up by Trollehallar, there is a wide crevice in the cliffs still known as Freebooters' Place, where they used to hide their booty, and keep their prisoners chained; and quite near this the Ridge is broken by a long, steep ravine, crossed by a trout stream, along which they doubtless skirmished with the king's men, in the Spanish manner, using ambush and rolling blocks of stone. Possibly it will be my fate, sooner or later, to try to link up these happenings in neat, epic prose, in the classical style, to be contained in two volumes, if I can avoid becoming entangled in detail. I say to myself every day, when passing Guilty Conscience Point, that I should have begun on it long ago; but so far I have not succeeded in discovering how. With poetry it is always possible, in an emergency, to begin at the end; but there is quite another mystery attached to prose. Perhaps a novel is begun as life begins, lightheartedly, without principle and at random, to become gradually more concrete, taking form and consistency, or else to be thrown into the waste-paper basket. Novels should always, of course, end tragically, if they have any pretensions at all to quality; and there, at least, I am on the safe side as all my better freebooters are hanged, during the final act, to the roll of drums at Åby Assizes, only a few shady individuals from the lower orders being let off, and one particularly black sheep even receiving an annuity. Someday, after years of toil, when I have got as far as to this scene, I shall insist on an author's fee of precisely seventeen thousand dalers of silver, the exact amount of what is to be found in the casket; and I shall then endow the gloomy headland with a somewhat more cheerful name — the Silver Hump, or *Point de Trésor*.

Some distance further on from this trying spot, I come to a footbridge leading across a broad stream, and in connection with this, usually succeed in dismissing the troublesome affair of the freebooters from my mind.

In front of me, stolidly grunting, trots a little coal black French bulldog named Achilles. He is a faithful if occasionally rather troublesome companion on my solitary walks; and of all the animals with whom I have ever become acquainted, he is incomparably the most self-assured and unmanageable. It is a matter of principle with him never willingly to get out of the way for any approaching object, dead or alive, and whenever, as happens now and again, he makes use of a road that is frequented by traffic, he quickly becomes, despite his diminutive form, the terror of all wayfarers. He hates motor bicycles with an especial passion, and invariably flings himself at them blindly, his escape from many a sudden death being entirely due to the fact that embittered cyclists usually dare not run over him on account of the risk to themselves of overbalancing and landing in the ditch. With chained dogs five times his own size he fights gladly and furiously, often driving them to retreat in their kennels, partly by the fury of his assault, and partly through a certain icy, demoniacal undertone in the sounds he emits. Pedestrians interest him less; at the most he approaches them pensively, smelling at them with the cold, cannibalistic expression of a connaisseur; they in their turn treating him at least as seriously as though he were a motor omnibus in a narrow lane, and generally preferring to stand still at the uttermost edge of the ditch watching him waddle past, bloodthirstily growling, his lowered, pendulous face with its prominent eyes tracing the ground, his wide jaws half open, and his little thick-limbed body bobbing up and down in a short jerky jogtrot — the incarnation of brutal self-assertion and ever-ready wickedness.

At the footbridge he makes a halt. The bridge consists of a couple of long logs, laid out an ell apart, and sparingly joined together by occasional small pieces of wood, most of which have rotted and fallen away. Formerly he used to cross it by walking along one of the logs at his usual speed, without showing any sign of nervousness; but one day, when the bridge was slippery after rain, he plopped suddenly into the stream and was rapidly washed away towards a sandbank at the outlet, some distance further down. This adventure affected him deeply; he has always regarded water with distrust, and since that day he refuses to put his foot on the bridge. He sits calmly on his stump of a tail, as impervious to all coaxing as the pine root at his side, and with an appearance of such peaceful inward absorption that he might be reciting to himself Théodore de Banville's poem on the philosophical rabbits:

> Et dans la bonne odeur des pins
> Qu'on voit ombrageant ces clairières
> Nous sommes les tendres lapins
> Assis sur leurs petits derrières.

There is nothing for it other than to hook the handle of my stick around his collar and drag him across, upon which, in dumb fury, he resists with all his might, trying to free himself by means of frantic tossings and jerkings. Finally, and often on account of his own violence, he loses his foothold and tumbles out into space; and I balance myself ashore as well as I can, in the manner of a tightrope walker, his furious wrigglings, as he hangs from the stick handle, threatening at every moment to upset me into the water. As soon as we reach dry land and I put him down, he falls immediately into his customary surly trot, as though nothing had happened.

When we have crossed an open stretch of marshy field, full of rivulets and clusters of meadowsweet, and by way of rocky hillocks and sheer, concave hollows, filled by swampy pine, penetrated deeply into a region of grey wilderness, the path gradually bears northward; verging after a time on to the east side of the lake, over ledges and indentations, a few yards above the stony setting of its mirrored surface, curving forward, sand-yellow and sunveined, through wavering, leafy shadows, and down the steep incline of fir-covered slopes. Cool breezes from the west, which come in after sweeping the length of both lakes, are blended here with stagnated heat, quiveringly reflected from windfree hollows, and the aroma of damp, sundrenched vegetation from pines and marshes, to a decoction of languorous summer, sipped by some green-eyed, heavylidded Frau Holde; and the quiet lapping of the lakeside water, interwoven by reflections of green and gold, and rippling over polished stones, is like a half-slumbering murmur, and the sound of drowsy kissing.

A little way towards the northern strand, on the edge of a low, exposed rock, an outpost heron may sometimes be seen, neck against shoulderblade, deep in contemplation of some chapter in the philosophy of the filled gizzard, or occasionally, with lightning beak, spearing a wandering pike, which is subsequently conjured down the working, snakelike throat with voluptuous elaboration; and from the top of a pine tree, a startled raven may suddenly break away, croaking and fluttering, to steer, after a few moments' dizzy manoeuvering in unwieldy circles, a cumbersome course along the Ridge, its shadow floating slowly away over the contours of the trees like a forgotten flake of desolation and black magic from the days of yore.

The atmosphere of hot slumber and epicurean drowsiness is not, however, all-prevailing; creatures unfamiliar with every form of indolence are here industriously engaged in the plying of tasks which do not allow of postponement, and it is here that we meet the only wayfarers for whom my forerunner considers it advisable to step aside: columns of ants, in close formation, who belong to a hill on the outer side of the path nearest the lake. Some experience has evidently taught him to respect them, depending perhaps on their ability to bite through his pads, the fact that he is ticklish between the toes, or simply because they have a smell which he dislikes. Instead of trotting ahead straight through their ranks as he did at first without noticing anything unusual, he has now learned to recognize the unpleasant spot, and prefers to leave the road, which they occupy in its entire width, and with an appearance of troubled care continue his way by means of a steep hollow along the inner side, amidst sliding gravel and pebbles. I myself am obliged to take similar precautions in order to avoid these singular creatures, who have chosen their thoroughfare and place of habitation with such complete disregard for every consideration of life and limb. The path is certainly unfrequented; but in view of the fact that their military highroad coincides with it for at least a hundred yards, in addition to which they are a compact swarm, every wanderer who passes by without specially observing them, must necessarily massacre them by the thousand. This, however, does not seem to crush their zest for living in any way, nor does it prevent their community from flourishing.

The place that they have chosen for their hill is both impressive and extraordinary. I saw it at first without being particularly struck by the strangeness of its position; but with the passing of time this ant hill has begun to present itself to me as more and more intricate and puzzling, and has gradually come to be the outstanding phenomenon of nature on my daily walks. Who has ever heard of an ant hill at the very edge of a lake, firmly attached to two blocks of stone and a dwarf pine, at a distance of a mere yard or two from the water? In any case I never have. What business have ants there at all, when there are a thousand acres of forest all around in which they can colonize freely? Here is mystery indeed; and to complete the picture they have settled down just at that end of the lake which is most exposed to the wind and the waves, in precisely the most risky spot which, by a process of systematic exploration, they could have discovered for themselves. A more literal fulfilment of the old Nietzschian programme of living dangerously could scarcely be imagined. Perhaps they are superants, the result of some recent mutation, a *lusus naturae,* over which Nature herself has reason to rub her hands — gallant, light-hearted creatures, immune to everything, and filled with wisdom and happiness, who, from their adventurous abode on the narrow, sloping strip between the path and the lake — between the devil and the deep sea, as one might say — would seem content to murmur, quietly and with grim humour: O, grave, where is thy sting? Where, death, thy victory?

After a week of bad weather and storm during which I had not been that way, I expected to find them wiped out — drowned and washed away by the waves which, in a westerly gale, arrive at the beach in mighty form to break in foaming fury. Submerged they had certainly been; the hill looked suspiciously flattened out, pine needles and gravel had been drained away between the small stones on the shore, and countless grey cocoons had followed with the deluge. Business, however, was going on as usual; architects and masons tackled their problems as before; invalids crawled cheerfully about in the heat of the stones; fishers after wreckage rummaged on the beach; and in the warmth of the returned sunglitter along the path, the legions continued magnificently on their way as though for them no Capua existed, in close formation, and determined as ever, unaffected by a weeks imprisonment in the darkness of their cellars, impervious to leaking roofs, rheumatic pains and boredom.

Sometimes, when contemplating the hill, I have imagined it to be the result of a revolt against hygienic conditions in the depths of the wood to which the race has hitherto been accustomed, such conditions having in all probability been characterized by a certain primitive stuffiness. In their ordinary surroundings wood ants do not have much opportunity of coming into contact with the elements in the wider sense. Now and again, by climbing on to a tree root, they are able, certainly, to lap up a little pure sunlight, but that is about all. Generally they crawl about in semi-darkness, among fusty pine needles and damp moss, pottering about in the rich earth and drinking out of stagnant pools. Possibly some wandering adventurer among them, intoxicated by "fresh woods and pastures new" has come home to establish himself as a prophet among his own in the dim forest with legends of fresh air and water, and has gradually succeeded, after heroic effort, in rousing the enthusiasm of a group of listeners, whom he has then enticed with him to the edge of the lake. When I think in this way, my feelings for these ants acquire a flavour of temperate respect, without any actual warmth; they appear to me rather as rootless visionaries, ordinary rebels against tradition, capable but misguided, full of ingenuity but without wisdom; creatures who through some tragic blunder have exchanged intrinsic values for those more superficial. Whereupon I wish them, the sooner the better, an effective drowning.

Occasionally, however, I picture them to myself as unwilling emigrants, exiles as the result of some great catastrophe of war — the sole survivors of some assaulted Ilion, high up where the fir trees grow most thickly, who, despite an adverse fate, are now growing to new strength after having succeeded in attaching themselves to the edge of a barren and stony Latium. I am supported in this view by the fact that the hill shows, if not seven, at least three distinct mounds, due to its uneven foundation of hummocks. These exiles are, admittedly, numerous and well-disciplined, and give no impression of being at a loss to account for themselves; but who can tell what larger states and still more terrible armies may be lurking up there in the darkness? Seeing them in this way I follow their fortunes with interest, wishing them continued salvage from storm and flood and such contentment in their daily tasks that the time may come at last when they will see fit to put an end to their state of exile, and turning their backs on the lake, climb up the slopes to win back their place of origin, and even, perhaps, to conquer others; after which they will enter upon a superior existence, surrounding themselves with slaves, riches and an atmosphere of respect; rulers, mayhap, of a hill of hitherto unattained dimensions, grim dispensers of *jus gladii* over an area of up to half an acre. In this way, finally, surfeited by toil and battle, they will allow the sun to go down upon them in imperial decadence, only listening with indifference to scanty reminiscences of their heroic kingdom on the beach.

As a boy I once witnessed a great and complicated ant war. It was fought on a sunny August afternoon in a garden, along the creeper-covered wall of an old grey stone house, around a windowjamb — the Thermopyle of this particular war — and in its final stages across the floor and furniture of a little parlour behind the window. The battle was waged between an attacking host of large red ants from under the stonework at the back of a stable, and a defending army of black ones, also fairly large, and possibly of the species known as *Fusca Nigra*, which came from the wall underneath the creeper. The red army marched along a garden path, proceeded in under a hanging ash, passed by a group of asters and one or two fuchsia plants, rounded some verandah steps, thereupon swinging up through a rosegarden, and finally advanced on the wall, to disappear in a jungle of runners and intertwined branches. The actual storming of the blacks' fortress took place in the unseen; but after a little while, someway up the wall where the creeper grew less thickly, groups of retiring black ants began to appear, carrying with them what personal property they had been able to rescue; and when the attackers, not satisfied with their achievements during the first assault, had crowded after them through the troublesome thicket, their red columns debouched at breast height from the ground, and went immediately to attack across a piece of open wall up to the windowjamb, where the blacks had concentrated themselves for a final effort, and where a murderous battle began. It was strange to watch this drama of violence and epic fury, enacted without a sound in the clear stillness of the afternoon, amid the scent of warm leaves and roses. Sunshine lay over the battlefield, idyllically scattered in sprays and splinters among the shadows of the overhanging creeper; and all that could be heard was the noise of tiny clickings against the leaves, as slaughtered warriors tumbled downward. The refuge of the blacks, consisting of a row of bricks which stuck out somewhat at an angle from the wall, could only be scaled from either end; filled with the lust of battle, the blacks stood there, prepared to throw themselves head downwards upon every climbing enemy, while the reds advanced untiringly, regardless of their losses. No crazy bravado of ancient wars which I may have happened to have read about since has made a stronger impression upon me than this battle of the windowjamb, waged with such bitter determination by both sides. Finally, in spite of all, the ascent was achieved by the reds; and owing to the fact that the window could not be shut properly on account of the masses of creeper, the two armies now swarmed across one another into the room, which soon became crowded with combatants. The blacks did what they could to the end; duellist met on the floor, on cushions and on tables, manoeuvred in raging clusters up the legs of tables, and among books and albums; hunted each other in the Homeric manner around photo frames and flower vases, or staggered, locked in a deadly embrace, on the edge of the abyss presented by the antimacassar embroidery of armchairs. After an hour or so the tragedy was over, and the destruction of this black Carthage so complete that even a Cato Major among the reds must have declared himself satisfied. The visitors retired by the same way that they had come, leaving many of their numbers on the field, and could be seen after a time on their way home along the garden path, dragging with them booty and wounded. Feelings of victory ran high in their ranks; but under the hanging ash a little further on, as though a step in the direction of poetic justice, a bitter epilogue awaited them. On the grass verge of the path there happened to live a small community of bright red pavement ants; and suddenly these, whether roused by the sight of the homewardbound booty or else irritated by the marching and songs of victory, rushed out of their nest like a streak of lightning and went to attack on the victors' flank. They were few in number but caused, none the less, a tremendous commotion. Panic broke out at once, baggage was deserted, and the injured left to their fate; and the same companies which had so recently and intrepidly taken part in the great assault, now promptly turned their backs in the face of these thunderous pygmies, and fled in terror, *ventre à terre*. The tiny red furies, however, did not trouble to engage themselves in further adventure, nor did they appear actuated by any tendency to aggression; and after tidying up the stony ground in front of their abode, and forcing the large army to veer off in a wide semicircle, they returned contentedly to their interrupted pursuits; — upon which the legions, lately so impressive, their glory now considerably diminished, meekly trudged back home.

This was a great and harrowing battle, a drama the equal of which I have never witnessed, and in the role of the only war correspondent present I followed it during the course of nearly three hours; this is my attempt — somewhat late from the point of view of reportage — to preserve its outlines for posterity.

In the case of the exiles on the beach, I have, as yet, never seen any such enterprise; for the time being these are content to fritter away their lives under more peaceful conditions, doing this in a manner so lavish that it would seem to be a matter of complete indifference to them whether war were going on or not. On the pathway they are crushed by pedestrians; from the hill they are washed into the deep by the least disturbance of the waves; and when the weather is calm they climb up into a small oak tree which has grown out over the lake, and fall from its branches into the water. This way of coming down from a tree may have been expedient when they lived in the forest, and there was soft moss on which to fall; but the same course of action is probably only upheld here for the reason that none of those who fall into the water ever return to the hill to point out the drawbacks of the system, now that a treacherous green mirrored surface lies below. A few save themselves by climbing on to isolated stones, there to perish; most of them float slowly out to sea. In course of time, perhaps, an ant-eating race of blay and roach will come into existence in this lake — shrewd epicureans, who need make no effort to obtain their dinners, and who, in a pleasant attitude of loafing, are able continuously to stand and sway with folded fins in the rippling shorewater, serenely confident of the bounties which some surface god permits to rain into their mouths.

The settlers in the ant hill, however, do not pay heed to small matters of this sort. Majestic in their strength, they may waste royally with themselves; and where no fear exists, there can be no calamity. Calmly and as it were triumphantly, they can, from their inexhaustible reserves of life, pour themselves out in both directions — on the one side to be crushed under the feet of some passing Juggernaut, on the other to be swallowed by the hungry lake; and it is as though some unquenchable spirit of philosophy still remains theirs, even as regards those members of the race who in the stillness of the afternoon are in process of drifting slowly away, like souls in the wake of the planet, across the Waters of Forgetfulness, towards oblivion.

After I have contemplated all this for a while, and when Achilles has thoughtfully scratched an ant or two from his neck, we resume our walk, and begin, in philosophic mood, to climb the slopes of the Ridge.

Translated by Elspeth Harley-Schubert

THE OLD OAK

*A*ND that one," I observed intelligently, "that one must be very old indeed." I am a newcomer to these parts.

My wife was born in the district. "It is five hundred years old," she replied.

"Five hundred years," said I: "Then it must have started life about the time when Christopher of Bavaria came to the throne — planted, perhaps, by some zealous Christopherian desirous of commemorating the occasion. We should find out whether Christopher had any active partisans in this area: hopeful characters who looked forward to a brave new world with the aid of a professional touch from the Continent. If so, we might christen it King Christopher's Oak: it should be ripe for baptism by this time. But I wonder, all the same, if it is not even older. How do you know that it is five hundred years old?"

"My mother always used to say so; she had it from the old people."

"And she, you may be sure, heard it when she was a little girl. That gives it another seventy years already. Which would put its birthday some time before the Black Death. And the old people who told your mother had doubtless also heard the figure five hundred in *their* childhood, and had modestly forgotten that their own little span was to be reckoned in. I think it is extremely old; even older than it looks. As Pan Zagloba says in one of Sienkiewicz' novels, 'Gentlemen, did any of you know Pan Dieviontkiewicz the Pandour? He did not look a day more than a hundred and forty, but he was a hundred and forty two, and still in harness.' It is the same with the old oak, I don't doubt."

The first feature of the landscape to delight me when I
came to this country was the Gullspång River, stretched majestically between broad banks of reeds at the bottom of the
garden; for if a man is to live happily he must have water to
look at — and Sweden, in all her infinite variety, can count it
not the least among her charms that she seldom stints us of
water. The second feature was collective, and comprised the
garden's apple-orchard — twenty-eight varieties, if you include
the Paradise-apple. For an apple is a lovely thing, and lovely
is all that pertains to it. Apple-blossom, the ruddy bloom on
the ripe fruit, the scent of apples, the loaded bough, an apple-
orchard — all these are the stuff of poetry; and the apple remains irreproachably poetic until we get down to apple-pie,
apple-sauce, and apple-charlotte, which on the contrary are a
sufficiently malignant kind of prose, to be tolerated only for
the poetry from which it derives. Add to this that my twenty-
eight varieties grew, not on those young, depersonalized sap-
lings which are the beau ideal of the horticulturist, but on
ancient, knotted, massy trees, whose gnarled shapes recalled
(though to be sure they were much more fruitful) a totalitarian
orator in an ecstasy of indignant eloquence; while among them,
leavening the mass of apple, grew fourteen sorts of cherries,
and a good many other things besides.

It was only in the third place that I noticed the old oak.

It stands in one of the remoter corners of the wide-spreading
garden, where the grassy hillside runs down in sweeps and
undulations to the river. The soil at that point does not seem
particularly rich: the rock breaks the surface at the very tree-
foot; the slope, too, faces north — no very favourable conditions
for strong growth. Yet it was there, for all that, that it struck
root, at some indeterminate moment of time, far back in the
Middle Ages; there it flourished exceedingly; and there, to all
appearances, it is resolved to grow and flourish for unnum-
bered years to come. Ashes and elms, noble old trees all of
them, stand in its immediate neighbourhood and do their best

to appear its equals, as in pillared majesty they guard the
bowling-green at their feet; but in the oak's calendar they are
but the striplings of yesterday, shrubs and bushes with hardly
more than a century to their credit, and the wisdom of years
is not in them. Of all that my oak surveys, nothing is really
old, save only the river.

I am not a great authority on giant oaks and their dimensions: in the poor soils of my own corner of Skåne the pines
overtop the oaks; but I am disposed to count my oak as at
present only among the minor giants. Three men cannot en-
circle it, but four can do it easily: its circumference must
be between six and seven metres at the height of a man's
shoulder, and that, perhaps, is not much. In an encyclopaedia
I find a statement (with photograph) concerning an oak at
Norra Kvill in Kalmar Province, which may be presumed to
be the portliest in Sweden: nearly fourteen metres. A depressing figure, this, which makes my giant dwindle suddenly into
fragility; but I comfort myself by looking at this Kalmar giant's
picture. For a lamentable picture it is, of impotence, dissolution, rottenness and decay; with the trunk a mere carious shell
surrounding a cavity, so formless and bloated that its circumference might be anything you pleased. For myself I prefer
giants with more life and heart and less senility, even though
their abdominal measurements should fall below approved
standards. And my little giant, I rejoice to say, is well-grown
and healthy from crown to foot, without the smallest sign of
rot, or hint of dropsical habit — a consequence, probably, of
its having grown on poorer land, and thus having escaped the
phenomena attendant upon a course of high feeding.

What is it that gives the oak its peculiar poetic quality? The
poetic appeal does not come from the great trees only (though
of course most forcibly from these): the very concept *Oak* is
in itself poetic in quite another fashion than (for example) the
concept *Rowan* or *Aspen*. That the pine is a highly poetic tree
needs no explanation: it is the characteristic tree of the wild-

erness; its autumnal sighing is a music inimitable; and against an evening sky — especially if the season be winter — a solitary old pine is beautiful beyond all other trees. The birch is poetic because its bursting into leaf tells us, more than any other sign, of the coming, and the comeliness, of spring; and the linden is the poetic tree of folk-song — less, perhaps, by reason of its own loveliness, than because rhymes for linden (in Swedish, at all events) are easier to come by than for any other tree. Mere beauty, in fact, seems to have little to do with whether or no a tree is to be considered poetic; for such trees as the larch or the sycamore may be as handsome as they please, and lack the poetic quality for all that.

The oak and the pine, indeed, are the only trees we have of which it may be said that on occasion they enter the category of the sublime, and thereby attain the highest level of poetry. The sublime is that form of the beautiful which produces in the observer a feeling — it comes near to being a physical sensation — of wonder, awe, reverence, piety; and in the case of natural objects it is clear that one very important factor in inducing this feeling is *size*. There are some animals — the tiger, the eagle, possibly the whale — which can be accounted sublime; but, as an acute theorist once remarked, you will look in vain for a sublime insect: the requisite attribute of size is lacking. But if we confine our attention to trees, it becomes apparent (upon reflection) that mere size alone does not suffice to make a tree sublime. Even when confronted with the most gigantic horse-chestnut or beech, I at least receive no impression of sublimity: such a tree may well be called stately, splendid, or even magnificent, but hardly sublime: some element of strength or majesty is wanting. It is not only that they lack age, for a beech may be at least as old as any pine; but a beech never succeeds in giving the *appearance* of age, as a pine or an oak does: these two are the only trees which by their very shape and stature produce the impression of being at one with the ages — with the firmament, with solitude, and with fate. The yew, which it is thought may attain the greatest age of all living things in these latitudes, must also (strictly speaking) be reckoned among the sublime trees, at all events such yews as Wordsworth sings of in his poem *Yew-Trees,* where the sublime is evoked with rare power; but his yew-trees seem to have been giants whose equal this country can no longer show — though in former times there may have stood by the temple at Uppsala a holy yew-tree of such dimensions as to play a part in the evolution of the myth of the Yggdrasil.

The oak, above all other trees, is venerable: the only tree (if we ignore the rare yew-tree) which can lay claim to the epithet "primaeval". When Keats refers to "those greenrobed senators of mighty woods", we have no need of what comes after to tell us that it is of oaks that he is singing. How anyone can ever cut down a really old oak (provided that the tree is not dying already) I find difficult to understand; but to plant oaks — trees which shall stand in their glory and strength long after the planter is dust and the very record of his name has perished — that must be an inspiring occupation for those who own land where oaks do well. I have a friendly feeling for that old English admiral who during his spells ashore was in the habit of planting oaks: I do not recall at the moment just who it was — possibly Sir Cuthbert Collingwood, who led the van at Trafalgar, and took command after Nelson fell. Whenever he was at home on leave (he was mostly to be found on his flagship in the Mediterranean) it was the Admiral's custom to take with him on his daily constitutional a stick provided with a pointed ferrule, and a bag of acorns which he slung from his belt. When he came to a suitable spot, he would bore a hole in the ground, and push an acorn into it; and thus he did what he could to ensure that in time to come the British Navy should be provided with the right sort of timber.

A few years ago someone counted the annual growth-rings of a couple of felled or fallen old oaks in Denmark, and found that they must have germinated about the time when Gorm and Tyre built Danewirke. Now I am admittedly prejudiced in favour of the oak in my garden, but I am not just prepared to believe that it is as old as that; and I trust that it may yet be centuries before anyone has an opportunity to count its rings. I very much doubt whether it was in existence when Olof Haraldsson of Norway passed hard by, a fugitive from his own country; and perhaps not even when the three princes were murdered on Älgarås. But at the time of the next notable event in these parts — the battle of Hova and the game of backgammon in Ramundeboda — why then, maybe, it had begun to show modest growth; and when Engelbrekt's men were about their business here it must have been a fine tree.

At the mouth of the river lies the island of Amneholm; and it is odd to think that smoke from Amneholm may have drifted through the same branches that I look upon to-day, on that occasion when the enthusiastic henchmen of Erik of Pomerania were interrupted in their plans for endowing this district with an economic New Order. These royal bailiffs of Amneholm seem, when you come to think of it, to have been men of strikingly modern mould, with concentration-camps for the recalcitrant upon a number of barren islets in Lake Vänern (whence their later name, "The Hunger Isles"); but with all their eupeptic methods it turned out that there was some error in their calculations; for old-fashioned folk came down from the North with axes and cross-bows, stormed their stronghold most expeditiously, and burned it to the ground; and I dare say the prisoners liberated from The Hunger Isles danced a turn or two around the bonfire, if they still had the strength for it. And of Amneholm, as of other similar centres of the New Order up and down the country, no more remained thereafter but a blackened ruin.

Whether since those days the old oak has witnessed any major historical drama at close quarters I cannot say: but it may still live to see a thing or two, long after we who dwell in its

shadow have ceased to concern ourselves with the vicissitudes
of existence "under the mutable disk of the moon". At present
its lines are cast in quiet places, with only the annual dancing
on the green at midsummer for interruption. On these occasions, it may be, it so far unbends as to afford a certain
measure of practical aid to the dancers; for behind its trunk
at least two pairs of lovers can be about their kissing in comfort, without fear of jostling one another.

But for the rest it is mostly alone with the river, on whose
banks it stands like some frontier watchman from an earlier
age, and upon whose waters it bestrews its leaves, when the
autumn storms blow off Lake Vänern. And of those leaves a
few, perhaps, make landfall first upon the further bank — in
Svealand.

Translated by Michael Roberts

THOUGHTS IN THE GRASS

I LIE on the grass, the rich, moist, sundrenched grass of May, warmly delicious and strewn with woodsorrel and forget-me-not, beside a book of verse which I am not reading, watching the budding apple blossom and thinking of the Assyrians. Wife, child, and maidservant have gone to town; nothing can disturb me. The telephone, charged with the busy formalities of the outer world, may ring as it will; no one can hear it. There is a great deal that I ought to be doing, and just because of that I lie here and enjoy doing nothing even more than usual.

One should not, of course, exaggerate; and, strictly speaking, I am not really thinking of the Assyrians, but only of the fact that I ought to be thinking about them. This reflection, however, does not trouble me overmuch; one takes things easily, thinking on the grass. Why, I wonder, am I continually promising delightful friends in editors' offices to write articles for them, when I know, in the depths of my being, that I do not want to write articles, and when, furthermore, my financial requirements do not compel me to the said depressing occupation. With the passing of the years I have often speculated on this problem, and I am still far from a solution of it. Although never having approved of unnecessary self-torment, my life is, to a great extent, made up of it, as the result of promises such as these. Now I have promised again; and for the moment I am not equal to anything in article form other than the Assyrians. These ancient pioneers of well-organized political and military rascality, mass torture, transportation of entire peoples and the like, have a certain topical interest; and for the momentary diversion of the thoughtful reader, a parallel might well be drawn, containing both psychological and historical points, between the years 1945 A. D. and 612 B. C., between Prussia and Assyria, Berlin and Nineveh, and the coalitions which laid them in ashes.

Today, however, I prefer to lie on the grass, a pastime which, to me, is one of the real pleasures of existence, besides being one of the simplest and most reliable.

When one is getting old (I am fifty, and was born in a prehistoric world) it is sometimes a delightful surprise to reflect that there really are a few simple pleasures in life which keep their charm, undiminished, through the years. Outside the world of books (mark well I mean real books) there are no sources of delight so completely satisfying as those which come straight from the cycle of Nature, unaffected by human fads and fancies. Long after one has ceased to feel any inward satisfaction over Christmas and Midsummer, in their character of patented seasons of goodwill, the budding of birch trees and the coming of the swallow are phenomena which remain at their true value, unchangeably joy-bringing. One never gets tired of the cowslip; one is never bored by the monotony of constantly recurring springs, nor does one sigh impatiently for a May in purple or in blue. No one yawns over the chaffinch or the willow warbler, secretly wishing that another year their melodies would be newer, or more original and up to date. Offer me parties, ceremonies, intellectual soirées, brilliant discussions or the society of clever speakers, and my heart sinks immediately at the very thought of all that characteristic boredom, emptier in itself than the space between extragalactic nebulae. Never, on the other hand, have I recoiled at the sight of the grebes in the river below, with the same feeling that I have attended this sort of unprofitable gathering quite sufficiently often.

It must be confessed, nevertheless, that a few small things are not the same as before. I can no longer experience the scent of apple blossom, for instance, not even in the early morning when the dew is still fresh and I am surrounded by blossoming apple trees. By taking a sprig and burying my face in it where the bloom is thickest, a faint suggestion of the smell comes to me, but that is all. In the beginning I thought that this particular scent was gradually being cultivated out of modern apple blossom, as being valueless from the point of view of political economy; but alas! — I have been obliged to give up this theory, it being obvious that bees and butterflies would in all probability go on strike were such a thing to occur. It is, instead, tobacco and increasing age which are to blame for the degeneration of my powers of smell, a fact which I must try to face philosophically. For a matter of that, apple blossom is not absolutely necessary to me, as it does not come into the category of really important smells.

Of these there are two kinds; one which is merely delightful scent, and another which is magic. Apple blossom, violets, lily of the valley, and ripe wild strawberries all belong to the former kind; they are just delicious scents, and require no further comment. Lily of the valley reminds one of lily of the valley, wild strawberries of wild strawberries, and nothing more. Even the exquisite fragrance that comes from a large, newly-picked, coffee-brown stone morel, and which, in itself, from the point of view of mere scent, is perhaps the most aromatic I know, is without associations — perfect of its kind, but one dimensional.

Scents of the other kind are entirely different; they go straight to the heart, stirring it in the strangest manner, arousing slumbering feelings and forgotten memories, bringing back horizons of the past, timeless worlds of fantasy, and hallucinations of space, woven in marble-veined iridiscence. To be suddenly confronted by a scent of this kind may be compared with going through "The Door in the Wall", H. G. Wells' admirable story of the same title. For me, memories are brought back by such things as the scent of bog myrtle leaves, crushed in the fist; the smoke of a distant peat fire; wild thyme, mint, and ripe corn in damp fields on a misty August evening.

The reaction to different scents is in all probability highly individual; the odour of incense, and the smell of a mulatto woman's hair appears to have had a strong effect upon Baudelaire, whereas Schiller, as is well known, had to have rotten apples in his vicinity in order to become poetic.

The fact that there are more painful losses than the scent of apple blossom was brought home to me recently by a conversation with my son.

"Father, what is it that squeaks in the grass?"

There was a silence, while I strained my ears to their uttermost. Nothing could be heard.

"Squeaks in the grass? Can you really hear something squeaking in the grass?"

"Yes, of course. Something that says i-i-ih all the time. What is it?"

Not the faintest trace of any sort of noise was registered on my hearing.

"Oh, you mean that noise," I said carelessly, "that's a grasshopper. They draw up their hind legs against their wings, like a bow on the strings of a violin. It's amusing to listen to."

And while we talked on about grasshoppers, and of how boys with warts on their fingers have great fun hunting up a certain kind of grasshopper and letting it bite the warts, which is a much better idea than the method of using bacon fat, I sat on the grass listening vainly; only to realize at last that the music of the grasshopper was silenced for me. Incipient stalactite growth, I presume, among the cells of the brain which are qualified to register these particular vibrations while those designed for the interception of the telephone bell, and which I should infinitely prefer to be without, still go on causing me to jump, on occasion, as though I had been stung by a hornet. I imagine that the next sound to fade away will be the voice of the lark.

The contemplation of all this is somewhat melancholy; but as Wordsworth wisely says (it is Wordsworth whose poems are with me on the grass):

> ... may thy Poet, cloudborn Stream! be free
> (The sweets of earth contentedly resigned,
> And each tumultuous working left behind
> At seemly distance) to advance like Thee;
> Prepared, in peace of heart, in calm of mind
> And soul, to mingle with Eternity!

These are the last six lines in the last but one of his sequence of sonnets on the river Duddon; the sonnet in which the river reaches the ocean. Wordsworth begins, in an orderly manner, at the river's source, following it step by step to the sea through thirty three sonnets, many of which are supremely beautiful. I know of no river in Europe which has been so successfully and conscientiously serenaded as this otherwise inconspicuous waterway in Lancashire. Wordsworth, who at his best is one of the great poets, concludes his sequence with a particularly good point in the thirty third sonnet, which he calls "Afterthought". In the previous ones he draws a comparison between human life and the course of the river; uneventful childhood, gay and turbulent youth, followed by increased stability and even useful work; finally, the great quietude and understanding, flowing out into the ocean of eternity. At this point, however, he seems to reflect that the parallel may not be strictly accurate; and the result has been a sonnet which I, for my own part, without any attempt at absolute objectivity in judgment, have long thought to be the best of all the sonnets I know. Although there may not be many nowadays who trouble to read this sort of thing seriously, I cannot refrain from quoting it here. And who knows; perhaps someone who reads the sonnet here may become the richer by a lasting quality of beauty, and even go so far as to buy himself a suitable selection of Wordsworth's poems, for a further study of real poetry. It is the river to which the poet speaks:

I thought of Thee, my partner and my guide
As being past away. — Vain sympathies!
For, backward, Duddon, as I cast my eyes,
I see what was, and is, and will abide;
Still glides the Stream, and shall for ever glide;
The Form remains, the Function never dies;
While we, the brave, the mighty, and the wise,
We Men, who in our morn of youth defied
The elements, must vanish; — be it so!
Enough, if something from our hands have power
To live, and act, and serve the future hour;
And if, as toward the silent tomb we go,
Through love, through hope, and faith's transcendent dower,
We feel that we are greater than we know.

It is a curious thing about the great poets. The thought expressed here is not unusual, the subject by no means new, the choice of words straightforward, and the verse strictly conventional; yet, taken as a whole, it becomes great and majestic poetry, of a quality to which no living poet can attain, try any modernized recipe he may.

The composition of sonnet sequences on waterways — as well as on other things — has quite gone out of fashion. Below the slope on which I am lying flows the peaceful Gullspång river, which I have come to love; as far as I know not even a limerick has ever been written about it, much less a sonnet. Yet, in its way, it is rather a superior stream, marking as it does the border between the old Kingdoms of Svealand and Götaland. Apart from this it used to possess a name of honourable antiquity — Amn. This word is so old that it can probably be traced back to the Bronze Age, or even farther; the ancient people of Latium had the same word, amnis, which means a great river. I like murmuring the word Amn to myself as I lie watching the stream and trying to picture the sort of people who came here first and gave it the name. The only thing I am sure about is that they were not engineers. They must have been fond of fish; not only did the river abound in ordinary kinds of fish, but on occasion it became full of salmon which

came up from Lake Vänern. They could catch as many as they
wanted and still be sure there were just as many left. The
Bronze Age passed, and the Iron Age, the Viking period, the
Middle Ages, and the centuries after them; and still there were
salmon to be caught in unlimited numbers in the river, and
still there were plenty left to catch. "Give us this day our
daily salmon," said the inhabitants of the shore piously; and
it was often according to their wish.

At last, however, and fairly recently, the second immigration
took place. Engineers came to the place, cheerful and terrible
men with slide-rules, giants of strength and ruthlessness, who
looked at the river and found it to their taste; and in their
delight they immediately began chewing up both stream and
salmon-falls with jaws of iron. They had no time left over in
which to put up a salmon-ladder, such men being rationalists,
always in a hurry, and for the most part unable to think of
anything that is not dictated by their instruments; with the result
that we, the real inmates of the shore above the waterfall, are
no longer able to fish our daily salmon from the stream, but
have to journey, with a sigh, as far as Vänern, in order to buy
the commodity there. This is a sad business, but nothing really
worth grumbling about, because engineers are now the accepted
lords of creation, and able to do as they think fit; what is more,
they understand their work and do it well, and that is saying a
great deal in these days.

From farther down the stream comes the sound of discordant
shrieks, as though the souls of betrayed salmonfishers were
circling above the water in baffled fury. Worse, however, than
this; the noise is the noise of seagulls. I may say here that
there are no creatures on earth which I dislike more heartily
than these inland gulls, which increase in number every year,
break all boundaries, cover fields and gardens in thick clouds,
and are, by reason of their excessive stupidity, as good as safe-
guarded from human attack. No one considers it worth while
wasting shot on these wood lice of the air. The common crow,

which from early childhood one has been taught to regard with suspicion and dislike, becomes a highly superior type of pest in comparison with the seagull. It is to be presumed that Parliament and bureaucracy have no official knowledge of the existence of seagulls, otherwise something would be done to keep them in check, as, for instance, the taking up of collections for the purchase of unlimited ammunition. Enterprising children might be generously rewarded for collecting eggs; machine guns of direst capacity, suitable for the destruction of gulls, would be constructed by engineers and distributed to the armed forces for shooting practice, now that foreign bombers are no longer an objective. Chosen intelligentsia at the Ministry of Agriculture would be appointed to tackle the problem; even the Medical Board might be called upon to intervene. This admirable body has, with remarkable precision in truth, discovered and decreed — amongst a number of other things — that it is dangerous to health, and consequently forbidden, for the inmates of a municipal community to drink unboiled milk from a byre in which the breadth of the gutter behind the cows is less than half a yard. It seems to me that the danger to health is just as great in the case of inmates of the community who become contaminated by the droppings of overhead gulls, a risk which grows daily greater. Impelled to action by such a train of thought, the body in question might set to work immediately on the mass production of scientifically poisoned pills for seagulls. How to induce the birds to eat such pills would be a problem for mutual intellectual resource, a battle of wits in which, to my mind, the Medical Board would not be without its chances.

Actually, the same thing applies to seagulls as to bureaucrats. Nature's equilibrium has been upset, and for this reason both categories are everywhere in evidence. Eagles, and other useful creatures which used to keep a check on seagulls, are gradually dying out, in exactly the same way as commonsense is disappearing from the world of bureaucracy; and as a result of this, both species of pest have perpetuated themselves unchecked, to hover, croaking, above human existence, like clouds of embodied idiocy. Quite probably they will continue to flourish in harmony for all time. Seagulls do not worry bureaucrats: why, then, should bureaucrats worry seagulls? The unfortunate human being has no defence against either of them, and is as helpless in the face of their attacks as a cow in its byre against flies and cowherds.

Poor, blessed, limitlessly patient, completely helpless, civilized being, in this our so-called land of enlightenment: poor little cow in its stall! Entered, numbered, watered, fed, groomed and milked by different bureaucratic experts, humming their age-old clichés about freedom. What freedom, strictly speaking, is left to the wretched creature? Exemption from the slaughterhouse, it is true, and — at least for the present — a certain freedom of choice with regard to the question of mating. What more? I do not know. Probably not much more than the freedom to sigh and groan a little over all this impertinent solicitude; and yet without the means, granted to a real cow, of lashing a tail across the face of its attendant. The tail is missing: and if it existed, such an unwarrantable liberty would certainly be penalized.

When, however, with noticeable relish in their tone of voice, bureaucrats themselves talk about freedom, it is possible that at bottom they mean another kind of freedom, namely their own supreme power of persecuting their fellow beings; and this, undoubtedly, would explain a great deal.

I scarcely know how it has happened; while I have been lying here, in the company of beautiful May, I have become melancholy. Reality, or more accurately a certain kind of reality, the actual situation of present day humanity, does not bear thinking of for more than ten minutes without inducing heaviness of mind. The only things that do bear thinking of are Nature, and the old books; and for a matter of that, it is high time that I went home and began to think about the Assyrians in real earnest. "And the cormorant and the bittern shall lodge in the upper lintels." Zephaniah's words about Nineveh. Bitterns and cormorants — a refreshing mouthful in truth, and assuredly better than if he had said seagulls and bureaucrats, although in the latter case the curse, as such, would have sounded even more fearful. This, however, may be considered as a possible alternative reserved for us. Be that as it may: I shall go home and read Zephaniah, who is a good author of the old school, and who may help me to ward off melancholy. I shall not leave Wordsworth behind me; one of the last of the fellowship of the prophets, he is also an antidote to melancholy. I can never tire of the last line in his great sonnet:

"We feel that we are greater than we know."

Nevertheless, I do not know whether this line is a true one, in a purely prosaic sense. For Wordsworth himself it was obviously true, and in his case the feeling existed with full justification. We ordinary folk, however, do we feel anything of the same sort as we sit and read of constantly recurring new developments in connection with our correct treatment as members of a community? Let us hope so, although it is far from certain. Should it ever happen, however, that the human being of the present day were to take the trouble to make a very slight alteration in Wordsworth's text, for personal application, he would be able to say without arrogance, and with a clear conscience:

"We feel that we are greater than *they* know."

For in the depth of our being, however much they may turn and twist us in our defencelessness, we feel ourselves to be something just a little greater than these industrious powers believe; — these powers of the community whose whole intensity of effort is concentrated from day to day upon increasing our similarity to cattle.

Translated by Elspeth Harley-Schubert

IN FRONT OF A BOOKCASE

*I*T may be a matter of conjecture as to which of all the wellknown authors has written the most. Probable calculation is made difficult, as is just comparison, by the fact that there are few individuals, or even public libraries, upon whose bookshelves the complete works of any of the greatest rivals in the field are to be found. Dumas the elder is a wellknown aspirant, a complete edition of everything that bears his name would amount to about two hundred and ninety volumes. He, however, had assistants, in particular the assiduous Macquet — whose descendants bring actions to this day concerning the partnership in question — and cannot therefore be seriously considered. Rather would one vote for Rétif de la Bretonne — lover of nature, erotomaniac, and shoe-fetishist, upon whose work Schiller and other great men set high value as being descriptive of "real life" and whose production had its own characteristic tempo. Rétif it was who encountered a friend in a Paris street one day, and gave as the reason for his noticeably bearded appearance the fact that he had sworn not to shave until some work that he happened to have in hand was completed; namely, a novel in fifteen volumes, of which three were already written.

"Good Heavens," said the friend, "twelve volumes left: you will be treading on your beard long before that time."

"Calm yourself, my young friend," answered Rétif majestically. "It is my habit to write half a volume each day. In twenty four days I shall be as beardless an Adonis as yourself."

No entirely reliable sum total of his collected works exists, but without doubt he must have written well over two hundred books, and possibly three hundred or even more. Edmund Gosse, however, with his wide knowledge in this particular field, did not consider Rétif de la Bretonne to be the most prolific of all book producers — if so the latter must have had considerable periods of idleness — but that more probably the well-known literary critic Émile Faguet, who died a few years ago, had a stronger claim to the title. Émile Faguet said of himself that during the whole of his life he only stopped reading in order to begin writing, and only finished writing in order to begin reading again, — with a sort of exception one evening a week when he went to the theatre, and during the pauses achieved a long article on what he saw there.

The full extent of his writing has not, as yet, been ascertained, nor has it been possible to make even a reasonable calculation; in any case Gosse gives no figures, but contents himself by conjuring up the vision of a mountain of tomes in which one might pick and choose at will without causing any noticeable lessening of the pile, like those who, in their day, used the Coliseum as a stone quarry. If much of what Faguet has written is as good as his Cult of Incompetence (the only book of his which I know) this industrious professor of literature is beyond all doubt a highly estimable writer, even though he may not hold the record with regard to quantity.

My own belief is that one could guess equally well at the Scottish allround scholar Andrew Lang (who died in 1912) whose numerous books and articles about learned and curious things — history, strange life stories, antiquarian mysteries, hauntings, Homer, the Maoris in New Zealand, and Joan of Arc (probably the best, and certainly the most readable book on the latter is his), primitive religion, pirates, troutfishers, ballads of the Middle Ages, and many other things, were achieved, even at their most erudite, with the same ease and speed with which ordinary people carry on thoughtless conversation. Andrew Lang was in every way a delightful writer, amongst other qualities, of extreme modesty, who did not consider the writing of a large number of books on general topics anything out of the ordinary, always provided that one were interested in one's subject and knew how suitably to limit one's occupations. For his own part he favoured only three forms of the latter, namely writing, reading and fishing: a combination which, in contemplation of even a few fragments of his total production, one is tempted to believe that he must have been able to execute at one and the same time.

The true philosopher in this sphere, however, and himself one of its strongest aspirants to the place of honour, is beyond all doubt Edgar Wallace, a man whose name to an even lesser degree than Rétif's will blazon in serious literary history. Wallace did not deal in learned subjects, but with a simple and tangible apparatus of revolvers, poisonings, cardsharpers and the like, variated his popular theme (according to the information of connoisseurs) to the tune of at least three hundred volumes. It is said that he dictated his books at the rate of two or three novels simultaneously when working at full capacity, and for this reason had no need to follow the example of the prominent Victorian novelist Anthony Trollope, who, in his autobiography, announced that he always kept a reliable stopwatch on the desk in front of him while writing; if, during an eight hour day, an average speed of two hundred and fifty words every quarter of an hour was not kept up, he considered that he was wasting his time. In spite of this method, Trollope's books were mostly good (*The Last Chronicle of Barset*, probably his best, is quite excellent) and even to this day he has enthusiastic admirers among the most critical experts in England, who place him at times on a par with Dickens. Wallace, on his simpler plane, and with his Caesarian methods of dictation, did not, however, produce only rubbish; a short series of his with Africa as its subject, which deals with the adventure of Sanders of the River and Lieutenant Bones in their lively cannibal surroundings is, of its kind, fairly good. Towards the end of his life, Wallace was once asked how he had managed to write so many books. His answer was philosophical in the extreme:

"It is only the first hundred that are troublesome; after that it becomes an easy habit."

Lope de Vega would undoubtedly have agreed with him. Lope, the great Spanish dramatist, was considerably taken up during his youth, and well on into life, by a series of love affairs, often both complicated and tedious, which included duelling and even exile; but through it all he retained and developed a gift for dramatic authorship, leaving, at the time of his death, according to reliable information, fifteen hundred comedies, four hundred other dramas, a number of lesser pieces, and in addition enormous quantities of lighter material in the form of lyrics, novels and fiction. These dramas and comedies were in themselves by no means trivial things, but on the contrary of the best quality, and in verse; students of research who have read some hundreds of them at random always appear to have received the best impression. Lope himself, if asked how in the world he had found time for all this, would probably have answered that the whole thing was very simple. If only (Lope would have said) one took the opportunity in youth, during moments of relaxation, or when there was nothing more important on hand, of writing a few hundred comedies, the result would be a gradual conversance with the profession, a feeling of technical security and a sense of habit; after which, on reaching years of maturity, there would be no difficulty about becoming a dramatic author in earnest, and for all time following the example of Lope himself, who, after having finally settled down, punctually produced three three-act dramas in verse every week.

When a habit becomes sufficiently formed and ingrained, it is usually termed a vice. The word vice, however, contains a palpably censorious inference, and is only applied to bad habits. What, then, should an equally ingrained good habit be called? Virtue is scarcely the right word, as this implies a characteristic

or a condition of mind rather than a habit. Possibly the wise
founders of the language considered that good habits never
become so well ingrained that a special word for them would
become necessary. Let us, for want of a better, use the somewhat inadequate word virtue; in which case, the habit of
writing, more and more freely formed by the abovementioned
industrious authors, must certainly be called a virtue. Their
books were not always particularly good; most of them humanity could very well do without: none the less, and according
at least to conventional Western ethics, the achievement as
such, and the energy, driven to the point of automatic function
and life essentiality, is in itself deeply impressive. The irrepressible writing of books is, therefore, a virtue, but books are
obviously written in order to be read; does this mean that the
corresponding, although far simpler function of unrestrainedly
reading books, is also a virtue? I should like to be sure about
this, but find it difficult to decide. The probability is, despite
all, that this particular form of reading more nearly approaches
vice.

The habit of reading begins in the same way as all other
habits: hesitatingly, haltingly, and with considerable feelings of
doubt, even with actual reluctance, gradually to gain in ease
and speed. It is the same thing as with Edgar Wallace's writing
— the difficulty is at the beginning; then the habit becomes
established and there is no further trouble. The first cigar or
whisky of adolescent youth is an undertaking which sometimes
demands a considerable degree of heroism and self-conquest,
often leaving as its aftermath a certain lassitude. — Carry on,
says the devil genially; do not despair, my young friend: in due
course it will be easier and far more pleasant, without any
disagreeable squeamishness to follow. And in his own way the
devil is obviously right. The same thing is true with regard to
books; people who become exhausted by reading are still at
the faltering pupil stage: when the habit has been formed
weariness will disappear, — provided, of course, that one only

reads that which one wishes to read. It is obvious that reluctant reading must tire; but gradually, as the habit grows, the spontaneous voracity has a tendency to increase. For my own part, it is as necessary for me to read as it is to breathe (and I do not say this in order to brag, inasmuch as I strongly suspect it to concern a habit which has been allowed to grow into a vice); and nowadays I am able to read almost anything that is at all humanly written and has subject matter. I can also read, with equal pleasure, certain kinds of literature which have no subject matter, but only consist of words, artistically arranged; or primitive descriptions, however simply put together, of important or curious things.

There are, of course, definite exceptions over which I cannot prevail, in the same way that some people of otherwise good appetite become sick at the thought of eel or mussels. I cannot read jurisprudence (apart, of course, from popular reproduction of selected crimes); neither can I read political economy, proletarian novels, the prophet Paul, nor free verse, other than Heine's in his Poems of the North Sea. Certain kinds of overwhelming quasi-psychology, literary or otherwise, are abhorrent to me, as are pompous discussions on general topics of the popular type "we live (*bien entendu*: as distinct from the people of any other historical epoch) in a period of transition". If I try to read this sort of things, the kind of beginners' phobia which sometimes attacks wretched and unwilling schoolchildren asserts itself with undiminished force; the universe collapses into grey pulp, and my soul fills with agony; reason writhes as though it were on a gridiron, my brain turns to water, and within five minutes a weariness, more compact than any which can be induced by any sort of work or amusement, has penetrated every fibre of my being like a slowly-rolling tide of lead.

These, however, are strictly limited idiosyncrasies, of the same sort as the reactions earlier mentioned with regard to certain foodstuffs; and having accepted the situation as it is, inflictions of the kind are easily avoided. That is to say, unless one happens to be a reader of manuscripts at a publisher's; once, long ago, I met a man like this (though not in any manuscript errand of my own), and during the evening we chatted unforgettably for some time about his profession. He was a powerful man of great spirit, and he spoke with philosophic restraint, and did not go greatly into detail; but his voice had a hollow tone, and he silenced me with a gesture of resigned tragedy when I tried to suggest the existence of possible compensations. He seemed well acquainted with the state of mental weariness outlined above, though finding it in his own case even deeper and more inevitable. Worst of all, he said, was having to try to retain the necessary degree of consciousness which would enable one to sort out that which was not quite so bad from that which was even worse. From his point of view irrepressible writing was anything but a virtue, and the assiduity shown by budding followers of Rétif and Edgar Wallace aroused no feelings of respect in him. He suspected the itch to write as being in itself a serious communal illness, in concrete cases usually a form of debility or dementia; and he implored me, if I *must* go on writing, not to become, at some future date when I had failed in the line of authorship, a reader of manuscripts. I was able to make him this promise so much the more fervently as it so happens that from very early days I have always considered myself a passable stable hand; and after his remarks, this line of retreat seemed, in comparison with his own fate, a combination of light and happiness. Cases of subversive reading such as this are, of course, rare; and one may be comforted by the reflection that there can scarcely be more than ten thousand or so professional manuscript readers in existence – a profession which, since that occasion, has always seemed to me to be shrouded in the darkest shades of the Inferno.

Contrary to arousing feelings of this sort, books are actually intended to bring out those of quite another nature. We acquire them, often with difficulty and at some personal sacrifice, collect them and put them on our shelves, in the pleasant consciousness that they contain enough diversion to be worth quite a good deal. Many people, however, put the wrong books on their shelves, or rather, have no principle as regards what they put there, filling the shelves with everything they can get hold of, and in this way never achieving a real library. The only books which should be put on shelves are those which one intends to read over again. The mere fact that a book is not worth while reading more than once, does not necessarily imply a criticism; newspapers and periodicals are not ordinarily read more than once, admirable though they may be, and the same principle may be applied to certain books, which thereafter have as little claim to be placed on a bookshelf as have newspapers.

It is always entertaining to look at other peoples bookcases; if one is at all interested in the subject one can see immediately whether the contents make up a real collection, with which their owner is in personal contact, whether they comprise a mere sporting array of good bindings, or whether the bookcase is simply an abstract piece of furniture. If sequences of the collected works of different novelists occupy a prominent place, the first category is obviously ruled out. Complete works usually belong to public libraries, impersonal institutions where it is expected that everything should be available; but for those who really read and love books, such things — with a few rare exceptions — should not be allowed to take up space; the fact of the matter being that amongst the most prolific writers there are probably not more than five or six whose entire collection is worth setting up. A man like Fitzgerald, the translator of Omar, went perhaps a trifle too far by his method of making a personal selection of literature: from the good books he had read: he extracted the chapters and passages which did not interest him, binding in what was left, to represent a concentration of literary perfection. This would seem to be taking things too seriously; but it is nearly always possible to delete a good deal from the pages of collected works before arriving at the best they contain. As far as I can see, the novelists whose complete works I own personally are Smollett, Flaubert, Joseph Conrad, J. P. Jacobsen and Gogol; but considering that the last-named only wrote a single novel, and furthermore is known with certainty to have burned up the second half of it, there is nothing remarkable about having him complete; while the whole of Jacobsen's work is contained in two volumes. I have, admittedly, Apulejus and Petronius too: demi-gods of a volume each, neither of whom one thinks of as being a novelist. From this point of view — as from every other — the great French moralists, Larochefoucauld, La Bruyère, Vauvenargues and Chamfort, are utterly satisfying authors: they did not write for a living, and never to excess, one volume each being sufficient for their complete production. They fill their small space on the shelves extremely well. The poets, too, are often equally considerate; as, for instance, Baudelaire, whose verse and prose, sketches, diaries, publishing comments and all find room in two volumes of thin paper; not to speak of the considerably terser Heredia, who never wore out his readers with trivialities. Supreme among them all, however, is Villon, the sum total of whose works occupies ninety nine pages in Longnon's edition.

In order to be sure of having one's books in peace, so that irritating gaps do not appear, either through borrowing or simple appropriation, one should go in for different kinds of awe-inspiring, so-called learned works; history, archaeology, chronicles, topical commentaries, thick biographies, and whatever else of the sort which, on closer acquaintanceship, may have an appeal. This type of book has the worst possible reputation as reading material, and even fairly gluttonous readers consider them, for the most part, as being solely of interest to students of the various subjects in question; this is, of course, quite a wrong impression, but has, at least, the advantage with it that no one pockets them. For a matter of that, such books cannot generally be put into even the largest pocket. My own treasures of the sort are humble enough, a mixed bag in their way, and with nothing out of the ordinary about them except that they are intended to be read. Two bulging volumes, however, bound in leather and pigskin, in the middle of a shelf, look so enticing that they have actually been known to rouse the covetousness of one or two observers, despite their character of learned works; and I have only saved them from seizure by telling the barefaced lie that their whole attraction consists in a deceptive outward appearance. One of them is a singly-bound edition of professor Diez' two works on the troubadours and their poetry, and the other a magnificent and beautifully illustrated German translation of Philippe de Commynes. I bought them quite honestly, for nothing, in Germany during the extraordinary currency period, but had to smuggle them home in order to avoid a troublesome Customs duty of about 600 %, if I remember rightly, — the only occasion on which I have succeeded in being courageous enough to attempt such a thing.

Close beside these is a little curiosity containing a phrase which has always delighted my heart. Outstanding among Sweden's orientalists is Carl Johan Tornberg, professor (two generations ago) of Arabic at the University of Lund. His great life work, which occupied him over a long period of years and earned him his reputation among those interested in the subject, was an edition in fourteen volumes of the famous historical work written by the great Arab chronicler, Ibn-el-Athir, which, at the time, only existed in manuscript form, the scattered volumes of which had to be hunted up in Uppsala, Paris, Constantinople and various other places. This chronicle is called by Arabian scholars "the Complete", as it contains everything and covers a period from the Creation until about 1230 A.D. From a western point of view, the eleventh part, dealing with the Crusades, is the most interesting; and this was translated by Tornberg (Lund 1851) into a characteristic, almost cubist Swedish — his natural languages were Arabic and Latin — which lends the translation its unusual, somewhat rugged charm.

In his foreword to the translation (an attractive book, printed on thin linen paper, which, despite of its insignificant size, contains 590 pages) Tornberg writes in a delightful manner of his planned edition of the Arabian text to cover the whole of the great work: how long drawn out and complicated the preparations have been, to what an extent learned friends in Paris have helped him with corrections of the text, so that much of the honour is due to them; how at last he has been generously supported by an enlightened government, which continues to give its approval and powerful encouragement to all forms of enterprise within the field of Eastern literature; and how, at the final moment, unexpected delays have arisen with regard to printing. In spite of all, he continues, the printing of two parts of the work is now so far advanced that "the first one can be put into the hands of the public before the end of the summer". To me, this last sentence is both wonderful and dazzling. The great scholar sees before him a public, chafing with impatience at being unable immediately to satisfy its longing for Ibn-el-Athir in the original; if only this same public will restrain itsel a little longer, a first volume of the longed-for work shall be placed in its eager hands before the end of the summer. In this simple sentence of Tornberg's lies a great and beautiful humanistic dream.

Not far from Tornberg in my bookcase are the two professors of whom, amongst all learned writers, I think most highly: W. P. Ker and August Müller. The former was professor of poetry at Oxford (a fine subject, of which there is, perhaps, no other professorship), the latter professor of Arabic at Königsburg. Ker wrote about the literature of the Middle Ages, old epics, ballades, icelandic sagas and a great deal more, and amongst all those who had written of such things, he is the best; August Müller wrote the History of Islam, and I guess him, too, to be the best in his particular genre, although he himself, in several notes, obstinately insists that the great Professor Dozy of Leiden (immortal author of Histoire des Musulmans d'Espagne) is vastly superior. What these men wrote about, no matter how interesting the various subjects which they treated, is not of so much importance — it is the authors themselves who are so incomparably admirable. I shall not write about them in this connection, as it would be a hopeless task; but some other time, and given plenty of space, I will attempt to praise them as they deserve.

They are not unlike each other, these two great men: wise, calm, deeply learned, melancholy, ironic, and magnificent; and as far as I know there is little, written by true scholars, which gives one quite such complete inner satisfaction as the reading and re-reading of Ker's *Epic and Romance*, and August Müller's *Islam im Morgen- und Abendland*.

It is difficult, however, to arouse the interest of one's fellow-men for reading of this sort; as a rule they stick heroically to their novels, even when these contain nothing but the most ordinary, banal and uninteresting trash.

A special corner which I never really succeed in organizing, although I often try, is the little shelf which contains the Literature of Pure Delight. The lightest kind of reading should be found here, but only that which brings real and ecstatic joy to the reader. I do not know whether many books of this sort exist; I have tried to collect all those which, from time to time, I have come upon, but they gradually disappear again, for very obvious reasons. Among their number are books which, I expect, are known to most people: *Huckleberry Finn*, *Tom Sawyer*, J. K. Jerome's *Three Men in a Boat*, *Diary of a Pilgrimage*, by the same author, Herzec Ferencz' *Gyurkovicz Stories*, Murger's *Vie de Bohème*, Hermann's *Kubinke* (an exceptionally brilliant book), Meredith Nicholson's *The House with a Thousand Candles* (I have owned four copies of this, and the last one has long since vanished), Morley Roberts' *The Mad Hatter*, everything of W. W. Jacobs, all or nearly all of O. Henry, P. G. Wodehouse's Mulliner Stories, and a good deal more. Among Swedish authors, Hans Zetterström should, naturally, be well represented as well as Albert Engström, above all *Through my goldrimmed Spectacles* by the latter, on account of the story of August Carlsson's Return, which, every time I read it, strikes me as being the most stimulating humoresque in Swedish prose; several things by Frank Heller, in particular his two masterpieces, *The Archduke's Finances,* and *The Emperor's Old Clothes;* and further, a large number of academic letters of protest, which are a special literature in themselves, almost un-rivalled as pleasure-reading now that the passions of the actual moment of writing have faded into oblivion. Among the most epic, and at the same time fiery efforts in this connection are considered documents concerning the frenzied battle over a pro-fessorship of ophthalmics in Stockholm during the nineties. According to information given to me by a learned librarian, the ultimate collection of dossiers giving reference to this fight amounts altogether to eighty seven printed numbers; a sort of Iliad of the literature of written protests with which I am not yet acquainted, but which, some time or another, I shall optimistically try to borrow from the University library. It has long been a dream of mine one day to write a really good treatise *On Academic Letters of Protest,* a copy of which will thereafter be found on the bedside table of every thinking individual.

Chief among, and surpassing all Swedish works in this joy-bringing group are, however, Strindberg's Blue Books, to which there is probably no equivalent in world literature. They are tremendous things, inexhaustible as Nature itself, and to say of them that they are amusing and entertaining is to use sadly inadequate words. Strindberg's attitude, in these books, is both serious and at the same time full of relish; to all appearance he is quite mad, with his arguments that the earth is flat, that cuneiform is nothing more than the traces of straw in bricks, that certain dialect words of Scania reappear in Hebrew, that the multiplication table is in need of examination and reform, and a hundred other such things; but at the same time he is

wiser than ten ordinary people, and writes with incomparable
and masterly precision.

"Why, this is nothing but unscientific madness, the whole
thing is pure nonsense," say sensible people faced with these
things; and of course it is nonsense, but the most incredibly
brilliant nonsense that has ever been achieved. During a literary
epoch, or amongst a literary people, works such as the Blue
Books would be worshipped as treasures of untold worth, frequently published in special editions for which everyone ought
to fight. Tame and boring nonsense is not difficult to produce,
a fact which we often have the opportunity of establishing both
as regards ourselves and others; but appoint a mixed committee,
made up of ten intelligent people and ten prominent lunatics,
offer them rewards, daily sustenance, and five years to go, and
it will be beyond their power to achieve a single thing which is
even as good as the less brilliant expositions in the Blue Books.
These are probably the most completely original works in
Swedish prose; with all certainty they are the highlights on that
shelf containing the Literature or Pure Delight which I can
never fill.

Translated by Elspeth Harley-Schubert

*T*OWARDS ten o'clock on a dark evening just before Christmas in the year 1456, five silent figures helped to raise a ladder against the high wall of a garden behind an untenanted house in the precincts of the Sorbonne University in Paris. Such an action, in conjunction with the lateness of the hour was, to say the least of it, suspicious; and in consideration of this, the nocturnal toilers had chosen a sheltered spot to which it was reasonably certain that no wandering patrol of the town watch would penetrate, armed with pikes and awkward questions. When they had placed the ladder safely in position, four of the company removed their outer garments, and laid them in a pile beside the wall; leaving the fifth to guard these, they climbed with agility up the ladder and disappeared into the darkness on the other side of the wall, where lay the College of Navarre, whose chapel served as the treasure house of the Theological Faculty. The raiders, obviously young and active folk, were a miscellaneous collection, and included the profligate son of a burgher, Colin de Cayeux, onetime student at the university, now a professional criminal, and already more than ripe for the gallows, on which, a year or two later, he was to end up; two academicians of shady origin, François Villon and Guy Tabarie, thoroughpaced rascals both; a specialist called Petit-Jean, particularly handy at the picking of locks — fortis operator crochetorum —; and finally a miscreant priest from Picardy, probably brought along in his capacity of namesake to St Nicholas, the patron saint of thieves. Once inside the chapel, the four concentrated themselves upon an enormous ironbound chest, two of whose many heavy locks quickly yielded to Petit-Jean's artistic coaxing. The lid was then forced up by combined effort, until the remaining bolts burst apart; and when a smaller case, contained inside, had proved even more accommodating than the chest under the hands of the clever expert, the thieves soon found themselves, by the carefully shaded light of a lantern, in possession of five hundred écus of gold, which were hastily divided and stowed away. About midnight, four satisfied men climbed back down the ladder; a deducted gratuity was pressed in to the hand of the guardian of the clothes, after which the entire company slunk off into the night. The Theological Faculty slept on in peace, and did not miss its lost pieces of gold until the following spring.

This little episode, preserved in the records of a lawcourt, and discovered by a learned admirer of Villon's amongst the centuries' old lumber of a Paris record roll, is, in itself, by no means remarkable. The song of the sirens, or the name taken by Achilles while he hid himself among the maidens — two things which the Emperor Tiberius amused himself by asking of his men of learning — would have seemed comparatively important subjects of human interest beside the details of this nocturnal visit to the College of Navarre, had it only concerned an enterprise of ordinary simple rogues. Considering, however, that in this case one of those involved was a great poet, beyond question the greatest of his century, a certain significance attaches to the matter and gives it colour. The episode itself, as it now appears, having been dug up and polished by energetic scholars, may also serve to illustrate, in some degree, a particular characteristic of Villon's, — namely, the complete familiarity with every aspect of a crooked existence which is mirrored in his poetry, and which stamps the latter with its hallmark of peculiar authenticity.

The planning of a burglary by a great poet, together with a band of thieves, is strange enough in itself — probably no exactly parallel case can be found in literary history — but it is an even more curious fact that when as in this case five

people, among them a poet, set to work on an undertaking
which must certainly have appeared to be both arduous and
risky, it is by no means the poet who is detached from the
company as being unequal to any responsibility greater than
that of mounting guard over the discarded clothing, while the
central organisation is taken over by the more practical element
in the group. Guy Tabarie, the second academician, was the
one to be left outside the wall; while the poet was obviously
deemed, by experts such as Colin de Cayeux and Petit-Jean,
a valuable and active assistant, in all respects their equal, and
one in whom they had complete confidence. No danger that he
might fumble or be nervous, or become a prey to poetic fancies,
was considered to exist; nor was it feared that through some
wine-drenched impromptu in the cellar of La Mulle he might
at any time show ill-timed loquacity. Despite his youth and
comparative inexperience — he was at this time twenty years
of age, and had just committed his first murder and his first
long poem, fairly innocuous things both —, this swarthy
little academician and versemaker was, in the opinion of his
professional comrades, by no means a being to be looked down
upon with friendly indulgence, and pushed aside when the
game became earnest; no spirit dulled in the very least by his
departures into the mysteries of ballade-making, but a man
well worth his salt even among those of an entirely practical
turn of mind.

Most of the famous lyrical poets of the world would naturally, in such a situation, have been set to guard the clothes,
in so far as individuals like Cayeux and his satellites had considered them capable of even such subordinate work; for, as
the poets themselves often point out, in different variations of
pride, melancholy or fury, their accustomed lot in life is to
sit alone and meditate —

> We are the music makers,
> And we are the dreamers of dreams,
> Wandering by lone sea-breakers,
> And sitting by desolate streams; —

while the true children of the world, the incomprehensibly stupid and incomprehensibly shrewd, are occupied elsewhere — above all in the search for current coin in a universal College of Navarre. A few of the greater lyricists can be mentioned as having, with all certainty, been permitted to come in; men such as Byron, Runeberg, and Robert Burns, probably Keats, possibly a few more —, individuals with a certain clearness of vision despite their continued existence among dreams and melodies; but the vast majority, after a cursory examination by Colin de Cayeux and Petit-Jean, would have been enjoined to remain outside, helplessly entangled in their poetic wings, like the albatrosses in Baudelaire's poem.

Villon himself was no changeling; he was seldom at a loss to cope with the problems and situations of a bewildering Bohemian world, and thus far had obviously no sensation of having landed on a wrong planet. "I know everything except myself," he declares in his *Ballade des menus propos,* a poem which he dashes off in playful barrel-organ mood, without any particular attention to artistic conscientiousness: ... "I can tell a crow from a donkey, and a good opportunity from a bad one; I know the man by his coat, the master by his servant, and the wine by its barrel; I know where to find Bietris and Belet, the ladies of the town, and I know how landlords tot up their accounts; I have wit enough to associate with fools in rich places *(fols nourris de cresmes)* and the jargon of cardsharpers is not unfamiliar to me *(je cognois quant pipeurs jargonne)*: I know what is meant by dreams and visions; I know the power of Rome, and the heresies of the Bohemians; in short:

> Prince, je cognois tout en somme:
> Je cognois coulourez et blesmes:
> Je cognois Mort qui tout consomme ...
> Je cognois tout, fors que moy mesmes.

Poetic gifts and scholastic learning do not occupy much space in this catalogue of Villon's accomplishments, in which he boasts

chiefly of his practical wisdom. As he himself confesses, with
pious mien, at a point in the Testament where he laments
his wasted youth, he was never industrious at his books; and it
is difficult to imagine him in any position connected with eru-
dition and science, except possibly in the rôle of leader of an
institute for thieves' slang. Speaking generally, one may well
hesitate between two opposite, but almost equally justifiable
alternatives in connection with a final summing up of his
strange case. When reading an account of his life with the
vision of his poetry foremost in one's thoughts, it seems natural to think of him as a poet and a scholar, tragically laid low
by his own hasty temperament, and the snares of an un-
kind world; on the other hand, when returning to his literary
production with his adventures and escapades in fresh memory,
it seems even more natural to think of him as a professional
criminal who occasionally permits himself a short holiday —
when he is not actually supplied with one by the long arm of
the law — and who, during such a holiday, for want of a better
pastime, amuses himself by writing poetry.

In the long run, however, he has not been able to escape
capture and examination at the hands of scholastic learning —
that learning which, during his lifetime he so studiously
avoided, preferring to go about, like Gustaf Fröding's Poor
Monk from Skara, in the company of harlots, cheap fiddlers,
and even worse; — and it is this same learning which has since
adopted him, with the greatest love and understanding and
without any trace of rancour. If it is true that God's angels
delight more in helping one lamb that has strayed from the
fold than in associating with those who have always gone their
way faultlessly, something of the sort must also be true with
regard to the attitude of mind among the learned interpreters
of Villon and his works which our later days have produced.
Patient investigators, quiet but unswervingly devoted enthu-
siasts such as Longnon, Marcel Schwob, Pierre Champion and
others, have penetrated deeply into his world, trying with the

help of thousands of documents to instil as lifelike a semblance
as possible into his environment, and by using the acutest per-
spicacity have combined in arriving at an explanation of the
veiled allusions, and a knowledge of the ancient Parisian
scandals, which served as a background for his poisonous darts
and witticisms. It would seem as though for his sake alone
these indefatigable admirers have read through what amounts
to an unlimited number of archives (on studying a book such
as Pierre Champion's great biography of Villon, one is overwhelmed with respect for the ability of the human being to
drag official papers with him through the centuries); and in
their devotion to their subject, they appear to feel themselves
amply rewarded for their pains if they are able in due course to
bring to light even a few minor details which may, however re-
motely, be connected with his name, — delighted, so to speak,
over the faintest trace of a last year's Villonian snowflake.
Never, assuredly, on any Doctor Subtilis or Seraphicus — produced with pride and seen to shine in their day by the Sorbonne University — has a tenth of so much loving and learned
care been expended by the afterworld as upon this dark
banterer and incorrigible *gibier de potence,* this knave, expelled
from his university and native city, and condemned on the
stern parchment of the Châtelet Court to instant exile, this
wretched little student so hopelessly at loggerheads with his
world, *povre petit escollier,* as he wistfully calls himself. Every
imaginable alleyway through which he may have roamed has
been mapped out and described; every tavern which he honoured by a mention has been localized: la Mulle, where the
burglary at the College of Navarre was planned; Pomme de Pin,
his favourite haunt, and in which he owed the landlord, Robert
de Turgis, large sums of money; les Trumilières, where he was
obliged to pledge the pair of trousers later bequeathed in the
Little Testament to Maître Robert Valée, writer in Parliament,
for the latter, in the interests of respectability, the better to
clothe his mistress. The portrait gallery of his poems — a fan-

tastic collection, all wholly fascinating individuals for the Villon-
bewitched — has been re-opened and arranged in his background, clothed, whenever possible, in flesh and blood; knaves
and shabby creatures for the most part, with one or two of a
better sort, but none of them remembered now for any reason
other than that he happened to have come in contact with
them. Some of those whom he has immortalized would themselves have scarcely been flattered by the attention. Thibaud
d'Aussigny, Bishop of Orleans, in his day a brilliant and energetic prelate, would assuredly have been more than sceptical
had some prophetic voice, during the summer of 1461, foretold that he was to become a figure of interest to the afterworld
for the sole reason that an unfortunate wretch, at that time
confined in the deepest dungeon of the ecclesiastical prison at
Meung after having been caught in an attempt to steal the
church silver at Baccon, was to perpetuate his name through
the centuries, showered by abuse in immortal verse. Messire
Robert d'Estouteville, provost of Paris, would have been equally
surprised at his fate of being remembered in the world of
men after such a long period of time chiefly because Villon
once composed a ballade in his honour — not even one of his
best — engraving the name of his gentle consort, Ambroise de
Loré, in the form of an acrostic, down the margin.

People of this sort did not belong, naturally enough, to Villon's
normal sphere; in this were included simpler folk, who cared
but little for thoughts of their reputation, or the afterworld.
Research, notwithstanding, has been to some degree successful
in bringing most of them to light by means of documents. It
is a strange sensation at times to see figures whom one has
become accustomed to think of as part of some amusing tapestry
of Villon's, wander steadily — in a few cases, unsteadily — into
the foreground of reality, equipped with dates and lists of social
merit. Maître Jean Cotard, for instance, the old toper and man
of business who once helped Villon with a lawsuit, on an
occasion when the later had been "insulted" by a certain lady

of the name of Denise, and for the welfare of whose soul in
Paradise Villon dedicated, by way of thanks, the merry ballade
in which he prays Heaven's holy patrons of the vine — Father
Noah, Lot and architriclinus from the wedding in Cana —
to look well after

l'ame du bon feu Maistre Jehan Cotard:

it is difficult to picture an individual of this sort as existing
outside the realm of Villon's poetry. But he has actually been
discovered — and that in fairly recognizable form — in the
person of a lawyer of ill-repute attached to the ecclesiastical
courts of Notre Dame. His signature, shaky from the effects of
inebriation, may be seen in Champion's biography.

Strangest of all, perhaps, is the fact that research now goes
so far in the interests of curiosity as to produce biographical
notices regarding Villon's female acquaintances, most of them
loose creatures of all sorts and conditions, who, judging from
the human standpoint, should otherwise have had but little
chance of appearing in print. Conjured up by deft men of
learning, a crowd of barely discernible female forms emerges
from the names which Villon has carelessly strewn about him in
his Testament; and a fresh nosegay of Ladies of Bygone Days,
lifted from the dust and shadows, and made up of more realistic
flowers, is thus wreathed about the poet, who himself in his
most famous poem has woven an imperishable garland of
women's names from the echoes of ancient legend. These beings
in themselves are quite unsensational, and there is nothing of
interest to say about them; but the glow of Villon's genius
surrounds them for all time, endowing them with a certain
appeal to the curiosity and inner feelings of those who study
them. It is fairly certain that search has revealed La Grosse
Margot, heroine of the terrible piece of self-revelation which
was the net result of Villon's partnership with her

in the brothel where we two have our being,

and one is even on the track — although without definite result
so far — of Catherine de Vausselles; it is she with whom he
relates having had a stormy lovescene which ended by her
beating him, naked, in the presence of his friend Noel le Jolis
"in the way in which washerwomen thump their garments".
Concerning Marion l'Idole, whose name Champion finds, with
good reason, "gentle and mysterious", one is fairly well informed, thanks to papers pertaining to a lawsuit with her
souteneur, the clerk Colin de Thou. Marthe, on the other hand,
who appears to have been his one serious infatuation, his
chière rose and faulse beauté, and who placed the jingle of
coins higher than the devotion of a pauper poet, still dwells
undiscovered where Villon left her.

No reader of Villon's poetry has ever questioned the existence
of these women, and others of the same sort whom he names
in passing, with a possible exception in the case of La Grosse
Margot — which is a special story in itself, where subtleties
concerning literary influence play a part —; there appears in
the Testament, however, a stately and awe-inspiring figure, in
the shape of the only woman represented therein as speaking
(apart from Villon's mother, who recites his *Ballade pour prier
Nostre Dame*) and with regard to whom the inclination is to
feel oneself confronted by a universal type, created by Villon
himself, and here portrayed in order to give dramatic expression
to the philosophy of harlotry as seen from the point of view
of a former representative, rather than by a portrait with any
definite or living image. The figure in question is the wife of
the helmetmaker, Villon's immortal Belle Hcaulmière. He
begins his poem about her with the words "I heard the old
woman, the helmetmaker's wife, lament her youth and wish
herself a girl again — and this is what she said . . .;" upon which
follows, in verses of sheerest beauty, the wonderful litany in
which she reviews the desires and triumphs of her youth, and
the glories of her body, and ends with a final melancholy
scrutiny of the ruins that remain. After concluding this piece

of selfcontemplation in a verse which Matthew Arnold quotes somewhere as being an example of "the great style" in poetry, she addresses, in somewhat lighter tone, the young women of easy virtue in her neighbourhood; exhorting them with tragic fury (and, naturally, with a background accompaniment of Villonian irony) to take their fill of life on the broad highway while there is still time. Her final appeal, *La Belle Heaulmière aux filles de joie*, runs roughly as follows:

> Glovemaker's wife, I pray yóu turn
> To me, your counsellor by years;
> And you, Shoemaker's Blanche, to learn
> One thing, I beg you through my tears:
> Catch while you may each willing swain,
> Remember, as your thirst you slake,
> That years will turn you, soured and plain,
> To worn out coin that none will take.
>
> You, Hawker's lass, so white and fair,
> Tripping the dance with dainty feet.
> And Weaver's Jenny, have a care
> Your obligations well to meet!
> Up to your windows, coy beguiling,
> Arms to entice and hearts to break!
> Soon, all too soon, come caps and veiling
> And worn out coin that none will take.
>
> Be, Tailor's Netta, for your lover
> More than a bonbon or a toy!
> Sweet Catherine, your embroidery cover,
> Give while you may of love and joy.
> Let lusty manhood claim at last
> Its own, for youth's and beauty's sake;
> What have you left, when years have passed,
> But worn out coin that none will take?
>
> Embittered, lonely, and heartsore
> I weep, who once had power to wake
> Desire and passion; now, no more
> Than worn out coin that none will take.

After this Villon bids her farewell, in a few lines of the kind that only he knew how to achieve. "This, then, is her teaching, she who once was beautiful and glorious; for what they are worth, and whether well said or not, I have recorded her words..."

> Ceste leçon icy leur baille
> La belle et bonne de jadis;
> Bien dit ou mal, vaille que vaille,
> Enregistrer j'ay faict ces dis...

Contrary to supposition, this figure was not merely a creation of Villon's imagination, but has been discovered by both Siméon Luce and Marcel Schwob, although her real name has always remained a mystery. She continued to be known as La Belle Heaulmière throughout her lifetime, even in official documents, from the time of her prosperity at the beginning of the century during the picturesque reign of Charles VI, when she was the mistress of the elegant and wealthy canon of Notre Dame, Nicholas d'Orgemont, until one memorable evening when, at the age of seventy or thereabouts, she appears to have discoursed on the happenings of her life in the company of the thinfaced homeless clerk with restless eyes, "dry and black as a broomstick", who had, perhaps, secured a night's lodging in her wretched hovel in the prostitutes alley.

Many an excursion might be made into this world of Villon's, which is both spacious and full of adventure, despite its fragmentary illumination, or possibly, to some extent, on account of this; ramblings of any length, however, would probably soon become tiresome for those who have not Villon's verses to guide them in the labyrinth. There is, nevertheless, one thing there all too significant to be ignored or passed over — namely, the headpiece and epitomizing symbol of the world of that time, the magnetic pole to which the greater number of Villon's friends are irresistibly drawn, and towards which he himself on several occasions feels that he is dangerously gravi-

tating: the place where all these *enfants perdus* reach fulfilment, thereafter to be left, like the prophet in the wilderness,
deserted by all except the ravens of Heaven. In the same way
that Dante's world is dominated by the gateway of the Inferno
and the inscription regarding justice which inspired its mighty
builder — *Giustizia mosse il mio alto fattore* — the world of
Villon is overshadowed by the gallows at Montfaucon with its
accompanying solemn sentence (which he in his turn once heard
mumbled)... "to be hanged and strangled on the city gallows
tree": *être pendu et éstranglé au gibet de Paris.* This gallows, an
enormous two-storey contraption of poles and beams, erected by
Saint Louis and capable of accommodating about fifty de-
linquents at one time, enjoyed a legendary reputation; and
the town hangman of Villon's time, Henry Cousin (known as
Monsieur Henry by his familiar public, and Monsieur de
Paris according to the private titulature of the Honourable
Guild of Hangmen), competed in public estimation with Tristan
l'Hermite himself, King Louis' favourite executioner. The
shadow of this lively gallows traffic falls darkly over the
period, which, indeed, was dark enough in every way; the
demoralization which had followed in the wake of the Hundred
Years war showed no sign as yet of growing less, and all
morale had sunk to depths which had probably seldom before
been reached. The liberal manner of dealing justice then prevalent does not, however, seem to have given rise to any particular
atmosphere of depression, this being due, perhaps, to the fact
that feelings of humanity lay for the most part completely
dormant, thereby causing little inconvenience either to the up-
holders or victims of the law; and as far as the spectators of
this same justice were concerned, these secured their gamut of
pleasure by attending an interesting execution — *une belle
pendaison* — in much the same way as most of us nowadays
enjoy an entertaining sports event. The existence of a criminal,
under such difficult circumstances, might indeed seem troublesome enough; but in the same way then as now, it was not

without opportunity for the intelligent and skilful. One could, by taking reasonable precautions, usually escape the legal consequences of a crime actually committed by oneself; but on the other hand there was always a considerable risk of being seized for the misdemeanours which entirely different people had on their consciences, and this was much more serious than being brought to book for one's own escapades, for the reason that the wrongly accused could not only anticipate ultimate hanging, but in addition had to endure divers forms of torture before a false confession had been wrested from him. Ordinarily, the special form of torture applied in such cases was the so-called ordeal by water, or *question de l'eau,* during which, with the help of a linen cloth made fast by some means in the accused's mouth, the latter was forced to swallow enormous quantities of water. Villon, who had once gone through this procedure, (though not as innocent) mentions with bitterness in the Testament the ruffians who poured more than sufficient water into him to last a lifetime.

Even though one had been caught and imprisoned, however, the chances of avoiding a closer acquaintanceship with M. Henry were by no means exhausted; and Villon's life story is an illustration of the various methods which could be made use of under such circumstances. To begin with, it was always possible in circles like his to plead the position of clerk, with its accompanying privilege of beeing judged only by an eccle-siastical court. This was an attempt which could never do any harm, and which was often effective, the church authorities being jealous of their rights, and at the same time held in great respect for their ability to retaliate against secular interference. For the reasonably literate criminal of the day, this way out had the same semblance of a reflex action as when knaves and lawbreakers of the present time, by means of certificates showing mental weakness, seek protection in the friendly arms of science. Should it fail — and in the case of specially notorious clients, the authorities could sometimes turn a deaf and obstinate ear — there were still other means to be tried. Prison guards, always figures of suspicion in Paris of that time, were often friends or brothers of their captives, and could occasionally be bribed or persuaded; upon which, quietly and without fuss, one simply left the prison, to be regretfully reported missing at the ensuing trial. There was also the precedent of prisoners having been released and sent into a gaily-decorated outer world with the indulgent approval of the high authorities themselves, for the simple reason that the king happened to be visiting the city. Fortunately for Villon, this occurred while he was in Bishop Thibaud's tower, and the newly-crowned Louis XI passed through Meung. Yet another way out was the obtaining of a royal letter of pardon — *lettre de remission* — which was a sort of document which could be induced to rain impartially upon the good and the naughty through the help of influential friends in the Royal Chancellery, or by an inner knowledge of the winding paths which led thereto. A valuable letter of this sort was secured by Villon, then sought for his first murder, in the summer of 1456. While resting one evening on a stone bench behind the church of St Benoit-le-Bétourné, in the company of a girl named Ysabeau, he became involved in a quarrel over the girl with a drunken priest, by name Philippe de Sermoyse, and ended the altercation by thrusting his dagger through the body of the latter. It is entirely thanks to this letter, of which there are two copies, the one addressed to Maître François de Montcorbier, and the other to Maître François des Loges, *autrement dit* Villon (he invariably used several names) that the episode has been preserved to posterity.

No one can say how many times Villon succeeded in extricating himself at the last moment from the snares of justice, but they must have been numerous. Some of these escapes are common knowledge, but concerning the most adventurous phase of his life there is little or nothing to go on as, for instance, after the burglary at the College of Navarre, when he wandered

about the countryside in the company of the rogues and vaga-
bonds who flourished there, and who were known as *les co-
quillards;* but everything points to his having had an unusual
capacity for taking advantage of the smallest loophole of escape
when he got into any sort of trouble. *Fluctuat nec mergitur* —
though tossed by the waves, yet does not sink — runs the inscription on the city arms of Paris, and a similar motto might
well have been adopted by this versatile citizen: threatened by
the gallows, but still unhanged. Nevertheless, on one occasion the dark shadow came so close to him that, despite
all his luck and ingenuity he was almost overtaken by despair. This is the last picture of his life, and the event which
led to composition of his well-known *Ballade des Pendus.*
After his escapades in the country had ended by landing him
in Bishop Thibaud's prison, he returned to Paris, where he
immediately wrote his Testament, still exhaused by his imprisonment, and with violent feelings of hatred for the bishop
as *poetic stimulus.* During this time he kept himself well
hidden, as in spite of *lettre de remission* and the coronation
pardon it was still extremely risky for him to be seen in the city.
Two of his closest friends, Colin de Cayeux and Regnier de
Montigny, had recently been hanged; and in the account books
of the Theological Faculty his name was entered against the
sum of one hundred and twenty écus of gold, this worthy body,
thanks to the drunken babbling of Guy Tabarie, having now
been apprised of the nocturnal raid on its chapel. None the
less, confident in his luck and his exceptional powers of
discernment, possibly, too, relying on the absentmindedness of
the Faculty, he gradually ventured out of his hiding place, and
seems, at this point, to have seriously considered the suitability
of turning over a new leaf.

Nothing of this sort became possible for him, however, before
really serious difficulties began to arise; and before long he
found himself imprisoned in le Châtelet, accused of some
theft or other. This accusation had scarcely had time to prove

itself groundless, or at least impossible to drive home, before the Theological Faculty suddenly put in appearance, having discovered that Villon was to be found in prison, and demanded a squaring-up of the now five year old debt to the College of Navarre. The Faculty insisted, not so much on the hanging of Villon, as upon the recovery of its money; and as the poet was obviously without means, a somewhat curious agreement was reached. Villon was made to sign a document in which he bound himself to repay by instalments the sum which, at the time of the burglary, had fallen to his lot, namely forty écus yearly over a period of three years — after which he was set free for the time being in order to facilitate the carrying out of the terms of the agreement. As his own signature can scarcely have had any value, it is probable that some friendly soul vouched for him, possibly his uncle and fosterfather, the pious chaplain of St Benoit-le-Bétourné, Guillaume de Villon.

One can hardly imagine a more pitiable figure than the liberated poet at this time; not only was he obliged, as before, to earn his daily bread, this in itself a sufficiently arduous task, but it was now expected of him that he should begin to pay off mortgage on old burglaries. Staggering under the weight of these obligations, he hurriedly withdrew to his former haunts in the darkness of the alleys; and it is there that court documents permit the curtain to be raised for the last clearly illuminated scene of his life.

One evening in November 1462 Villon appears at the house of his friend Robin Dogis, residing at Parchmentmaker Street, and asks, in all probability starving, to be allowed to have dinner there, which request is granted; other guests include Hutin du Moustier and Rogier Pichart, the latter a clerk of uncertain temper. After the meal Villon invites the company to go with him to his lodgings, address unknown. On the way there they pass some lighted window, behind which Maître François Ferrebouc, the papal notary, is sitting with his secretarial staff, absorbed in writing. The clerk stops, and begins to insult the writers, using strong language; and when an altercation is in full swing, he further emphasizes his points by spitting at them through the window, whereupon the entire company rushes out into the street and a wild scuffle takes place. Two of the secretaries overwhelm Hutin du Moustier, while the papal notary himself comes to grips with Robin Dogis, and receives a comparatively serious knifewound. A great scandal follows, as Ferrebouc is a highly respected individual, who had taken part some years before in a revision of the trial of Joan of Arc; and when the mischiefmakers are tracked down and called to account, Villon, too, is seized and brought with them, despite the fact that, once bitten twice shy, he had been wise enough to remove himself in good time from the scene of action. When his well known features appear again in the Châtelet lawcourts, which have so recently released him, the patience of the authorities is definitely exhausted; and without taking much trouble to find out the extent of his share in the mischief under examination, they consider it now high time that the affairs of this unsatisfactory academician are settled, once and for all. The water torture is immediately applied to him, and he is thereafter sentenced to the gallows. This time it is in deadly earnest. The wellmeaning old Robert d'Estouteville is no longer provost, but instead one of King Louis' new brooms, who is bent on sweeping clean. Villon appeals against the sentence to the Paris parliament, but he has a feeling that his chances are very few. In spite of all, M. Henry is clearly to get him in the end.

While waiting in some dark corner for the final scene, he composes two poems, one of them a thing of four lines, and the other a formal ballade, constructed in masterly style according to the most exacting pattern for this difficult form of poetry. The four-lined poem was long bandied upon the lips of Parisians as being Villon's most brilliant witticism, and is quoted by Rabelais: without any doubt it is still a high light in the sparsely cultivated genre of gallows humour. "I am François, which is worst for myself, born in Paris, a town in the neighbourhood of Pontoise; and with the help of a rope, three ells long, my neck is soon to be taught the weight of my buttocks."

The Ballade which he wrote at the same time is unique, in consideration of its nature and its psychological background. There are not many who have been able to compose poetry in the shadow of imminent and violent death. The old Scandinavian poets who improvized verses as the price of their heads in the presence of some irritable monarch cannot be cited as parallel cases; for, apart from the fact that their achievement under such circumstances have scarcely come to be reckoned as poetry, in the case of these poets the actual compositions themselves were a sure means of saving their lives, and in no way to be considered as a final accounting in the face of the inevitable. Sir Walter Raleigh, executed in the Tower of London in 1613, by reason of the displeasure of James I, and the Marquis of Montrose, hanged in Edinburgh in 1650 as an incurable royalist, can be mentioned on the other hand as being among those capable of writing noble verses in a similar situation. In addition, on a plane nearer Villon's, there are the classical poems composed by André Chénier immediately before he was sent to the guillotine by Fouquier-Tinville. Both Chénier and Villon could still entertain some hopes of a reprieve when they wrote, Chénier's chances being considerable, and Villon's infinitesimal. Chénier's lot was to die, and Villon's to survive; but from a psychological point of view, Villon in his poem is much closer to death than Chénier in his. He has made his peace with the world, is reconciled to his fate, and to all intents and purposes already hanged. Chénier's last poem is incomparably the more harrowing, dependant on the fact that its author is overcome by the fear of death, with his face turned towards life; a Laokoon in more supreme anguish than his marble counterpart. Villon's achievement is the greater and more incredible because he, despite his hunger for life, has passed beyond the regions of lamentation and stands, calmly

gazing, face to face with death. Supreme among gallowsbirds,
and prince of all ballade-makers, he is himself to the last; the
steady hand does not tremble; and however seriously the piety
of expression may be meant, no feature of his countenance is
changed. Without hope, indomitable, and impossible to dis-
concert, he triumphs, like Lucifer suddenly raised from the
gutter, over the darkness into which he stares.

Epitaph in the form of a Ballade.
Written by Villon for himself and his companions, while
he was waiting to be hanged with them.

Ye brothers left on earth, judge not with blame
As ye pass by: with pity mark our fate.
For each one shall, who doth revile our name,
Himself, of God, be judged at the same rate.
Five, six, of us, strung up in piteous state,
The flesh we pampered, in indulgence free,
Now ravaged, torn and rotten; soon are we
As dust and bones upon the earth to fall.
Pass not with jesting, nor with mockery,
But pray to God that He receives us all.

Be not affronted, ye to whom we say
The name of brother; for although we here
By law are punished, t'is not all who may
Live well and wisely, and in godly fear.
Remember this, now that our end is near,
And plead for us before Our Lady's Son
That our abode be not a fearful one
Where burning torments hold the damned in thrall;
Cast not upon us jeering scorn alone,
But pray to God that He receives us all.

The beating rains have washed us where we swing,
Snow, frost, have blackened us; foul ravens tear
Our eyes out with their sharpened beaks, and cling
To hairless scalps, nor even beards do spare.
No peace is ours; we spin, now here, now there,

Through rain or shine, the playthings of the wind,
To noise of croaks, and flapping wings behind
Each peck and hack. O, brothers, hear our call!
To follow our sad path be not inclined,
But pray to God that He receives us all.

Lord Jesus, Prince most High, whose grace makes free
Our souls from gaping Hell, we turn to Thee.
Under its threat, before Thy Face we fall.
And fellow beings! Pass, without mockery,
And pray to God that He receives us all.

In this attempt at translation, the title is retained in accordance with the superscription with which Clément Marot,
Villon's 15th century editor furnished the poem, and which
has first become an object of criticism in the learned editions
of recent times. No title exists for this ballade, or any other,
which can be shown as having originated from Villon himself,
and it is difficult to understand why even the most erudite of
latter days cannot accept the inventive genius of Villon's humorous old colleague, and leave things as they were, instead of
drawing on his manuscripts and first publications for unsatisfactory alternatives. Both the Ballades of the Ladies and Gentlemen of Bygone Days appear, for instance, in Longnon's latest
edition (which in all other respects is undoubtedly as good as
an edition can be) under the titles *Ballade,* and *Autre Ballade,*
a return to original chaste simplicity which is unquestionably
good scholarship, though not of the kind which makes either
for pleasure or understanding. This, however, is only a sigh
in parenthesis.

Contrary to all belief, and as though equipped like the cat
with nine lives, Villon once again escaped the noose. In an
access of good humour Parliament took pity on him and
cancelled the death penalty, though at the same time, on account of his "evil way of living" condemning him to ten years
exile from the city and provostry of Paris. When informed of
this pardon, Villon burst forth into a gay impromptu, addressed

to the doorkeeper of the prison, and sent to Parliament a tottering ballade, obviously written in great haste, full of rambling thanks, and with a request for three days respite in which to prepare himself for his exile. This is his last sign of life; and from this moment he disappears entirely, swallowed up by a darkness so impenetrable that no efforts of research have since been rewarded by so much as a trace or an echo of his name. All that is known is that he must have been dead in 1489, when his poems were first published.

From a strictly compositional point of view, Villon should naturally have been hanged in connection with the writing of the great ballade; one may say that he was hanged, for the reason that it marks the end of his biography. From the beginning, his life points towards the gallows; and having come as near this end as possible, he reaches in this ballade his supreme height as a realist, in that he here masters poetically the greatest and most serious reality of his life, — a reality even more difficult to transform to poetry than the most intimate aspects of his life with La Grosse Margot. From a purely poetic standpoint, however, the ballade itself is not among the greatest of his achievements; there is nothing really gripping or magical in this narrative of the hanged, no lines which, of their own accord, become once and for all a part of the reader's consciousness, returning time and time again to ring in his ears with an enchantment that can never die. His greatest poem, the Ballade of the Ladies, was not written in any autobiographical connection, nor on the basis of any particular experience, but during a period when he had completely extricated himself from the trials and difficulties of his existence, and, poetically speaking, shaken off the coverings of the flesh.

The Ballade of the Ladies of Bygone Days contains nothing, explains nothing, presents no problems, and probes no depths of the soul; it preaches neither morals nor immorality, and sets forth no striking points of view concerning any phenomenon under the sun. Its constituents are the simplest possible: a few rhymes, an intonation, a group of names, and a refrain. In its simplicity the poem should be easy of analysis, and what Villon achieved therein possible for translators and imitators in some degree to interpret. No one has succeeded, however, although many have tried; no hand may touch this poem. As in the case of the royal apparition which appeared to Hamlet:

> We do it wrong, being so majestical,
> To offer it the show of violence;
> For it is like the air, invulnerable,
> And our vain blows malicious mockery.

With its harmony of colour and etherealism, its veiled shimmer, and its tone as of bells among blue mountains on the other side of time, this may be called true poetry, the embodiment, in purest form, of its platonic idea; an "insubstantial pageant" that melts into thin air, like the fairy drama on Prospero's island.

> ...La royne Blanche comme lis
> Qui chantoit à voix de seraine,
> Berte au grand pié, Beitris, Alis,
> Haremburgis qui tint la Maine...

Perhaps it came to him in Thibaud d'Aussigny's tower, where he had plenty of time; in which case the sungod's horses, as once those of the moon goddess, had to trot for a while on their own that day, while their driver paid a visit to the bishop's dungeon.

Translated by Elspeth Harley-Schubert

THE SILVER SHIELDS

*A*S LONG AS Alexander lived, men called them *the Hypaspists:* "the shieldbearers", we should say. They were then a picked regiment of the heavy-armed footsoldiers, led by Nikanor, Parmenion's son; and in the battleline stood to the right of the phalanx, next the cavalry and the Cretan archers, on Alexander's own wing. After his death they had the reputation of the best, most haughty and most terrible of his veterans, and bore more costly arms than the others. And then men called them *the Argyraspids,* which is "the Silver Shields".

Once, when they were already old, they fell into error. They did it with their eyes open, acting to the best of their judgment: out of concern for themselves, that they might preserve their wives and property, and out of concern for all Macedonians, that they might no longer destroy each other in war. They were forced to choose between two laws of different character: the law which says that the soldier shall be true to his lord, and the law which says that peace should reign on earth — or rather, according to the more modest aspiration of the Silver Shields, that peace should reign between Macedonian men — and they believed themselves to have chosen the better. But Antigonos — he who was surnamed "the Great", and also *Monophthalmos* or *Cyclops,* which being interpreted signifies "the One-eyed" — Antigonos punished them, since they had chosen wrongly; and sorrow, tribulation and destruction became all their portion. This was when they betrayed to Antigonos their general Eumenes, a Greek from Kardia, who formerly had been secretary to Alexander. And of this the historian Hieronymos of Kardia has written, in a work no

longer extant, and after him Plutarch, in his biography of
Eumenes, which is included in the *Lives*.

To Alexander they were faithful, for him they loved; and
they knew that he was so much greater than other men that
it was vain to try to understand him. It was his foible to
fare over the world's face and conquer the kingdoms of it; and
when once they had become used to this, it did not appear
to them as a thing to be amazed at, especially if it were recollected that he was of divine birth. For it was common
knowledge — and the Silver Shields who followed him saw
it daily confirmed — that Zeus was his father. Had not King
Philip once through the crack of the door seen a great serpent
in intercourse with Queen Olympias, and had not Zeus thereafter stricken one of the King's eyes with blindness — the
same eye which had through the crack beheld the holy mystery? And even if there were those who were unwilling to
believe this story — for it was reported that Queen Olympias
laughed harshly and stamped with fury when anyone applied
to her for corroboration — the question of his divine birth
was little affected thereby; for all knew that through King
Philip he descended in the direct line from Hercules; and
that Hercules was son to Zeus, no man was known to have
ventured to deny. Certainly it was from Zeus and from Hercules that he derived the heritage which drove him to press
on to the uttermost parts of the earth — farther even than
his great ancestor had fared for the girdle of the Amazons
and the man-eating horses — and forbade him ever to feel
that he had reached his journey's end. What he sought for
on these his journeys, the Hypaspists never rightly could make
out, though they followed him constantly, and often spoke
thoughtfully of it by their camp-fires; for the girdles of queens
made little appeal to him, and for horses he cared only in so
far as they were needed for his cavalry; the golden talents
of the treasury of the Persian King he gave away, and his
companions (whom he made satraps) had the most good of

the lands he conquered; and the sparrows and herbs which
he caused to be collected and forwarded to the learned in
Athens could be no satisfactory explanation. But perhaps it
was his superhuman ability in war which led him always to
hope that somewhere, in the furthest corner of the world, there
might yet be some terrible King with an army worthy to be
matched with his own, and which filled him as it were with
the impatience of a lover, in his longing to measure himself
against him. For on the battlefield he could with his Macedonians draw out harmonies as rich as ever musician struck
from his cythara; and perhaps this was the greatest of his
felicities, and one which Zeus vouchsafed to him alone.

Since the Hypaspists were among his best men, and could
most easily endure hard marches, it fell to them to follow
him everywhere. The phalanx at times marched with Krateros
by other roads, the cavalry with Hephaistion or Perdikkas:
the Hypaspists went always with Alexander. It was their fate
never to be permitted to rest — their fate, but also their boast.
They could never be left behind; for them, however far they
went, there never dawned the day of ease in quiet quarters;
wherever the King's desire might point, there always lay their
line of march, and the King's desire took no account of fron-
tiers. In their young days in their own country they had made
their way into every corner of Greece and Macedonia, in the
course of campaigns against the Thracians, the Triballi, and
the Boeotians — useful little exercises, these, which expanded
their lungs and hardened their legs. Thereafter they had said
farewell to Antipater's men, who were left at home to guard
the land; and turning their faces eastward had moved off to
more serious work. Eight years later, as they struggled wearily
through the desolate marshes east of the Indus, they had long
ceased to reckon the parasangs they had traversed; but we,
who have more time for such things, have caused our learned
men to calculate that they had at that time some 18 000 kilometres behind them, not counting minor excursions from the

main line of march. Nikanor, Parmenion's son, then led them
no longer: in a happy hour for himself — just before his
brother Philotas, commanding the cavalry of the guard, had
been condemned to death by the army for concealing a plan
for Alexander's murder — he had fallen in battle in Iran, and
had been succeeded by Seleukos, a great man, and a man
to command respect, who could hold a bull by the horns, and
was at last to be King of Asia.

Many others, comrades and commanders, had they left behind them as they marched; some dead, some installed in conquered satrapies. Antigonos and Kalas, with many of the allies
and the hired soldiers, had been settled in Asia Minor, while
the Hypaspists raced with Darius for the Cilician Gates, and
succeeded in getting there before him. Thereupon they had
fought with the Greek mercenaries of the King of Persia at
Issus, and endured seven months' tribulations by land and
sea before Tyre, and then gone to Egypt, a land where ale
was brewed of strange grain, and where they helped to mark
out with flour the plan of a new town named Alexandria, in
the black bog-lands by Pharos. It was there, too, that it had
fallen to them to accompany Alexander through the desert,
where eyes smarted and the skin on their faces drew tight
as a plaster, to the oasis of Ammon, where he desired to com-
mune with his father through the mouth of the oracle. On
their return march through Syria they sat sometimes together
with their former comrades, who spoke of their life in garrison
there, and of good victuals and light labour, and an easeful
existence of fencing-halls, baths, and women's quarters; but
after a brief interval the Hypaspists were again on the road,
veered to the right and passed the Euphrates, and watched
above lowered spears the scythe-wheeled chariots of the Persians bearing down on them over the green fields of Gaugamela. They had now come further even than the men who in
the time of Cyrus the Younger followed the Spartan Klearchos
to Kunaxa and were thence led home again by an Athenian

scribe named Xenophon. But for the Hypaspists the road
went on to the horizon: they turned southward through Babylon, where winged bull-gods with curled beards stared at them
from terraces and temple-stairways, and so through a moist
and sweaty land filled with canals and grainfields, where the
wheat stood twice the height of a man, and the ears were
half an ell long. Leaving behind them the plains of the Land
of Rivers, they traversed Susiana the Red, saw the mountain
peaks towering ever nearer with snow upon their brows,
stamped their way through the defiles of Fars — in air ever
thinner, which at first gave them palpitations — and at last
halted on sun-swept highlands round a great group of fair
buildings with rows of unusually slender pillars, under a
heaven more blue than any they yet had seen. Here, behind the guardian lions at the gate, had dwelt until quite
recently the King of Kings, who was now a wanderer in the
unknown.

One evening, as they leaned upon their spears, they watched
the burning of this proud city of Persepolis. Many in the army
were glad at that sight. "This now is the end," they said. "It
is fulfilled. The empire of the Achimenides is destroyed. Hel-
las is revenged for the expedition of Xerxes. Now we may go
home again." And indeed all the Hellenes in the army were
permitted to return home from that place, even to the Thes-
salonian cavalry, for their war was now over; but when the
snows melted, Alexander moved to Ecbatana, where once the
Kings of the Medians dwelled, and the Hypaspists heated
their gallipots in quiet angles of the city's seven-fold ring of
parti-coloured walls. Here Parmenion was established with the
rearguard; and here he was permitted to stay, until by the
King's command he was hewn down, after the condemnation
and killing of his son Philotas. The Hypaspists held it for a
grievous thing that the King should be constrained to kill Parmenion; for he was chief among all the generals, and had
himself done no evil. But it was easy for every man to see that

the King could not leave him behind him, now that it had
been necessary to put Philotas to death; and he was besides
an old man, whose life was not much shortened thereby; and it
was certain that the King himself best understood such high
matters.

From Ecbatana they went up to Hyrcania to hunt for
Darius, and their marches grew longer and heavier than before. But the Hypaspists made no complaint; for they perceived that for so long as Darius roamed the frontier dis-
tricts, there could be no peace and order in the land. At last
they found him, dying by the roadside, and watched the King
cover him with his cloak. They drew a breath of satisfaction,
believing that now they should have rest. But Alexander took
them with him afar off, to the uttermost parts of the earth, to
Bactria and Sogdiana and other lands so distant that they
had hardly even a name. Once they even crossed the Oxus,
close by the world's end, and fought with the Massagetes
of the outer wilderness, who bore woollen armour and high
caps of lambskin which it needed a stout sword-hack to cleave.
And in these regions they long abode, that they might war
against a multitude of rebellious old Persian satraps, whose
long names they learned to recognize, and to curse.

When at last all was quiet, a rumour ran around the army
that they were to go to India. At this all rejoiced; for India
was a land where the rivers ran upon sands of gold, and the
gems burst from the rock-face as blossom from a spring meadow.
Recruits who arrived from Macedonia brought the ranks of
the Hypaspists once more up to full strength, and received
tacit instruction at the hands of the veterans, as touching their
own great awkwardness, and concerning all that was required
of them that they might fill the honourable places to which
they had been called. After which the army moved off to
India, over the mountains called *the Paropamisadian*, which
are far higher than other mountains, and seldom trodden by
travellers; and there many of the young men fell swooning

to the ground. Having descended to the hot lowlands, the
Hypaspists looked around them for golden sand and precious
stones; but all they found were armies who came against them
with great noise of cymbals, and long lines of war-elephants
with towers upon their backs, from which naked men with
red turbans showered stones and small poisoned spears upon
them. The Hypaspists felt themselves deceived in this country,
and found the war-elephants far more troublesome than the
Persian scythe-chariots at Gaugamela. Then, after they had
beaten King Poros, it began to rain, and the torrents of warm
rain fell ceaselessly and ever faster, swamped their camping-
places and caused the leather on their cuirasses to be covered
with a luxuriant mould. The army thereupon began to murmur;
and when they had reached a river by the name of Hyphasis,
all the footmen drove their spears into the ground and refused
to go further, for in the Kingdoms that lay beyond were only
rain and fevers and war-elephants; and even the Hypaspists,
whose boast it was never to complain and always to go where
the King went, said, there at the Hyphasis: "It is enough." For
three days they saw not Alexander: in his grief he kept himself
within his tent; but they did not allow themselves to be moved.
Then he built twelve great altars at the limit they had forced
him to fix, and thereupon turned back, and all were filled with
joy. On the fleet which he had caused to be built on the Indus,
the Hypaspists sailed with the King towards the sea, after he
had sacrificed to the gods of the river and the ocean; but at
the city of the Malli they went ashore and fought, and beheld
him borne from the battle, deathly pale, with a long arrow in
his breast; and then they stormed the city of the Malli and put
every living thing therein to the sword. Alexander was now as
cicatrized as themselves; and they did not cease to be troubled
lest he might be killed, and leave them abandoned in a far
country.

Then, when the fleet under Nearchos had sailed away over
the ocean, the Hypaspists fared westwards for seventy days

through lands accursed by the gods called Arachosia and Ged-
rosia; and as they went they recalled, as though it had been
some pleasant memory of their childhood, their earlier desert
march to the oasis of Ammon. Men fell dead in the ranks,
stricken by the sun, and many of their wives and slaves in the
baggage died of heat and thirst. The Hypaspists could indeed
buy new ones in the future, if the King gave them money, or
take them for themselves in cities carried by assault; but nevertheless they grieved much both for the women and for their
children, for they were no longer in their first youth. But their
heaviest care was for the King, who was still pale after his last
wound; and when on the worst marches they found a little
water, they brought it to him in their helmets.

Their tribulations ended at last, and they came again to in-
habited regions, where they celebrated with rejoicings their
meeting with the crews of the fleet. As they moved off towards
the great Land of Rivers, Alexander punished his satraps, who
had done things very unmeet while he was away in India. And
then they witnessed the burial of Hephaistion, which was more
splendid than that of any other man, and grieved for his death
— not for his own sake, for he was a man severe and haughty,
and little esteemed by the army in comparison with Krateros,
whom all the Macedonians loved, but for the sake of Alexander,
for Hephaistion had been the friend he held dearest. When
in Opis the great mutiny broke out in the army, which was
filled with sorrow and fury because the King favoured Persian
men, and all cried aloud that they would go home to Macedonia, the Hypaspists alone remained faithful. Then Alexander
commanded, after that the disturbance was settled, that henceforward they should bear shields overlaid with silver, since they
were more faithful than all the others. And thereafter men
called them the Silver Shields.

They came again to Babylon, where the bull-gods were;
and there, twelve days before midsummer, in the thirteenth
year of his reign, in the great palace where once had dwelt a

mighty King named Nebuchadnezzar, Alexander was taken
from them. When his strength failed him by reason of the
sickness, the Silver Shields came together in anger before the
palace, and demanded to see him, for they mistrusted those
that were about his person. As he lay dying he commanded
that they should be admitted to his presence. They went in,
through dim galleries where physicians hurried about and generals whispered together, and filed mutely through the room in
which he lay, propped on cushions and half-turned towards
them. His eyes, which were very clear, met theirs; but he could
no longer speak. They went silently away, and this was the
last they saw of Alexander. When the news of his death reached them they slew all the physicians who had come near him
and all the prophets who had prophesied his recovery, till a
sense of impotence overwhelmed them, and their weapons fell
from their hands in the bitterness of their sorrow.

After Alexander was gone, the Silver Shields comprehended
nothing of what passed in the world in which he had left them.
When the generals began to quarrel about his empire, they
sought to stand by the best and the wisest of them; but even in
them they found infirmity of purpose and little wisdom, for
the Silver Shields had now grown grey in arms and had followed Alexander too long. Their new masters spoke to them in-
sinuatingly, and often gave them great gifts, but they served
them with sorrow and scorn, and now and then in their impatience slew them. They would have preferred to obey the
two Kings of Alexander's blood; but his son was a new-born
child, and his half-brother had since childhood been stricken
with insanity; and the Silver Shields saw naught but unending
care before them, unless the armies themselves (to whom it
fell to order affairs when no King ruled) should resolve upon
a general peace till Alexander's son grew to be a man. In Babylon was Perdikkas: he had the greatest power, and strove for
peace and the cause of the Kings; but soon he was forced to
war with Antipater, who ruled Macedonia, since Antipater had

shown himself an enemy, and had seduced Krateros, who before the King's death had brought the time-expired veterans
from Asia, persuading him to join with him in disobedience.
Against Ptolemaios also, Lagos' son, who ruled the country of
the Nile, Perdikkas was compelled to do battle; for Ptolemaios
had stolen Alexander's body, and caused it to be buried in
Alexandria, and seemed afterwards to intend to steal Egypt
also. The Silver Shields considered it to be proper to chastise
Ptolemaios; but against Krateros they were not willing to fight,
for he was accounted the best of the generals, and was of all
of them the most beloved. Then Perdikkas sent to Asia Minor
Eumenes of Kardia, who was faithful to the royal house, and
had been secretary to Alexander; and to him he gave money
and elephants and Cappadocian horsemen, and bade him do
what he could against Krateros and the others; but himself he
went with the Macedonians to Egypt.

When the Silver Shields came with Perdikkas to Egypt, they
marvelled among themselves that he was not able to cross the
Nile, whose further bank was held by Ptolemaios and his men;
they remembered how they had gone over the Hydaspes with
Alexander when King Poros stood against them with a numberless host. They began then to murmur against Perdikkas; and
when he led the army southward to Memphis, and there also
failed with his crossing, they were ashamed of his incompetence,
and slew him in his tent. But to the two armies, who had immediately concluded an alliance (since they held it unseemly
that war should be waged between Macedonian men) there
came two days later word from Asia Minor that Eumenes, the
scribe from Kardia, with his Cappadocian horsemen and other
loose foreign folk, had vanquished Krateros in a great battle,
and killed both Krateros and another of Alexander's generals
named Neoptolemos, a distinguished man of the royal house
of the Epirots. The army was amazed that this Eumenes, who
was esteemed a mere quill-driver, should be capable to do such a
feat; but all grieved for Krateros, and found it wrong that the

best men of the Macedonians should be slain by a Greek; and they accordingly doomed Eumenes to outlawry.

Thereupon the Silver Shields went with the army out of Egypt to Triparadeisos, which being interpreted is "The Three Paradises", a place on the Orontes in Syria, and met there Antipater and Antigonos the One-eyed, with their troops; and here for the last time all the Macedonians were united, and Antipater was made regent of the Kingdom and Protector of the rights of the Kings. But after the Silver Shields had contemplated Antipater for some days, they grew weary of his countenance, and fell upon him in The Three Paradises, and cast stones upon him, and forced him to keep himself hid in his own quarters. They were now also tired of marching about in Asia, as for thirteen years they had done without ceasing, and longed for the rewards which Alexander had promised them. With much difficulty the generals turned aside their wrath, and gave them a task worthy of their rank and fame: with their new leader, Antigenes — a man who had earlier commanded a regiment in the phalanx — they moved off to the royal treasure in Susa — a long journey beyond the Land of Rivers, by roads they had travelled before — and brought thence Alexander's Persian gold westwards to Kyinda in Cilicia, where it lay nearer at hand for Regents and others who might wish to dip their fingers into its riches.

The road there and back was long, and the transport of the treasure took time for the Silver Shields, who now moved majestically through the countryside with women and servants and much baggage in their train, no longer hastening as in the days of Alexander. Soon after their arrival at Kyinda they received most unexpected tidings. They heard with equanimity that Antipater was dead and that Polysperchon, a tried veteran, well-known to them, had succeeded him as Regent; but they were filled with amazement when messages came to them from Macedonia with Polysperchon's order that the treasure should be given over to Eumenes, and that they themselves should be placed under the command of that same scribe from Kardia whom in Egypt they had helped to declare an outlaw. Antigonos the One-eyed had now shown signs of a serious intention to appropriate Alexander's Asiatic empire for himself; he was now a mighty man, with elephants and heavy infantry, and very violent in all his undertakings; and Eumenes was the only man in Asia with whom Polysperchon could ally himself, that he might essay to preserve the realm for the Kings. Eumenes had elephants and Cappadocian horsemen and a great reputation for generalship, now that he had beaten Krateros; but he lacked Macedonian infantry, which were the most needful of all; and all that Polysperchon could give him in that kind was the three thousand Silver Shields. All men knew that the Silver Shields were invincible, supreme among the veterans of Alexander, and this they themselves knew also; but they were now sated with glory and would fain have dwelt in peace by their treasure. Yet though they murmured at the order, they obeyed Polysperchon, and broke up from Kyinda for fresh battlefields.

No contemporary poet hymned the fate of the Silver Shields; but had any such epic been written, it might well have begun, in a Macedonianized Homeric strain

Sing of Eumenes' fall, and the Argyraspids' hard fate

by launching into a description of their tranquil sojourn at Kyinda, before Polysperchon's order reached them. Here, in Kyinda, was rest at last, after all their battles and exertions; here was the glory of Alexander, embodied in them and enshrined in the memories of those that had followed him and won his victories; here was his treasure, the tangible recompense for all his labours. It was very meet, the Silver Shields considered, that the guarding of the treasure should fall to them, for they were the last of his soldiers to hold together in their old units, and who could really have a better title to the treasure than they? For the first time since Alexander's death, they

saw the world falling into a rational pattern, and our sup-
posititious epic would have painted, in accents austerely idyllic,
their days in the Cilician rock-fortress, as they watched over
his hoard.

But Eumenes came, and took with him the treasure, and
themselves along with it, and the Silver Shields found themselves once more adrift in an unintelligible world. From Phoe-
nicia to Media, from Babylon to Gabiene, they played their
part in events which convulsed Asia; enduring more, and fighting harder, than ever before, in battles where Macedonian
grappled with Macedonian, and the war-elephants waded among
the shattered battalions, in the mighty swaying struggle between Eumenes and The One-eyed. The Silver Shields were
often refractory, but in the end they always allowed Eumenes
to pacify them, and to persuade them to continue faithful to
him; and by and by they began to look upon him with respect,
finding him most like to Alexander in resource and ability to
win battles. He reminded them often that it was for the Kings
that they fought; and when that no longer sufficed them, he
caused a throne to be set up in his tent, whereon were laid
the sword and diadem of Alexander, and declared to them
that Alexander himself, who had now become a god, was still
among them, and continued to exercise the supreme command.

Of Eumenes, who "by nature loved war and dangers", and
of his stubborn fight for a desperate cause, the old epic would
have had glorious things to tell. His audacity, nerve, and
abounding resourcefulness, would have been shown forth by
many examples; he would have shone illustrious as the best of
all Alexander's generals, and an honourable man to boot, the
last who fought for the royal house. But he had one thing
against him: he was utterly alone. There was no man in Asia
inclined to put much money on Eumenes or the cause for
which he fought. To his own soldiers he was a foreigner and
an outlaw, a "Chersonesan disaster", who caused the deaths of
good Macedonians; to his subordinates he was an upstart, a

man who had served Alexander with the pen rather than the sword; to the eastern satraps on whom he had to rely he was an interloper in their petty dynastic affairs. His generals constantly sought to betray him, and sometimes to murder him; to prevent which he hit upon the device of borrowing large sums of money from them, and so obtained a certain ease of mind, so long as the debts remained unpaid. But to his intimates he complained that he lived among wild beasts.

In the intervals of peace — in camp, or in winter quarters — the Silver Shields lent a willing ear to those generals and satraps who conspired against Eumenes, and from such they took gold on friendly terms; declaring that they perfectly understood that Antigenes or Peukestas, leaders of Macedonian birth, ought by rights to have the supreme command; but when the army was on the move, and came unexpectedly upon the foe, they halted and called for Eumenes, and clashed their spears upon their shields when he was seen among them, in token that he was still the only man they would hear of when a battle was in the wind. Under him they continued to maintain their old reputation for invincibility. They went forward against the finest battle-lines of The One-eyed with a mien of contemptuous confidence, trampled all resistance under foot before their onslaught, and overthrew even his choicest Macedonian infantry, crying "Urchins, would you fight with your uncles!"

The years passed; the great tide of battle rolled back and forth across Asia; through many adventures Eumenes contrived to maintain himself against guile and arms, and in encounters with his terrible opponent he was always the victor. They fought on the Pasitigris in Mesopotamia, where Antigonos sought to come to grips with him, and Eumenes filled the river with the bodies of the slain; later, at several places in Media, where Eumenes stirred up the wild mountain tribes against his enemy, and came near to destroying Antigonos altogether. After which, in the country called Paraitacene, near the place where the Persians of a later age were to build their capital Ispahan, they came to a pitched battle, with phalanxes of heavy spearmen, much cavalry, and long lines of war-elephants on both sides. Eumenes was strong in elephants, which he had managed to obtain from the satraps of the Indus country, but Antigonos was superior in heavy infantry, and had good store of Macedonians among them. But he proved once again unequal to the Silver Shields, the elephants, and the skill of Eumenes, and was constrained to abandon to Eumenes the coveted winter-quarters in Gabiene. But The One-eyed was not easily discouraged, and in mid-winter he advanced against Eumenes again.

This winter Eumenes had had such trouble with his generals and their conspiracies that he was seized with melancholy and was minded to withdraw from the struggle. He knew his life to be so threatened that he made his will and burned his letters, so that they might not compromise his friends after his death. But when Antigonos drew near, he felt a desire to measure his weapons once more against his old antagonist, and in this resolve he was confirmed by the Silver Shields, who promised him certain victory: did not victory always abide with them and him? And on a wind-swept plain in Gabiene the two mighty men of battle were for the last time locked in a trial of strength.

Where the Silver Shields attacked, the event fell out as always: they thrust roaring through Antigonos' lines, and scattered the greater part of his infantry in flight. But on the other wing Antigonos' horsemen had the better of it, and swept round to Eumenes' rear. Peukestas bore himself lamely and half-heartedly, and the army's baggage fell into the hands of Antigonos. In the baggage-train were the women and children of the Silver Shields, and all their possessions — everything that they could call their own after so many laborious years of service. Eumenes, who held that nothing was lost as yet, was for renewing the battle; but by this time the Silver Shields had already sent word to Antigonos, with a request that their belongings might be given to them again. Antigonos made answer, that they should obtain what they asked, and more also, if they would give up Eumenes in exchange.

There stood the Silver Shields, in anguished cogitation, impaled on the horns of a tragic dilemma, in a situation from which there was no way of escape. They were Eumenes' men. He had led them better than any other leader, save Alexander himself, and he had always been to them a good lord. To betray him would be an evil deed. But it seemed to them yet more evil and unfitting that the oldest soldiers of Alexander should be bereft of everything, and perhaps go begging in their old age. And with a sudden anger, born of the difficulty of decision, they asked themselves what claim this Eumenes could justly have upon their fidelity. Why should they suffer so much for his sake? Had not the Macedonian army, in legally constituted assembly, once doomed him to outlawry — a sentence which Polysperchon had never troubled to declare annulled? Was not there now an opportunity to carry this sentence into effect, and at the same time put an end to the war and assure themselves for ever of Antigonos' favour? The longer they considered, the greater became their rage against Eumenes, and soon they saw their way clear, and in the decision they had taken found nothing that was not meritorious.

They approached Eumenes with respectful mien, seized him swiftly and bound his hands behind his back with his own sword-belt. When the emissaries of Antigonos came to fetch him, he begged that he might be allowed to say some words to his men. He was led then through the army, and stopped before the Silver Shields.

"Hitherto, O Silver Shields," said Eumenes, "you have been esteemed the best of all the Macedonians; but by this deed you have made yourselves the most contemptible. Though you were victorious, for the sake of your chattels you have pronounced yourselves vanquished. But I for my part am unconquered, though I stand here now a prisoner: the vanquisher of mine enemies, stricken by my own people. One boon only I ask of you now: I adjure you by Zeus now to kill me, here, with your own hands. Antigonos will make no complaint; for it is not the living Eumenes he desires, but the dead. Kill me now, or give me a sword and one free hand, that I may do the deed myself. But perchance you are afraid to give me a sword: cast me then bound before an elephant. I pronounce you then free of all guilt of my death; and bear witness that you have borne yourselves as honest men towards your general."

So spoke Eumenes; and the others in the army wept when they saw him bound, and heard him speak thus. But the Silver Shields cried in fury that there had been enough of babbling, and that he should at once be led to Antigonos.

Antigonos caused him to be set in strait custody, and was at first doubtful what he should do with him. Two who were near him begged for the prisoner's life: Antigonos' young son Demetrios — he who later won the name of the Taker of Cities — and Nearchos, former admiral to Alexander; but the voice of wisdom at length prevailed, and he was put to the sword in his prison. The Silver Shields thus perceived that all proper safeguards were being taken, and looked forward to a brighter future. But when in this expectation they came into the presence of The One-eyed, they were cast down to observe that his gaze did not rest upon them with kindness. Once again they had fallen in with something which they did not comprehend, and their reward was to be otherwise than they had imagined it.

"For the divine Justice," says that wise moralist from Chaironeia who told the story of Eumenes' life, "did not leave it to any other to punish the commanders and soldiers who betrayed Eumenes, but caused it to be done by Antigonos himself, who was filled with loathing of them by reason of their despicable and inhuman deed. Therefore he caused them to be sent to Sibyrtios, who was satrap in Arachosia on the borders of India, and ordered him by every means to harry and destroy them, so that not a man among them might return to Macedonia, nor ever catch even so much as a glimpse of the Grecian Sea." Thus perished the Silver Shields, because they betrayed their general, Eumenes.

Translated by Michael Roberts

*T*HOSE mediaeval poets who from the time of the Crusades onwards set themselves to sing of feats of arms, or composed lays in honour of their noble patrons, drew up for their convenience a standing list of heroes, to serve them as a yardstick and standard for knightly virtue. The superior beings who were included in this list they called "The Nine Worthies"; and with that feeling for orderliness in these matters which was characteristic of the age they grouped them into three triads: three pagan — Hector, Alexander, and Julius Caesar; three Jews — Joshua, David and Judas Maccabaeus; and three Christians — King Arthur, Charlemagne, and Count Godfrey of Bouillon. Even after the Renaissance these Nine Worthies crop up with some frequency in English literature; while in French, even as late as Brantôme's *Vies des Grands Capitaines*, the highest praise the author can bestow upon (for instance) Charles de Bourbon or Anne de Montmorency is that he was not inferior in valour to *Les neuf Preux*. From time to time during the later Middle Ages, as some great popular hero emerged in this country or that, the claim was advanced for him that he should be incorporated as a tenth member of the sacred circle. Thus the English contended for the Black Prince; the French, even more zealously, for Bertrand du Guesclin, and later for the Maid of Orleans; while the Scots considered Robert Bruce, the victor of Bannockburn, to have a title superior to all other pretensions. And in one historical work by a Swedish author it is written that somewhere in Germany there is, or was, an old picture of this band of heroes in which the tenth place is occupied by a Swedish King — Magnus Barnlock.

Magnus would probably not receive many votes to-day: to the layman of a later age he appears — perhaps in virtue of his nickname — a good and solid, but not a particularly heroic person; but if the Nine Worthies had chanced still to be a matter of topical interest, there can be no doubt that more than one vote would have been cast for the inclusion of Charles XII among them.

His title to a place among these heroes of the nations would be held to rest not only upon his purely personal qualities, nor upon the great exploits he performed, but also upon a quality extraneous to these, which he shared with some of the immortal Nine, but of which he alone of his contemporaries possessed the secret. Like Alexander, like Charlemagne, he is in some degree the generator of a mythology, a man with whom the imagination of men will never weary of concerning itself. True, no Carolingian cycle of legend grew up around him; yet it can hardly be denied that in his case a certain tendency towards something of the sort, despite the unpropitiousness of the times, has always existed. He has always appeared as a lonely, mist-shrouded figure, over whom broods a mystical majesty which is utterly different from the historical aura of any of his contemporaries; and partly for this reason all accounts of him (and in this also he differs fundamentally from the great majority of historical personages) have been strongly coloured by emotion and poetic feeling. His personality is, indeed, recalcitrant to strictly scientific treatment. Every historian finds himself irritated by the Charles XII-legend: he passes his hand over his eyes as it were to brush aside a web, a mist, an illusion, which has interposed itself between him and the object of his researches; he is vexed by the figment of the poet's fancy, by the stock figure of popular tradition, by the idealized monarch. There is hardly any other personage in our history of whom this is true. We have had other heroes; we have had romantic rulers such as Eric XIV and Christina; great soldiers, more fortunate than he, such as Gustavus Adolphus or Charles X; but they

are not romantic after his fashion, nor soldiers after his fashion
either: their power over the imagination of men is insignificant
in comparison with the power which he wields. His men are
called "the Carolines", and it is a word with a specific and
limited application; but for the men of Breitenfeld, or the men
who marched with Charles X across the frozen Belt, we have
no special name, and the light of history which falls upon them
is not a light peculiar to them alone.

What is it, then, that gives this legendary quality, makes of
him an object so inexhaustible to the imagination? His character and his career are no doubt sufficiently extraordinary and
sufficiently grand to secure him his place in history; but this
is not the whole explanation. The impression of limitless power
which he induces, of tremendous ambitions, of capacity for
endurance and ability to succeed — these are such that all un-
consciously, as we follow in his footsteps with names and dates
from Narva to Fredrikshald, we see before us not only the real
figure of history, with its pursuit of shadows and its ultimate
harvest of failure, but also another, indefinite, ideal figure
— the image of what he would have become if Fate itself had
not gradually passed over to the camp of his enemies. He is
greater than any of his works; and for the imagination, which
is not concerned to judge, or reckon, or assess, but only to
contemplate and sympathize, he remains for ever and essentially
the Invincible.

He grew to be a legend even in his own lifetime. The
eighteenth century does not naturally suggest itself to us as a
very congenial soil for the cultivation of hero-worship: on the
contrary, it is usually represented — and perhaps with justice
— as being in many respects a period as dry, cold and utilitarian
as our own, but to him everything, even the eighteenth century,
capitulated. He stood high above all others; and those who came
nearest to him followed at a great distance. In some curious
fashion he appeared from the very first to every casual observer, to every reader of news-letter or student of *Haupt- und*

Staats-actionen, as so "singular and incomprehensible", so strangely provided with a certain "I know not what of *venerandum* and indeed *horrendum*" (as the student Alstrin writes in a letter from Altranstädt) that he was in some degree emancipated from his age and milieu, and even for his contemporaries appeared an antique figure, timeless, inaccessible, utterly alone. He was daemonic, in the Greek sense, as no other man. Men marvelled at him, enthused over him, adored him, were drawn to him even while he held them inexorably at an arm's length, by something in his modest and taciturn bearing which was unfathomable and even terrifying, something unspoken, undisclosed, elemental. Merely to see him for a moment was accounted a matter for congratulation. Maurice, later famous as Marshal Saxe, who can scarcely be supposed to have acquired much in the way of admiration for Charles XII from King Augustus or Aurora von Königsmarck, and who never had the slightest taste for Spartan living and strict morality, made while still a youth a pilgrimage to Stralsund, merely in order to catch a glimpse of his hero under fire on the battlements. In Turkey he became a mythological figure; in Holland a sect worshipped him as the Messiah. It is not on record that any sect worshipped His Grace of Marlborough, either as the Messiah or in any other capacity; nor does Marlborough's military reputation appear to have been comparable with Charles'; although strictly speaking it ought to have been accounted at least equally creditable (and equally difficult) to deal with Villars and Vendôme, and to stand up to the Maison du Roi, as (to quote Charles' letter before the battle of Narva) to "dislodge the aforesaid scum and force the *canaille* to retire".

The age of Charles XII was not poor in striking personalities. A very notable one was Prince Eugene, with his romantic youth, his vendetta against Louis XIV, his intoxication with the fury of battle, his campaigns and victories over half a continent. Charles Mordaunt, Earl of Peterborough — "if not the greatest" (says Macaulay) "yet assuredly the most extraordinary character of that age, the King of Sweden himself not excepted" — waged war in Spain in a style which for spectacular feats of arms might well stand comparison with that of Charles XII in Poland: among other exploits he successfully applied at Barcelona the methods which Charles had invented at Lemberg — *i. e.* the storming of a fortified town, reputed impregnable, by a handful of dismounted dragoons. But over figures such as these there falls, in spite of everything, the cold, clear and sober light of the eighteenth century: they are more or less important, but they lack within themselves his mystic and unfathomable quality, they are ennimbused by no private firmament of their own; for their contemporaries they seem to have appeared interesting rather than admirable; and apart from professional historians no one now much concerns himself with them or their works.

Charles XII, on the other hand, was placed, even by the phlegmatic spirits of the eighteenth century, on a level with Alexander, as the highest exponent of military glory. Among the leading writers of the century it was not only Voltaire who responded to his magic. Henry Fielding, who in his youth translated Adlerfeldt's *Histoire militaire de Charles XII*, has a chapter, at the beginning of the eighth book of *Tom Jones*, in which he examines the nature of the idea of "the marvellous". He cites there Aristotle's dictum, that the poet should confine himself to the probable, and that it is no excuse for him, should he present his readers with the incredible, that it is in fact true, and that it really happened so. It is a dictum, says Fielding, which is valid for the poet and the novelist, but not always for the historian; who may on occasion be forced to narrate things wholly unbelievable, such as would not be tolerated in a work of imagination. "Such was the successless armament of Xerxes, described by Herodotus; or the successful expedition of Alexander, related by Arrian. Such, of later years, was the victory of Agincourt, obtained by Harry the Fifth; or that of Narva, won by Charles the Twelfth of Sweden. All which instances, the more we reflect on them, appear still the more astonishing."

Dr. Samuel Johnson, too, set down his view of Charles XII. If search were made for an individual entirely impervious to the bedazzlement of military glory, it would perhaps be difficult to find any less susceptible to its influence than this wise and sober representative of the culture of his age. In political history he took but little interest, in military, least of all. Of soldiers he personally had but a poor opinion, finding their conversation meagre and their interest in the humanities defective. Among heroes he assigned foremost place to philosophers, moralists and legislators, learned humanists, or reverend prelates productive in the field of high-church dogmatics. Apart from the isolated fact that on one occasion in his earlier days he felled a publisher with a folio, and that during his controversy with James Macpherson about the authenticity of Ossian he perambulated the streets of London armed with a stout cudgel, so that he might give the irritated poet something to remember him by if he should venture an assault, his biographer has not been able to trace any indications of a martial temper in the Doctor himself. But he contrived nevertheless to savour the peculiar bouquet of Charles XII.

"We fell to talking of war," says Boswell in this entry for 10 April 1778, when they dined with a man of law in the Temple; the great Doctor being then in his seventieth year. "Dr. Johnson: Every man thinks meanly of himself for not having been a soldier... No, Sir; were Socrates and Charles the Twelfth of Sweden both present in any company, and Socrates to say, 'Follow me, and hear a lecture in philosophy'; and Charles, laying his hand on his sword, to say, 'Follow me, and dethrone the Czar', a man would be ashamed to follow Socrates. Sir, the impression is universal: yet it is strange... Mankind reverence those who have got over fear, which is so general a weakness."

In his best work in verse, *The Vanity of Human Wishes,* a

poem modelled on Juvenal's Tenth Satire upon a theme which is sufficiently indicated by its title, he chooses Charles XII, as Juvenal had chosen Hannibal, as the grand exemplar of the mutability of the fortunes of war, and the inability of human foresight to provide for all contingencies or ensure invariable success; and although nowadays Johnson's poetry is not in general very highly esteemed, the verse of the eighteenth century has not often, perhaps, spoken in accents more majestic:

> On what foundation stands the warriour's pride,
> How just his hopes, let Swedish Charles decide;
> A frame of adamant, a soul of fire,
> No dangers fright him, and no labours tire;
> O'er love, o'er fear, extends his wide domain,
> Unconquered lord of pleasure and of pain.
> Behold surrounding Kings their pow'rs combine,
> And one capitulate, and one resign.
> Peace courts his hands, but spreads her charms in vain:
> "Think nothing gained," he cries, "till naught remain;
> On Moscow's walls till Gothick standards fly,
> And all be mine beneath the Polar sky."
> The march begins in military state,
> And nations on his eye suspended wait;
> Stern Famine guards the solitary coast,
> And Winter barricades the realms of frost.
> He comes: nor cold, nor want his steps delay;
> Hide, blushing glory, hide Pultova's day ...
> But did not Chance at last her errour mend?
> Did no subverted empire mark his end?
> Did rival monarchs give the fatal wound?
> Or hostile millions press him to the ground?
>
> His fall was destined to a barren strand,
> A petty fortress, and a dubious hand;
> He left the name, at which the world grew pale,
> To point a moral and adorn a tale.

The moral is the ancient moral which Solomon knew: "I returned, and saw under the sun, that the race is not to the swift, nor the battle to the strong, neither yet bread to the wise, nor yet riches to men of understanding, nor yet favour to men of skill; but time and chance happeneth to them all." Voltaire, if you will, expressed the same thought when he wrote: "Car où est le souverain qui pût dire: 'J'ai plus de courage et de vertus, une âme plus forte, un corps plus robuste; j'entends mieux de guerre, j'ai de meilleures troupes que Charles XII?' Que si, avec tous ces avantages, et après tant de victoires ce roi a été si malheureux, que devraient espérer les autres...?"

Voltaire's book, which did more than any other work to establish Charles XII's fame, is also, perhaps, the book above all others which in the long run did most for his own. It is a work which does equal honour to them both. Panegyric was in the ordinary course of things not much in Voltaire's way; and that the master and archpriest of mockery, who by his zest for contemplating historical personages with the coldly derisive smile of a valet so often revealed the inherent truth of the proverb — that Voltaire should for once find in Charles XII something which made him lay aside all his grimaces and his trenchant irony, and instead write simply and sincerely of a character which even to him appeared great, true, valiant and noble — this is not the least marvellous among all the marvels which attend upon Charles XII.

On the modern reader the book makes an impression of dilettantism, and to the historical expert probably appears as one tissue of inaccuracies. There are many obvious faults: the perspective is defective, the incidents are rhetorically stylized, the anecdotes are often dubious, the battles of Narva and Pultava, to mention no others, are particularly grossly mishandled and robbed of all colour and form. Sometimes, when his information fails him, he seems to embroider according to his own fancy (upon the storm of Lemberg he observes, in authoritative parenthesis, that *tout ce qui osa résister fut passé au fil de l'épée*, — conjuring up the picture of an epic massacre, though as a matter of fact few such enterprises have cost less bloodshed); and occasionally there are mere absurdities, as for instance the assertion that Charles was inclined to be jealous of Rehnsköld for his victory at Fraustadt. But some of these mistakes he corrected later on, as Nordberg and Adlerfeldt and other sources became available; and he always insisted that what he had written was innocent of romance, and was the truth in so far as he had been able to discover it.

And with all its deficiencies Voltaire's work retains special merits of its own. Herodotus, Froissart and Snorre are also full of errors; but they live in spite of them, and somehow or other communicate a truth which is perhaps not less valuable than any which their commentators are wont to elicit. As a historian Voltaire stands perhaps upon a lower level; yet he has something in common with them too, and above all this — that what primarily interests him is the personal, rather than any impersonal political process. He writes Charles XII's biography, not a history of Charles XII's reign — two things which though in part they may coincide are far from being identical. An author's relationship to Charles XII will naturally differ profoundly, according as to whether he is writing from the one viewpoint or the other: in the first case the King is himself an absolute value, is interesting and great in himself, is judged in terms of his tragic fate; in the second case he is but a factor in our history, a functionary and no more, and is judged exclusively upon the services or harm which he did to his country. For there is but one tragedy for the functionary as such, be he bank-teller or absolute monarch, and that is, if at the final reckoning he should be found unable to account for what he has received: in such a case he stands condemned. Such and such of our dependent provinces have been lost, so and so many men have been slaughtered to no purpose: he is therefore a bad king, a dangerous man, an adventurer, a committer of "errors". But this is merely another way of expressing an egotistical irritation at the fact that matters went ill for him. For had the winter in Ukraine been less severe, and had he not been shot in the foot at the Vorskla, then he had perchance succeeded; and then he might in time have wound up the whole affair, taken Moscow, and returned home to Stockholm with the Czar Peter and his crown in his baggage-train; and had he done *that*, there would have been no more talk of his "errors", no more of the dubious name of "adventurer" — precisely as Charles X rose above such censures and won the reputation of a far-seeing and responsible statesman, thanks to the timely freezing of the Little Belt. To approach him from one or other of these standpoints — the palliating or the condemnatory — is for us Swedes natural; Voltaire, on the contrary, could after the measure of his abilities see him and depict him in a purely epic light, since he was primarily interested in the King himself. In modern editions of his work are to be seen footnotes, in which this or that French editor corrects him, with references to Fryxell; and from one point of view such a proceeding is no doubt entirely in order; but from another it can be maintained that Voltaire, despite all his lapses and superficiality, had more of an idea of Charles XII in his little finger than Fryxell ever harboured under his venerable nightcap; for the one sought to portray the man, while the other apprehended him only indirectly, his eyes and attention being exclusively turned upon the material profit-and-loss account of his career.

Charles XII himself was certainly more inclined to estimate persons for what they were in themselves, than to measure them by the standard of success or failure. Once in his boyhood, when he was talking with his tutor of Mardonius, and the unhappy end of that commander, he had observed: "That an honest fellow should be unfortunate cannot affect the issue; and if he fell, at least he fell with honour." And of himself he might at the close of his life have said, like Aeneas and with no less justification:

Disce, puer, virtutem ex me verumque laborem:
fortunam ex aliis.

But heroical declamation about himself was not much in his line.

There are not many things which present at once so simple and so baffling an appearance, as the character of Charles XII. We lament his taciturnity, which causes his every aim and action to be veiled in an obscurity in which researchers painfully grope their way forward; we long to find some word, some hint from him, in which he opens himself without reserve, expresses a personal emotion, permits a gleam to light up the recesses of his mind. But this never happens: aphorisms and reflections were foreign to his nature; in his letters and recorded utterances he contents himself with a sober discussion of whatever matter may be in hand at the moment. But even had it been otherwise, even if he had been a little more loquacious, had had more intelligent listeners, had written more letters — would it have made much difference? Probably not. "The rest is silence," says the dying Hamlet, and departs with his heart's secret untold, after a whole tragedy in which he has laid bare his soul and explored its darkest recesses with a unique virtuosity; and the learned continue to debate uncertainly whether he was mad or sane, weak or strong, a man of action or a dreaming fantast, a warm-hearted nature or a disillusioned cynic. These two have not in general much in common, the philosophic Prince of Denmark and the warlike Majesty of Sweden — Scandinavia's only contributions to the first rank of tragedy heroes — but they resemble each other in that impenetrable and baffling quality which makes them for every generation always new, always controversial, always susceptible of every sort of hypothesis and interpretation.

They have, moreover, one odd fate in common, these two most masculine characters, and it is this: that the purveyors of clever commonplaces have discovered both of them to have been in reality women — Hamlet because his feelings for Ophelia were not warm enough, and because at the moment of death he thought of Horatio, Charles XII because of his unwillingness to drag a queen around among the Poles and Tatars, and because he took the sixth commandment too seriously.

Emerson has drawn a good character of Charles XII, in his essay on "Heroism". True, he does not mention Charles' name, and possibly was not thinking of him in particular; it is, indeed, far from clear which hero or heroes he had in mind, for though he refers to a passage in Plutarch, he also (with the transcendentalist's privilege of confusing his readers) mentions, as the best in Plutarch's gallery of heroes, the characters of Brasidas, Epaminondas and Scipio — none of whom are in fact to be found there. But however that may be, his words are worth noting:

> Towards all this external evil, the man within the breast assumes a warlike attitude, and affirms his ability to cope single-handed with the infinite army of enemies. To this military attitude of the soul we give the name of Heroism. Its rudest form is the contempt for safety and ease, which makes the attractiveness of war. It is a self-trust which slights the restraints of prudence, in the plenitude of its energy and power to repair the harms it may suffer. The hero is a mind of such balance that no disturbances can shake his will, but pleasantly, and, as it were merrily, he advances to his own music, alike in frightful alarms and in the tipsy mirth of universal dissoluteness. There is somewhat not philosophical in heroism; there is somewhat not holy in it; it seems not to know that other souls are of one texture with it; it has pride; it is the extreme of individual nature...
>
> Self-trust is the essence of heroism. It is the state of the soul at war, and its ultimate objects are the last defiance of falsehood and wrong, and the power to bear all that can be inflicted by evil agents. It speaks the truth, and it is just, generous, hospitable, temperate, scornful of petty calculations, and scornful of being scorned. It persists; it is of an undaunted boldness not to be wearied out. Its jest is the littleness of common life. That false prudence which dotes on health and wealth is the butt and merriment of heroism...
>
> But that which takes my fancy most, in the heroic class, is the good-humour and hilarity they exhibit. It is a height to which common duty can very well attain, to suffer and to dare with solemnity. But these rare souls set opinion, success, and life, at so cheap a rate, that they will not soothe their enemies by petitions, or the show of sorrow, but wear their own habitual greatness.

It would perhaps be sufficiently difficult to discover, either in Plutarch or anywhere else, a personality to which all this is more applicable than to that of Charles XII.

Patterns of virtue, ideal characters of every sort, are in general a great bore, whether in literature or in history, and most often yield pride of place in the interest of the reader to the picturesquely vicious or to those equipped with a sense of humour. It is impossible to contemplate Galahad or the young Siegfried for any length of time without a certain wandering of the attention; Gunnar Hâmundsson of Hlidarendi, the ideal character in *Njala,* is the only person in it who threatens to become a shade tedious; Aristides the Just and Cato Uticensis induce a certain apprehensiveness in the reader; even a figure like Gustavus Adolphus would, with his superfluity of excellences, become slightly oppressive if he were not redeemed by his periodical outbursts of choler. But Charles XII never becomes uninteresting, despite all his virtues — possibly because they sit so easily and naturally upon him that he never gives the impression of being pompous or artificial, never turns actor or moralist, but is genuine through and through, a nature whose inner harmony appears something inevitable, a character which needs no external props, but is indissolubly compounded of strong and pure elements.

And to these considerations may be added, that certain rare virtues, when they occur in an extreme form — as bravery and truthfulness do in Charles XII — produce something of the same sensational interest which is otherwise mainly associated with human failings and extravagances.

Apart from those "errors" which can be invented as an explanation of his misfortunes — selfishness, defective knowledge of men, small interest in diplomacy, and so forth — the sides of his character which have most frequently provoked unfavourable judgments are perhaps his harshness and his indifference to human suffering. The editor of his letters, for instance, paints a dark picture of him in this respect, basing his judgment especially on material from his famous directives to his generals about the pacification of the Poles, but also on examples drawn from his relations to his own people — his jest about priests and apothecaries who die of camp-fever at Lais, his light tone when speaking of the winter in Ukraine, and so forth. When his dog Caesar dies, he calls it a great misfortune; but when a foraging party is annihilated by the Poles, he declares that it is no great matter if only the Swedes bore themselves bravely in the encounter and maintained their honour to the last. The editor of his letters speaks of the enervating influence of camp-life upon humanitarian instincts; and no doubt there is much in this. War produces a certain habituation to suffering and to death in battle, as peace produces a habituation to death in bed; we die, after all, equally often in both cases — once each, in fact — but with death in its peace-time forms we have become familiar, and therefore find it less shocking. There have been ages — the age of the Vikings, for instance — when war and all that belongs to it was considered to be the normal, while a peaceful death produced a bizarre and terrifying effect because of its infrequency. "Array me," said a certain paralytic old Earl Sigvard of Northumberland, "in the shirt of mail that I was wont to bear, and lead me down to the strand where first I waded from the ships; for as a cow on the straw I will not die." But in such a case as that of Charles XII there are of course other factors at work than the mere habituation to war as a way of life. On the one hand it should be borne in mind that wars can hardly be waged by one who is for ever lifting up his hands to heaven in horror and grief that disasters and violent deaths should from time to time occur: however keenly the professional soldier may in fact feel these things, it is plainly best — from what may be called the point of view of pure technique — to try to take the news of them with as little fuss as possible. And on the other hand it is also clear that a man such as Charles XII, who was always prepared to throw away his

own life as he would throw away a bad penny, cannot in his
military enterprises have been predisposed to show any great
anxiety or tenderness for the lives of others. Our modern humanitarian viewpoint is of course no great matter for boasting,
being in fact no lofty moral attitude, but merely an objectiv-
isation of the desire of every man to extend, at whatever cost,
his own span of life to its uttermost limit.

Had Charles XII ever formulated his philosophy on this
point, he could perhaps have used words similar to those which
Sarpedon addresses to Glaukos in the *Iliad*, when he goes to
his last battle:

> Could all our care elude the gloomy grave,
> Which claims no less the fearful and the brave,
> For lust of fame I should not vainly dare
> In fighting fields, nor urge thy soul to war.
> But since, alas! ignoble age must come,
> Disease, and death's inexorable doom;
> The life, which others pay, let us bestow,
> And give to fame what we to nature owe;
> Brave though we fall, and honour'd if we live,
> Or let us glory gain, or glory give!

Which, though it is perhaps not the highest conceivable
philosophy of life, is yet a good one of its kind, and one
which views existence rather as a matter of quality than of
quantity.

It is remarkable, that commanders of strong religious feeling
and puritanical temperament, such as Cromwell and Charles
XII, should have had the reputation of being particularly harsh
and exacting, to their own men no less than to the enemy. And
it appears, oddly enough, that hardly any other commanders
are loved by their soldiers with a love so wholly fanatical as
commanders of this sort, although they have always demanded
the uttermost of their troops, and permitted few liberties in
their service.

That Charles XII should stir us, should speak powerfully
to our imaginations, when on some long evening we sit quietly
at home and read books about him — this is not wonderful;
for in him is found almost everything that fascinates in history
— personality, grandeur, romantic glory, epic deeds, high tragedy
(nothing in history — save perhaps the Sicilian expedition in
Thucydides — can be compared with Pultava in this respect)
— tragedy not only episodic, but tragedy which provides the
dramatic architecture of a whole period; and all this is now
but a drama unrolled for us at our ease, a moving drama certainly, and one which touches us Swedes more nearly than do
some others, but still something which is now but a play:
drums and salvos have long since died into silence, the dead are
forgotten, the old trails covered over, the last tears are dried;
and we — we who read — have but to turn the pages. What
we can feel for him, for all its intensity, is only a feeling which
is ideal, lyrical, the feeling of a dream; for to us he is but a
vision, a myth; and we accept him, as he appears to us now,
as an inheritance from the past. Of us he asks nothing. But
what those men felt for him, who followed him over half
Europe, without knowing whither, those soldiers for whom he
was no dream but the very incarnation of Destiny — and a hard
Destiny for most of them — those men from whom he asked
everything — what *they* felt for him was something infinitely
greater. That is their honour, but it is no less his. He lopped
an ell from their life-thread, often and often; but he added
more than an ell to their spiritual stature. In his company
there was nothing to which they were not equal; without him
they were only what we are in general — reeds shaken by the
wind. And this they themselves well knew:

> None left, now he is gone, to care what may befall us;
> Our Craft avails no more; our Master-Craftsman's dead.

So wrote a Caroline, prisoner of war in Russia, on the news
that he had fallen. It did not occur to him to think of what he

himself had done and suffered for the King, of his nine years' captivity, or of the chances of approaching liberation; all such things were for the moment unimportant beside the thought of what the King had been to him.

Translated by Michael Roberts

*M*Y BLOCKHEAD of a son", "my good-for-nothing boy": in such terms was his mother, Lady Mornington, wont to speak of him in his earlier years; and though there were five sons to choose from, the Mornington family never laboured under any uncertainty as to which of them she was meaning. "Food for powder and nothing more," she added gloomily, when at the age of seventeen he embarked upon his military career. Napoleon, some years later, was in the habit of alluding to him as "the Sepoy General", with a little titter of contempt which he strove to make as convincing as possible; and the English Whigs had also no lack of injurious nicknames for him, even after he had a long roll of victories to his credit. His soldiers during the Peninsular campaigns called him (when they were in a good humour), "The Beau", because of his invariably spruce appearance and irreproachably smooth-shaven countenance. But when their humour was not so good, which probably happened pretty frequently, they called him "the long-nosed bugger" — a satisfactory epithet, from their point of view, for a general who habitually referred to his weather-beaten, marauding and (especially after an assault) highly undisciplined soldiery as "the scum of the earth, enlisted for drink".

In course of time all these nicknames were laid aside, and men called him simply, "The Duke". England had a fair selection of dukes, some royal, some not, but nobody ever made any mistake about which of them was intended. "The Duke" represented the abbreviation — the very considerable abbreviation — of the full style by which he was entitled to be addressed on ceremonial occasions, supposing all the formalities to be complied with. His list of titles and dignities, when at last it was complete, is probably the longest ever borne by a single individual, or at least by any non-royal personage: Philip Guedalla, in his biography *The Duke,* uses it as a kind of interminable litany in the chapter on his funeral; and Richard Aldington, his latest biographer, fills his title-page with a closely-printed selection. For Arthur Wellesley (or in its original form, Wesley: the surname was changed to the more elegant form on the initiative of his eldest brother, the eminent Viceroy of India) — Arthur Wesley, his mother's backward boy, after beginning life as the untitled son of a piano-tinkling (but otherwise unremarkable) Irish Viscount, bore at last these titles among others: Duke of Wellington, Marquis of Wellington, Earl of Wellington in Somerset, Viscount Wellington of Talavera, Baron Douro of Wellesley, in the Peerage of the United Kingdom; Prince of Waterloo, in the Netherlands, Duke of Ciudad Rodrigo, in Spain; Duke of Vittoria, Marquis of Torres Vedras, Count of Vimiero, in Portugal; Duke of Brunoy, in France; Field-Marshal and Commander-in-Chief of the British Army; Colonel of the Grenadier Guards; Field-Marshal in the Spanish, Portuguese, Dutch, Russian, Austrian and Prussian armies; Grandee of the First Class in Spain; Knight of the Garter, of the Order of the Holy Ghost, of the Order of the Golden Fleece (and of innumerable other orders besides); Lord High Constable of England; Constable of the Tower, Constable of Dover Castle; Lord Warden of the Cinque Ports (not to mention sundry other gilded trifles); and, last of all, as a little touch of the humanities to finish with, Chancellor of the University of Oxford.

All these pomps and glories had been fairly earned. Consider the roll of his victories: in India, Assaye and Argaum (1803); in Denmark, Kjöge (1807); then the long list in Portugal and Spain: Roliça and Vimiero (both against Junot) in 1808; Oporto (against Soult) and Talavera (against Victor) in 1809; Busaco (against Masséna) in 1810; Fuentes de Oñoro (against Masséna) and El Bodon (against Marmont) in 1811; the storming of Ciudad Rodrigo and Badajoz, in 1812; Salamanca (against Marmont) in 1812; Vittoria (against Jourdan) and the Pyrenees (against Soult) in 1813; then the campaign in the south of France: the storming of San Sebastian in 1813; the Bidassoa, the Nivelle and the Nive, in 1813; Orthez and Toulouse in 1814 (all these against Soult); and next year the finale, in the ancient arena of the god of battles, away up in the north: Quatre Bras (against Ney) and Waterloo (against Napoleon). And this list of his victories (from which many of the less important are omitted) is identical with the list of his battles; for he is one of the very few commanders who never lost an engagement. There was only one occasion on which he was forced to admit a failure; and that was at the siege of Burgos (1812), which he was compelled to abandon for lack of heavy artillery. When in his old age he was asked how many guns he had captured, all told, in the course of his military career, he answered that he did not know exactly, but supposed it must be about three thousand (the correct figure seems really to have been far higher); but added, as a curious circumstance, that he himself had never lost a single one. There had indeed been one occasion, near Madrid, when three guns had fallen into the hands of the enemy after a surprise attack; but they had been recaptured the next day; and a battery which General Hill had been forced to heave over a precipice during the battle of the Pyrenees, in order to prevent its capture, had later been recovered.

It is not surprising that he never achieved real popularity in French military circles, and least of all with Napoleon and his Marshals: he had thrashed them too soundly for them to be able to endure his presence, or tolerate the mention of his name. From St Helena Napoleon in his will bequeathed a sum of money to an obscure individual who after the Restoration had discharged a pistol at Wellington in a Paris street: the deed was worth a *douceur*, he considered, even though the fellow missed. At one of Louis XVIII's levees all the Marshals who were present turned their backs on Wellington when he entered the room; the King mumbled some sort of excuse, but Wellington blandly assured him that it was a spectacle with which he was not unfamiliar: he had more than once, in the course of his campaigns, had the pleasure of viewing these same Marshals from the rear.

What more than anything else made Wellington's victories intolerably irritating to the Emperor and his men was perhaps the fact that it would never have occurred to anybody, whether English or French, to regard him as endowed with any very brilliant abilities. The Emperor, as all agreed, was a genius, — he was even the greatest military genius of modern times; and among those of his Marshals with whom Wellington had to deal, Masséna at all events (for all the defects of his character) could be considered to possess discernible streaks of genius too — not to mention Marmont and Soult, at least in their own opinion. Yet these, and others, and at last the Emperor himself, had all been laid low in the most lamentable fashion by this prosaic Englishman, who in his spare time on campaign hunted the fox like a simple country gentleman, who never dazzled anybody in his life, never rose to a brilliant proclamation, and possibly hardly knew what genius was. How was it possible? Neither strategic inspiration, nor *élan*, nor shouts of *Vive l'Empereur*, nor victory-laurelled eagles, nor terrifying assaulting columns, nor (to make an end) even the united irresistibility of Drouot's artillery, Milhaud's cuirassiers, and the bayonets of the Old Guard, had been able to make much of this man and his "scum of the earth". The thing was inexplicable: every thinking French soldier, memoir-writer and military historian, from the Emperor downwards, was liable to grow half frantic with exasperation and intellectual frustration when confronted with this inescapable and utterly ridiculous fact. Above all it was clear that the Emperor's own catastrophe at Waterloo must have depended on some other factor, on something accidental and ineluctable, on some incredible ill-fortune, on any and every sort of triviality subsequently raked up by desperate researchers: on rain which delayed the advance; on the fact that Soult lacked Berthier's training as Chief of Staff; on words of command misunderstood; on the Emperor's bladder-trouble; on Ney's nerves; on Grouchy's idiocy; and finally, (God help us all!) on the Prussians. The one thing which could not possibly have had anything to do with it was Wellington; and from that obvious starting-point all analysis of the riddle began its investigations.

Now it may possibly be the case that Wellington lacked what is usually understood by genius: he would himself probably have brusquely repulsed any attempt to encumber him with a quality so little suited to a gentleman. But there was one other essential quality which he possessed in fullest measure, and which never deserted him: the quality of common-sense. Not, perhaps, a very impressive asset, at first sight; indeed, an attribute which may reasonably be looked for, in greater or lesser degree, in every ordinary man. But as a rule the individual allocation of this useful characteristic tends to be infinitely less than its possessor believes it to be. When our tempers are cool and our personal interests are not engaged — when, for instance, we are pronouncing judgment on our fellow-men and their actions — we have all of us sovereign command of our common-sense; but on other occasions, when our ego is involved, or in personal crises, or when faced with the unexpected, or in situations where our instinctive selfishness asserts itself or our personal vanity is endangered — then our common-sense is very apt to cease to function, and the resulting activity is related to very different norms; — a phenomenon which, though we may have difficulty in detecting it in ourselves, we are daily in a position to study on a large and legible scale in our politicians and social reformers, as they elbow their way forward under every conceivable and inconceivable banner, save that of common-sense.

As against the secular genius Napoleon, Wellington was superior in this article of common-sense, and grew ever more markedly so with the passing of the years; and in the end it was this superiority which was decisive. They were born in the same year, and anyone who had encountered them as young men might easily have mistaken where their dominant inclinations were to lie; for while young Bonaparte shone at mathematics and geometry, young Wesley played the violin, until one fine day he put his instrument into the fire, that he might address himself with a proper seriousness to the humdrum side of life. His first known action as an officer is to have put on the scales first a private of infantry in uniform, and then the same man with the addition of musket, ammunition, greatcoat and full equipment; after which he made a note of the difference in weight. And when his fellow-officers expressed their surprise at this rash act, (not provided for in the drill-book), he answered that since he had started on a profession he had better try to understand it. It is the first significant gleam of Wellingtonian common-sense: there was something to be said for knowing what the infantry private had to carry, before arranging forced marches for him, and cursing him afterwards for being tired.

At the time when Bonaparte was already in command of an army, and was embarking on his brilliant Italian campaigns, Colonel Wesley (he had contrived to scrape together sufficient capital to buy his advancement to that rank) had just served his first apprenticeship to the military art in the Netherlands, in the course of an extraordinarily grievous campaign conducted by the Duke of York in his own exalted person. This was the Good Old Duke of York of the well-known song, one of George III's many disappointing sons. The Duke, who had the talents of a lead soldier and the obstinacy of a mule, and for many years discharged the duties of Commander-in-Chief of the land forces of Great Britain (ably assisted by his enterprising mistress, Mrs. Clarke), succeeded in destroying, rapidly and almost totally, the Netherlands Expeditionary Force, by a process of starvation and pointless marches. But despite this fact there was one item to be placed on the credit side, even of a campaign such as this: Wellington later said that he had here learnt many valuable lessons on "how not to do it". It sounds simple enough; but if we assume that young officers in general have throughout the ages learnt this much by serving under inefficient generals, then world-history ought in time to have shown a crowded galaxy of brilliant commanders — which can hardly be said to be the case. On the other hand it is possibly true that Frederick Augustus, Duke of York, was a more versatile and intelligible exponent of this indirect method of instruction than the great majority.

Wellington was to learn a thing or two from this instructor in after-years also; but for the moment, content with the lessons already acquired, he went to India, and devoted himself to arduous campaigning in that country; became a Major-General; and for some years practised himself in handling small forces in expeditions against fierce Mahratta chieftains. From the beginning he showed himself indefatigable in keeping his troops supplied with provisions and clothes, and in arranging for a proper care of the wounded; but he showed himself also not less concerned to maintain strict discipline. The disorder and looting which followed a storm was always a problem that vexed him, and it could on occasion drive him to outbreaks of cold fury: his remedy for such things was the lash or the gallows; there was no other practical method, he considered, yet the effect was never quite as satisfactory as it ought to have been. He had great difficulty in giving a patient hearing to humane persons who in his later years ventured to contend that soldiers might possibly be restrained from looting and rape by an appeal to their better nature: he considered that he knew his soldiers, and he had never observed that they had a better nature, except in the firing-line. All of which did not prevent him from maintaining no less positively that

British infantry, provided it were kept firmly in hand, was in a class by itself: "There is nothing like it," he said, "in the shape of infantry."

At that time the English in India, both civil and military, seem to have aimed at a short life but a merry one, seasoned by extremely high feeding; but Major-General Wellesley (as the name now began to be spelt) was in this matter also a man of common-sense. His drinking habits at Seringapatam were so spartan that a fellow-officer noted them down: "only four to five glasses at dinner, with a half-pint of port to follow." The result of this moderation was that he easily stood up to the tropical campaigns, and could return to England in 1805 in unimpaired vigour. He was now promoted Lieutenant-General; and might begin to ponder on the phenomenon of Napoleon, and his apparently unstoppable career. William Pitt, now very near his end — partly, perhaps, because he had never been able to bring himself to be content with half a bottle after meals — nevertheless lived long enough to make his acquaintance; and the sorely-tried Prime Minister, who for the most part had had to make do with military men of the Duke of York's type, expressed great surprise at a general such as this:

Sir Arthur Wellesley is unlike all other military men with whom I have conversed. He never makes a difficulty or hides his ignorance in vague generalities. If I put a question to him, he answers it distinctly; if I want an explanation, he gives it clearly; if I desire an opinion, I get from him one supported by reasons that are always sound. He is a very remarkable man.

Pitt judged quite rightly: he was in truth a remarkable man; among other reasons because common-sense such as his, when intimately associated with a fundamental integrity, and firmly rooted in the character, is a very remarkable quality.

Meanwhile that more dazzling celebrity Napoleon had contrived to learn a number of dangerous things: for instance, that for him everything came off, since he was so infinitely more talented than anybody else; that his boundless ambition had boundless limits within which to unfold itself; that in his case it was even possible to desert one's army when it had got stuck in a blind alley in Egypt, without any other consequence than becoming First Consul and master of France. At thirty-five he allowed himself to be made Emperor, and with that his common-sense sustained a blow which led to its progressive enfeeblement. The incense-clouds of self-deification began to be perceptible; the Imperial personality and its Olympian volitions came more and more to take the place of outward reality; the murder of the Duc d'Enghien marks the first collapse of his judgment; the habit of embracing vanquished Emperors on German bridges was not among the psychologically more healthy amusements; and after the Austrian marriage his eclipse is such that common-sense may be said henceforward to be absent from his handling of the great political and military problems. He could still win battles, with a sort of automatic virtuosity, but he was no longer able to make his actions accord with what was expedient.

Lord Acton, most learned, and perhaps also most profound of modern historians, in his day formulated a famous aphorism: "Power corrupts, and absolute power corrupts absolutely." It is a sentence as near true as an aphorism about humanity well can be, although it would be possible to point to cases where the converse might appear to be more correct: young Octavianus was a singularly repulsive rascal, but as Augustus he proved to be relatively innocuous. But the megalomania of Caesarism is undoubtedly no very unusual disease, and Napoleon remains one of the most impressive examples of it. In his manner of handling the Spanish business, for instance, it is difficult to discover any spark of his original talent. If we imagine that the young Bonaparte of 1796 had received the command in Italy only on condition that decisions about operations should be taken in Paris in every individual case that arose in the course of the campaign, on the basis of reports sent home from the front, and should be communicated to him by letter, then the still-unclouded Napoleonic intelligence would not have needed many minutes to demonstrate the crying absurdity of such an arrangement. Yet he himself attempted from 1809 onwards to direct his armies in Spain in this manner, by means of a correspondence which took three weeks in each direction between Spain and Paris. For a moment in 1810 he toyed with the idea of going to Spain himself, in order to bring some order into the ever wilder chaos there, but in the end he abstained, and contented himself with sending Masséna instead; and with the fatuous complacency of some half-idiot Habsburg or Bourbon he let it be understood that the reason for his abstention was that he and his newly-won Empress must first secure the succession to the throne. Almost as if a man should refuse to put out a fire in his front hall on the ground that he was busy with arranging the seating for a dinner-party that evening.

Despite all such symptoms of decline, Napoleon, with his terrible dynamic energy and his "income of 100 000 men", of course remained to the last an extremely dangerous man to have to do with; and Wellington always retained a healthy respect for him and his armies. After the final victory over Masséna at Fuentes de Oñoro he coolly observed: "If Boney had been here to-day we should have been beat"; and the worst he could say of the Emperor was that "the fellow is no gentleman". This, no doubt, was a very heavy indictment from Wellington's point of view — it seems to have been provoked partly by the stupendous mendacity of all the Imperial Bulletins whose accuracy Wellington was in a position to control — but for the rest it would be difficult to find in his writings any depreciatory judgments on Napoleon. But to the end Napoleon did not cease to express contempt of the "Sepoy General". Immediately before the opening of the battle of Waterloo he snubbed Soult, who had many memories of engagements with Wellington and his men: "You say that Wellington is a good general because he gave you a thrashing. But I tell you that he is a bad general and the English are bad soldiers. This will be a half-day match *(une affaire à déjeuner)*." It would have been wiser to defer this pronouncement — which indeed shows traces of a certain nervousness — for in this instance reality declined to conform to the Imperial dictate.

Even during the period of his service in India Wellington had begun to reflect upon the special French battle-tactics which had been developed in the armies of the Revolution and retained by Napoleon. The old linear tactics were impracticable for the revolutionary generals, who had to deal with untrained men, and instead they began to form battalions into attacking columns on a front of about fifty men and ten to twelve men deep. Protected by a thick cloud of skirmishers, who were to engage the attention of the enemy's infantry, these columns were calculated to reach the enemy's positions more or less intact, after which a short rush with the bayonet would permit them to break through his line. Against Austrians and so forth this system celebrated very great triumphs; but Wellington for his part very early came to the conclusion that when matched against steady infantry in line, with good fire-discipline, and with light-armed troops to send forward in good time against the enemy's skirmishers, the system must probably break down, especially since an English battalion in line (only two deep) could fire all its muskets at once — that is, five to six times as many as a French battalion-column, where only the two leading ranks could fire.

He had frequent opportunities to test this simple and lucid reasoning, and it proved in fact to be perfectly sound; for in the matter of steadiness on the battlefield his "scum" proved satisfactory from the beginning. The French infantry never succeeded in making an irreparable breach in the Wellingtonian line in any major engagement; neither did their cavalry ever break an English battalion which had had time to form square. In especially severe battles such as Talavera and Waterloo, battalions could stand losses of up to sixty per cent. of their strength without being shaken; and at the battle of Albuera, fought by his second-in-command General Beresford — in respect of percentage of casualties the most murderous battle ever fought between Englishmen and Frenchmen — when the action terminated one whole brigade (it was Hoghton's, and included the regiment named the Die-Hards) practically lay where it had stood, as the result of a half-hour's musket-duel at close range between 1 900 English in two ranks and 8 000 Frenchmen in twelve.

How it felt for even the bravest Frenchman to advance against Wellington's infantry was admirably described by one of them in his old age. This was Bugeaud, who ended his career as a Marshal of France under Louis-Philippe. In his younger days, when he was still a Lieutenant-Colonel, he had been through the Spanish campaign from beginning to end, and could therefore speak with some knowledge of the subject:

The Englishmen stood as a rule in good defensive positions, carefully chosen and usually on the crest of a hill, on the reverse slope of which a good part of their forces were held concealed. The usual cannonade took place on both sides; after which, in haste and without proper reconnaissance, without even investigating the possibility of an enveloping movement, we set off straight ahead to take the bull by the horns.

When we had got to within about 1,000 metres from the English position, our men usually began to show signs of uneasiness. They exchanged comments, increased their speed, and began to lose formation. The Englishmen, silent and motionless, with their arms ordered, stood meanwhile like a long red wall; the sight was imposing, and made a strong impression on recruits. The distance now quickly diminished; cries of "Vive l'Empereur!" "En avant à la baionnette!" broke from the ranks. Some put their shakos on their muskets, and began to break into a double; the ranks became intermingled, the excitement of the men increased; many began to shoot while they ran. And the English line, silent and motionless, even when we were within 300 metres, continued apparently to take not the least notice of the approaching storm.

The contrast was great. More than one of us began to reflect that the enemy's fire, so long withheld, would be extremely unpleasant when it came. Our enthusiasm began to cool: the moral effect of a calm which appeared unshakable, as against a disorderly rush which seemed to try to disguise its lack of steadiness by noise and shouting, depressed the spirits of all.

At this moment of painful expectation the Englishmen made a quarter-turn, and the muskets came up to the "ready". A nameless feeling paralysed many of our men, who halted and opened an uncertain fire. The enemy's answer — a salvo of split-second precision and deadly effect — fell upon us like a thunderbolt. Decimated by it, we closed our ranks; reeling under the blow, we sought to regain our equilibrium. But now the long silence of our adversaries was broken with three terrific "hurrah's!" and at the third they were on us and drove us back in disorderly retreat. But to our astonishment they pressed their advantage for no more than a few hundred metres; after which they calmly returned to their original position, to await the next attack. After reinforcements had been brought forward, we seldom failed to deliver one — with equally small success, and still heavier losses.

The sort of battle described above, which in many ways is reminiscent of the great English defensive victories at Crécy and Poitiers, Agincourt and Verneuil, during the Hundred Years' War, was admirably suited to Wellington. Among his victories, Roliça, Vimiero, Talavera, Busaco, Fuentes de Oñoro and Waterloo, are all of this type. Relying upon the weaknesses of the French column-tactics, and upon the endurance and superior fire-power of his own infantry, he always awaited actions of this kind with the greatest equanimity, and the result was always the same. The losses of the French in such battles were heavy, their morale was gradually undermined, their prestige in Europe suffered sensible damage. On the other hand Wellington never distinguished himself as a particularly effective pursuer after a victory of this nature; he was first and foremost an infantry general; his cavalry he tended to view with a certain distrust, and he was not anxious to give free rein to its initiative. This may in part have been the result of his lack of outstanding cavalry commanders; the best that England had, Paget, had eloped with the wife of Wellington's brother Henry — an event which was among the leading scandals of one London Season, and produced a certain coolness between the Wellesley and Paget families — and consequently it was some time before he could serve under Wellington's command. However, just before Waterloo the Prince Regent and the Duke of York, neither of whom was hampered by any excessive delicacy, at last sent out Paget (by this time ennobled as Lord Uxbridge) to command the cavalry and act as Wellington's second-in-command. Someone on Wellington's staff commented on the unsuitability of the appointment, in view of the old story of the elopement: "Never mind," said Wellington, "I will take damned good care he does not run away with me." Lord Uxbridge bore himself with credit at Waterloo, and subsequently attended the solemn interment on the battlefield of one of his legs, which a cannon-ball had carried off just before the close of the action.

Wellington's cautious strategy and mainly defensive tactics during the first four years in the Peninsula proceeded, at least in part, from his military position, which at this time appeared almost hopeless. With an army of at most 30 000 British troops (even less, at first) he had to hold Portugal, or portions of it, against the inexhaustible masses of Napoleon, who on occasion had as many as 350 000 men in Spain. The Whig party distinguished itself by the bitterness of its mockery of the whole enterprise; if any misfortune had overtaken him in the field the Ministry would have fallen, or at any rate the whole venture would have been abandoned. But Napoleon and the Whigs were by no means his only enemies: there was also the Duke of York, Commander-in-Chief of the British Army, and an uncounted number of inefficient Spanish generals, who impeded, with the haughty imbecility of Old Castile, any attempt at rational collaboration.

When in 1808 Castlereagh, the Foreign Secretary of the

moment (a great man, despite the appalling denunciations of
Byron and Shelley) hit upon the brilliant idea of sending an
Expeditionary Force to Portugal under the command of Wellesley — at that time a man of thirty-nine — the Duke of York
(among others) was seized with the direst apprehensions. In
the first place he considered that he ought to have been given
the command of the expedition himself; in the second, that a
youngster such as Wellesley could not possibly be equal to so
arduous an undertaking. By great good fortune it was however possible for a Commander-in-Chief to adjust matters on
a satisfactory basis; and two old Guardsmen, friends of the
Duke — Sir Hew Dalrymple and Sir Harry Burrard — both
of "tried incapacity", were fished out from their respective
corners and sent off as soon as might be to take over the com-
mand-in-chief, and the post of second-in-command, respec-
tively, thus reducing Wellesley to third place. From the point
of view of the Duke of York this arrangement seemed to offer
adequate security; but unforeseen circumstances caused the
dislocation of his plan. In the first place Wellesley obtained
a victory all on his own in the smart affair of Roliça; and since
Burrard, despite the fact that he had arrived in harbour, found
it expedient to stay aboard his ship for an extra day, Wellesley
won another and bigger victory against Junot's massed assault,
at Vimiero. Stimulated by the sight of an action in progress,
Burrard had himself put ashore, and did indeed, with great
presence of mind, succeed in preventing any attempt to follow up the victory; but it was unfortunately idle to deny that
the expedition had up to that point been conducted in ex-
emplary fashion without the assistance of the Duke of York's
commanders. Dalrymple now landed, cast a searching eye
on the situation, comprehended little or nothing of what he
saw there, and — since the beaten Junot sent over a flag of
truce — concluded first an armistice and then the notorious
"Convention of Cintra", whereby he politely undertook to
transport Junot's army (which had capitulated) by sea to France

— whence a wrathful Emperor straightway marched it off again
to the Pyrenees. Probably Dalrymple considered that by this
Convention he had assured his military reputation in the eyes
of contemporaries and of posterity; but this delusion was shattered by angry clamour for the heads of incapable commanders
from the public at home, which would have preferred to see
Junot's army in English custody until further notice; and Dalrymple, Burrard, and Wellesley were ordered home to appear
before a court-martial.

A court of the most aged generals the Duke of York could
collect sat in judgment on the affair, and all the accused were
acquitted. It was clearly impossible to condemn Wellesley,
since two splendid victories could hardly be accounted crimes,
and thereafter he had been in a subordinate position; but since
he must go free, the court found it logically absurd to condemn two officers who were older, and by approved military
standards also wiser. On Burrard's behalf it was pleaded in
mitigation that he had a large family, who would suffer if he
lost his pay and pension; and Dalrymple was found to have
acted to the best of his understanding — not, perhaps, a very
unreasonable verdict. But not all the Duke of York's influence
could send his two whitewashed friends into the field again
to keep an eye on Wellesley. Henceforward he had to content himself with harrassing that commander by means of
numerous unsuitable appointments to the less exalted ranks in
his army — up to the rank of Quartermaster-General or General of Division, for instance; — a form of entertainment to
which he was still addicted during the campaign of Waterloo,
in spite of ever sharper protests from Wellington. The conviction, which Wellington obstinately retained to the very last,
that practically all his officers, higher as well as lower, were
capable of every imaginable military blunder as soon as he
took his eye off them, was certainly less the result of an egocentric kink in him, than of his nerve-shattering experiences
with the many Incapacities foisted on him by the Duke of

York on grounds of seniority or for more personal reasons. The years 1810 and 1811 in this respect constituted a temporary alleviation from Wellington's point of view, since during this period the Duke of York was emancipated from his labours as Commander-in-Chief, in consequence of the revelation that he had permitted Mrs. Clarke to arrange the promotion of various officers on her own account.

The efforts of Napoleon and the Duke of York were certainly not to be despised; but in the long run the Spanish generals were if possible a greater trial than either. After Sir John Moore's unfortunate campaign came to an end at Corunna, where Moore himself fell; after Wellington had been once more sent to Portugal — now with a rather larger force — and had swiftly fallen upon Soult at Oporto, driven him out of Portugal and taken all his guns (a misadventure which forced the wily Duke of Dalmatia to renounce his dream of being promoted King Nicholas of Oporto) — came, in the summer of 1809, the first push into Spain. The invasion culminated in the great battle of Talavera de la Reyna, which was fought out with the greatest obstinacy on both sides. One of its consequences was that Sir Arthur Wellesley was transformed into Viscount Wellington of Talavera. There fought here on the British side a regular Spanish army, led by a certain Gregorio de la Cuesta, who bore the exalted rank of Captain-General of Old Castile. This Cuesta, with whom Wellington was thus doomed to collaborate, and who can be taken as a specimen of the Spanish generals of his time, was an aged paralytic, who was in the habit of being lifted into his saddle by two grenadiers and an adjutant (the latter with the special duty of correctly adjusting the Captain-General's right foot), after which he would show himself to his men "supported by two pages". Thus far, it is true, this Cuesta produces a somewhat tame and inoffensive impression, but the surviving wreckage of his mental processes was in reality neither tame nor inoffensive. On the contrary, having been commanded to collaborate with Wellington, he developed a most alarming activity, directed less against the enemy than against his ally, in the face of whom it was essential to uphold the ancient glory of Spain and the incomparable dignity of a Spanish Captain-General with sacramental care. His arrogance, in short, was as great as his military incapacity, and in respect of the latter he is rated by Sir Charles Oman (author of that superb work *A History of the Peninsular War*, in seven fat volumes) as the worst of all contemporary Spanish generals, which is indeed no small distinction. His military record as an independant commander amounted to the two crushing defeats of Cabezon and Medina de Rio Seco; but this did not prevent him from invariably trying to treat Wellington as a person of little consequence.

Cuesta and his army were now encamped before Talavera on the wrong side of the river Tagus, in a position where he could easily be surprised by the French: during the usual Spanish afternoon-nap, in particular — and this was an institution which was not to be interfered with — such a thing was always liable to happen, if no natural obstacles intervened. Cuesta took this sort of risk with much phlegm, since he rarely had any clear idea of where the enemy was; Wellington, on the other hand, was more apprehensive, and personally repaired to Cuesta's quarters, where he endeavoured by every means in his power to induce him to put himself in safety on the other side of the river, without a moment's delay. Cuesta declared at last that he was prepared to accede to this request, but only if Wellington, in recognition of Cuesta's position as the exalted representative of the King of Spain, repeated it on his knees. It was a situation in which Wellington had need of all his common-sense (and also of his sense of humour): without wasting any time in consideration, he came to the conclusion that Cuesta's army was worth more than a personal punctilio, and according to his biographer Gleig, he made no secret in after-years of the fact that he really did fall on his knees before the old imbecile. The Spanish army was thereby saved in time, and thereafter did its share when Marshal Victor launched his great attack. For some units, at least, its share did not amount to much. On the evening before the battle one of Cuesta's infantry divisions, which had heard some crackling in the undergrowth, let off a crashing volley, though there was in reality no enemy anywhere near them, and thereupon took to their heels, to the number of six battalions — "frighted by their own fire", as Wellington remarked in his report on the battle.

In the great crisis after the victory at Talavera Cuesta at first took no great part: inspirited by the victory, which he possibly considered to be his own work, he contented himself with pressing for more battles without delay, though the quality of his troops was already sufficiently obvious; and on one occasion really seems, by the prompt transmission of a captured French despatch, to have been of positive service to Wellington. But he was soon back to his usual form. The situation now was, that a combination of not less than three French Marshals — Soult, Mortier, and Ney — who for the moment found it expedient to cooperate, forced Wellington to retire to Portugal to avoid being starved out or surrounded. Cuesta lay in Talavera, and was entrusted with the evacuation of 4 000 British wounded along roads which were still open. It is conceivable that it was impossible to carry out this duty in full, for the transport resources of a Spanish army were seldom extensive; but however that may be he provided for this purpose a total of seven waggons and a handful of mules, and thereupon decamped with his army. After which the roads and tracks leading south-west from Talavera saw crowds of Wellington's wounded officers and men, bandaged, bloody and emaciated — all who could by any means use their legs (or leg) — hopping, lurching and tottering in the direction of the Portuguese frontier, where presently, by incomprehensible exertions, some 2 000 of them arrived.

There was one occasion later when the Spanish soldiers resorted to a faintly Biblical procedure against one of their generals by the name of Carlos de España: they tied a millstone about his neck and cast him in the River Segre. Cuesta escaped this fate, though he may be said to have done his utmost to deserve it. After causing the maximum of confusion and misery for a little while longer, his military activities were brought to a close by a satisfactorily severe stroke of apoplexy, and he retired to a watering-place, consoled by the testimonies of his government's gratitude, and there solaced his remaining years by the composition of a narrative of his services to the cause.

After his experiences with Cuesta, Wellington announced firmly that he intended never to collaborate with a Spanish general again. But he was not to escape so easily: Cuesta was only the first of many; and personages by the name of Venegas, Eguia, Areizaga, La Pena, Ballasteros (and several others) proved to be mainly of the same kidney as Cuesta. Among them all there was only one, La Romana, whom Wellington considered a tractable, honest, and reliable individual: other Spanish army-commanders seldom even made an attempt to keep their word, to aid a colleague, to manoeuvre rationally, or to provide their soldiers with something in the way of provisions. Hence when in 1812 Wellington was made supreme commander of all the Spanish armies the appointment was one which promised him little satisfaction. In the autumn of that year he could declare, in an access of intelligible ill-humour: "I have never yet known the Spaniards to do *anything,* much less do anything *well."* Spain's heroes in this war are to be sought elsewhere than among the generals in the field; they are to be found among the obstinate defenders of fortresses — Palafox in Saragossa, Alvarez in Gerona, and others besides; and among guerilla leaders — the two Minas, El Empecinado, El Pastor, El Medico (Dr. Juan Palarea), Baron Eroles, Julian Sanchez, Longa, Porlier and others — indefatigable men, who proved of far greater use than the generals, partly through their incessant blows against transports and isolated detachments, partly because they always kept large French forces busy on a vain hunt for them and their bands of fleet-footed mountaineers.

Constant maltreatment, constant hunger, and on top of it all the inexhaustible store of generals full of wooden-headed conceit, made it impossible for the Spanish soldiers, apart from a few exceptional occasions, to show what they could do. The Portuguese were more fortunate. Their original comic-opera army, excessively shaggy and moth-eaten, and in certain respects having a purely nominal existence (though fortified by the fact that for the last two centuries St Anthony of Padua had been entered on the muster rolls with the rank and pay of a sergeant) allowed itself in course of time to be transformed into a tolerable instrument, and was employed with effect on many a battle-field. First, and most important, Portuguese generals of the more hopeless variety could usually be soothed with courtesies and put out to grass as fortress-commanders somewhere in the background. Further, the Portuguese government came to understand — not, indeed, without some difficulty — that soldiers are improved by being drilled and given usable weapons, to say nothing of a little pay occasionally, and uniforms, shoes and food. These things Wellington took upon himself to provide them with, by means of certain financial operations, of which the subtle point was that the money should not find its way into the pockets of the Portuguese politicians. In return the soldiers were to fight under his command, and be incorporated into his army, with a few English officers to every Portuguese company. This system proved to work admirably; and when in the spring of 1813 Wellington launched his most spectacular operation — the great strategic march from north Portugal to Vittoria and the Pyrenees — his infantry was made up of 56 British and 53 Portuguese battalions. As he sat in Brussels in the spring of 1815, cursing the "infamous army" (as he called it), weak in numbers and scraped together in haste from all quarters, with which he was compelled to meet Napoleon, he tried to induce the government in Lisbon to lend him 12 000 men of his old Portuguese infantry. The attempt failed; but it shows how high a value he set upon these troops.

By his Portuguese Wellington was much beloved. It must probably have seemed very strange to them to march under a general who not only constantly led them to victory, but also did not require that they should starve to death; and when an action was in progress, as soon as he rode within sight of his Portuguese units, they always greeted him with a roar of *Douro! Douro!* For after Talavera he was in fact Baron Douro, because of his initial victory over Soult on the banks of that river, and his Portuguese clung to this, his first title, since it was taken from their own country. The uniform they wore while under his command — hessians, white trousers, blue coat — also included a high shako with a plume, which to judge from contemporary pictures must have increased the stature of the Portuguese foot-soldier by a good eighteen inches, and presumably increased his martial self-confidence in like measure. But to their great comfort in the long run — and to that of the English troops also — Wellington was never a stickler for the *minutiae* of dress. He could at times show great severity, but a button undone or a belt inadequately polished were never among the things to which he paid much attention. Here too his common-sense functioned unerringly: in his army there was but one standing order concerning dress, and that was a prohibition to appear in the uniform of the enemy. One of his colonels, by the name of Grattan, bears witness in his Memoirs to the great latitude enjoyed by officers in this matter:

Provided that we brought our men into the field properly equipped and with 60 rounds in their pouches, he never troubled to notice whether our trousers were black or grey or blue. There were scarce two officers dressed alike. Some wore grey coats with braid, others preferred blue; others by necessity or choice stuck to the old red. We were never harassed by the most tedious feature of service in the field — the compulsion to be dressed alike.

One of his oddest subordinates, Sir Thomas Picton, famous for his fighting spirit and his inimitably lurid oaths, led his troops, both at Vittoria and Quatre Bras, clad in a civilian frock-coat, with a top-hat of the voluminous and broad-rimmed type then in fashion, and was seen on one occasion in the Pyrenees waving a rolled-up umbrella, instead of a sabre, as the signal for attack.

In Gronow's Memoirs a single instance is recorded in which Wellington took action against umbrellas. It was outside Bayonne, and a newly-arrived Guards battalion had been sent forward to a half-finished redoubt. Wellington came riding by, to be confronted with the spectacle of a number of lieutenants of the Guards who were wandering up and down on the parapet of the redoubt *en grande tenue,* exposed to scattered fire from the enemy, and carrying enormous umbrellas, which they had opened in order to protect their bearskins and other finery from the drizzle. He at once sent an adjutant with an order that the umbrellas were to be discarded; pointing out that though they might if they pleased amuse themselves in this fashion while on guard at home in London, in the field the thing was not only ludicrous but unmilitary.

The severest test of endurance for Wellington and his men came in the autumn of 1810, when Masséna made his appearance on the Portuguese frontier with three army-corps, under Junot, Reynier and Ney, and totalling in all some 70 000 men. After some eight months of testing defensive warfare the issue was at last decided, and Masséna's retreat an accomplished fact. The responsibility for this result could not be laid at Masséna's door. When in after-years Wellington was asked which was the best of the French Marshals he had encountered, he unhesitatingly named Masséna: "He was always where I least wished to see him, and I could never permit myself such liberties against him as against the others." The failure of the French offensive in Portugal, despite Masséna's talents, was the result of Wellington's and Napoleon's totally different solutions of what was in some respects a mathematical problem. Wellington, who had foreseen in good time what was coming, had informed the English government that he believed he could hold Lisbon and its neighbourhood against a French invading army of up to 100 000 men, provided he had 30 000 British troops — together, of course, with his Portuguese forces. He was able to give this undertaking because of the quality of his troops and the extraordinary advantages afforded to a defending force by the Torres Vedras lines outside Lisbon, which he had reinforced in advance with the greatest care.

Napoleon on his side was firmly determined to "drive the Leopards into the sea", as he expressed it. He knew to a man how strong Wellington's British army was, for he kept himself always well-informed on this point through diligent study of the English press, which — in contrast to Imperial publications — was distinguished, on the whole, for the veracity of its information. Against 30 000 Englishmen, he considered, 70 000 men under Masséna ought to be adequate in all circumstances; indeed, more than adequate. There was one factor in the situation, however, which he did not take into account, namely the Portuguese; for at the period when he first took an interest in their country they had been a useless rabble in the field; and in that world of wishful thinking which he now preferred to inhabit, where reality had to conform to Imperial fantasies, they remained what they once had been.

As a result of this major error in his calculations, Masséna was doomed from the start: against Torres Vedras and Wellington he really needed an additional one or two army-corps. But even if he had had them, the problem would not automatically have been solved; for the larger the army, the greater the difficulty of supplies, and in the end he was not able to maintain even the 70 000 men he had with him. Napoleon's system was always to finish a campaign swiftly, and in the meanwhile leave the troops to live on the resources of the theatre of war. Already in Poland and East Prussia in 1807 this system had been very near to breaking down; and now, here in Portugal, came its first collapse, to be followed shortly by the Russian catastrophe. The hatred of the Portuguese for the French was no whit less than that of the Spaniards; and Wellington induced them to acquiesce in the evacuation and devastation of the countryside on the lines of Masséna's advance. The soldiers of Napoleon had, indeed, the great gift (improved by long practice) of making do with anything; but at last the task of victualling in a depopulated wilderness became an impossibility even for them, though Masséna, who saw his great reputation as a commander threatened with eclipse, defied starvation and held on with grim obstinacy to his positions before Wellington's lines for some weeks longer than Wellington had considered possible.

Masséna, who had once been honoured by the Emperor with the name of *l'enfant gâté de la victoire* (and of whom it was alleged by his detractors that he was of the seed of Abraham, and his real name Manasseh) is not a person who readily evokes sympathy: egocentric, intriguing, with no idea of honour, profoundly mendacious, a miser and despoiler of the grossest sort. Yet on this, his last campaign, one is almost constrained to feel sorry for him. Napoleon had set him an impossible task; and had in addition provided a collection of subordinates of whom Ney, wounded at being put under Masséna's command, was even more factious than usual, Junot already far advanced towards the complete insanity which broke out a year later, Reynier a mere nonentity, and only Montbrun, the cavalry commander, of high quality. Communications with France were sometimes entirely severed by Spanish guerillas and Portuguese militia; couriers to the Emperor had to be sent off with an escort of 200 horse. Hunger and misery were soon prevalent in the army, and at Headquarters were constant squabbles and sulks — the result, among other things, of problems of precedence concerning the mistress whom Masséna had brought with him. Masséna himself was growing old, and had lost some of his former dash; especially since that day, some years earlier, when at an Imperial partridge-shoot he had received at the hands of Napoleon himself (ever an incalculable shot) a charge of small-shot in one of his eyes. But despite all this and much besides, he showed himself a dangerous adversary to the last. With 20 000 men out of action from hunger and disease, he finally started on his retreat, slowly and with incessant fighting, over the border into Spain; collected reinforcements, with food, stores and horses, and gave his men a short breathing-space to recover themselves; and then, with something of the fury of a wounded boar, went to the attack against Wellington at Fuentes de Oñoro, where his excellent dispositions might possibly have given him the victory. But Marshal Bessières, who had now joined him, looked upon Masséna with professional jealousy, and had an old grudge against him too; and for these reasons found himself unable to send him the necessary aid at a critical moment. With that, Masséna's career as a general came to an end: he was recalled home and replaced by Marmont. And from this moment, in the early spring of 1811, the Imperial power in the Peninsula may be said to have passed its zenith. There would never be another serious attempt to "drive the Leopards into the sea".

Nevertheless, Wellington was to have a hard row to hoe in the next two years before he could begin to see the end of his labours in Spain. Marmont, with all his vanity and his almost crazy self-importance, his ancient and aristocratic ancestry, his princely manners, his magnificent service of plate and enormous kitchen staff, was by no means an easy man to get the better of in the field, although he was possibly handicapped more than any of his colleagues by Imperial orders from Paris, which spoilt his best plans and were never relevant to the situation when they at length arrived. He succeeded, partly by the aid of his hospitality, in making himself as well-liked among his officers as the parsimonious Masséna had

been disliked; and he was never at a loss for ideas. In spite of
the Emperor's blundering interventions, he contrived to give
Wellington more than one bad headache; and in the course of
their protracted manoeuvring in the autumn of 1811 and the
spring of 1812 there were minor actions in which Wellington
did not always come off best. For some time the strategy of
both generals centred mainly round the two key fortresses
still in French hands — Ciudad Rodrigo and Badajoz — whose
capture was indispensable to Wellington; but he was badly
off for siege-guns, and at Ciudad Rodrigo he was compelled
to employ, among other weapons, a number of two-hundred-
year-old cannon which had been disinterred from Portuguese
fortresses. Here as always it was his infantry which had to bear
the main burden: both these fortresses were in the end taken
by storm, with heavy losses for the English, and wild scenes
of drunkenness, looting, murder and rape, which Wellington's utmost exertions were at first unable to check, and which
elicited from him, in word and writing, expressions of the utmost acerbity. It was here that his conviction that he commanded the scum of the earth became unalterably fixed;
though this did not prevent him from taking very much to
heart the loss of so many of his best men in the storming-
columns.

It was during the terrible events in Badajoz that a fourteen-
year-old Spanish girl of noble family, half crazed with terror, and bleeding from the wounds inflicted when her earrings
had been torn from her ears, sought the protection of a twenty-
year-old lieutenant by the name of Harry Smith. Under his
care she soon recovered her composure, and presently began
to feel entirely at her ease; and as soon as Smith — who was
a dashing sort of fellow, addicted all his life to hasty decisions
— had found time to take in her extraordinary beauty, he married her on the spot, despite certain initial difficulties in the
matter of language. Thereafter she remained by his side, in
unbroken mutual happiness, through all his campaigns down

to the battle of Toulouse. She was with him at Waterloo, and afterwards in India and elsewhere; and finally accompanied him to the peaceful environment of the Cape, upon Sir Harry Smith's advancement to be Lieutenant-General and Governor of that Colony. A town in South Africa — Harrismith — is named after him; and another — Ladysmith (famous for its siege during the Boer War) — took its name from the romantic Juana Maria de Los Dolores de León.

After all their trouble with the fortresses Wellington and his men felt it a great relief to be able to give their undivided attention to Marmont; but Marmont proved remarkably spry, and it took time to deal with him effectively. On the contrary, there were two occasions when Marmont came near to dealing a blow at Wellington personally: once in the autumn of 1811 at El Bodon, when Montbrun's dragoons came within an ace of carrying him off while reconnoitring; another time during the affair at Castrejon, immediately before Salamanca, when Wellington was unexpectedly involved in a running fight between a few French and British squadrons. Of this episode a certain Lieutenant Kincaid writes:

I was sent out on picket on the evening of 17 July; and next morning, immediately after sunrise, the guns began firing. I was observing the shooting, when there suddenly arose without warning a most appalling shouting and din behind a rise in the ground to the left of me, and I lost no time in putting myself and my picket in a place of safety behind a broad dyke which was close at hand. I had hardly effected this before Lord Wellington, together with his staff, and a crowd of French and English dragoons, mingled with mounted artillery, came over the rise at full gallop, all laying about them in a general mêlée, and passed over the place I had just quitted. It turned out that Lord Wellington had ridden forward to reconnoitre, covered by two guns and two squadrons; by some mischance these had been surprised by a superior enemy force, which had driven them back upon us in the manner I have described.

The course of events in Europe would undoubtedly have run very differently, had Wellington received a sword-thrust in an affair such as this; but among the notable gifts with which the good fairies endowed him was not only that he was never ill and never tired, but also that he was never wounded. He invariably exposed himself quite unconcernedly, at outposts and in all his battles, and nothing ever happened to him; during the fighting in the Pyrenees he was once hit on the thigh by a spent bullet, and sustained a slight contusion, and we hear of a few harmless tumbles while out hunting in Portugal; but that is all. In earlier times men would have said that he had been made invulnerable to bullets, and it is not impossible that his veterans believed this; especially after Waterloo, when by the end of the day the whole of his staff was dead or wounded, while he and his horse, after nine hours in the hottest fire, remained unscathed. Such religious utterances of the Duke of Wellington as have been preserved must be remarkably few in number, and it is unlikely that they would provide adequate material for an anthology; but there is one, from the day after Waterloo, which is well-known: "The hand of God was upon me." It was in the circumstances a natural enough reflection, even for a rationalist such as he.

In the course of time his soldiers noted two other odd things about him. One was that Sunday was especially lucky for him, his victories frequently falling on that day; the other, that a major victory was generally heralded the preceding night by a terrifying storm of thunder, rain and wind.

After a month of manoeuvring in the country around Salamanca, there came at last the great nocturnal thunderstorm, this time of unprecedented violence, so that the terrified cavalry-horses stampeded in all directions. The next day, 22 July, was, sure enough, a Sunday. The armies were within sight of each other, skirmishing all along the front; and Marmont, too wary to attempt the frontal assault which had failed so often before, manoeuvred pertinaciously to outflank Wellington's right wing. Towards afternoon Wellington was sitting outside a farmhouse on a hill eating his dinner, with his spyglass lying handy: the best authorities inform us that he was making his meal of cold roast beef. Someone near him made a remark; Wellington rose from the table with his mouth full, and took another look through the glass. "By God! This will do!", he said; and ordered up his horse. Marmont had extended his left wing too far; and after a brief interval his forces were shattered, himself wounded, his army in total rout, and seven thousand prisoners taken.

The French escaped a complete catastrophe because of a hitch in the pursuit, as often happened with Wellington; but even so it was a glorious victory. Marmont was now out of the game; and in a Portuguese bivouac someone strung together a ditty — very popular with the English no less than with the Portuguese — called The Ballad of Salamanca, of which apparently only the first line has survived for posterity:

Hallo, hallo, Marmont! Where will you go, Marmont?

In London the news of the victory was received with delirious enthusiasm. The Whigs, indeed, preserved an unruffled selfcontrol, for they found it hard to swallow the obstinate and apparently unending good fortune which seemed to attend on Wellington, and which enabled the Tory ministers to keep their heads above water; and the good wishes of the Duke of York were conveyed by the sending out of a completely inefficient Quartermaster-General, who in the intervals of bungling his duties applied himself to the writing of confidential reports on Wellington's incompetence. But Walter Scott hailed him, in words which came warm from the heart, as the true hero of the age; the fat Prince Regent's enthusiasm was such that he got to the point of trying to delude himself and others into the conviction that he had personally led the heavy cavalry at Salamanca; Napoleon, apprised of the disaster by a confidential report which reached him on the way to Moscow, rained snuff and angry questions upon his entourage; and one of Marmont's generals of division named Foy (a gifted and knowledgeable person, later to be known as a military historian) noted in his diary that this was the most important and most glorious victory won by the English in recent times, and that it had put Wellington almost on a level with Marlborough.

Soon after Salamanca Wellington rode into Madrid, where he was in some danger of suffocation under the ecstatic embraces of the patriotic young women of that city. Wellington's taste was in all things simple and unstudied: he always submitted to the kisses of pretty young women with the greatest alacrity, and made no attempt to conceal his enjoyment, while on the other hand he appears to have beaten off any attempt at similar assaults from the more mature, with all the coolness of a master of defensive strategy. In Madrid he had, perhaps, too much of a good thing: in his off-hours he took cover with the great Goya, to whom he sat for a portrait. Wellington thought poorly of the likeness, and on this point quarrelled with the Master, who is said to have been so enraged that he fished out a pair of duelling-pistols, though he failed to obtain the satisfaction he desired. To judge from reproductions, the portrait was never much to boast about.

And indeed there are not many portraits of Wellington of such quality as to induce a prolonged inspection. The great hook-nose, the hollow cheeks, the wide-set eyes, the long upper lip, the thin mouth, the strong chin: these are all to be found in every portrait, but somehow they do not add up to a satisfactory whole. The most convincing face of those I have seen seems to me to be that in a full-length portrait by a certain Juan Bauzitt, painted in 1812: Wellington is depicted bareheaded, gloves in hand, wearing his ordinary field-uniform — a plain civilian greatcoat (certainly very well cut, though a shade awry in the picture) and short riding boots. The face has a look of composure which here seems authentic; the somewhat frosty stare gives the impression of being what in fact it was — a look which when it darted from beneath his

cocked hat upon some more or less obstreperous military delinquent was by no means easy to endure. It was thus that he
must have appeared, this man whose greatness was compounded of common-sense, indomitable will, and devotion to duty;
this man of whom Walter Bagehot once finely remarked that
"you can read a letter of his about draught oxen and horse-
nails, and still feel an interest, a great interest, because somehow among the words seems to lurk the mind of a great
general". In Muriel Wellesley's *The Man Wellington* this
portrait is reproduced, and provided with the legend "Beau
Douro".

Considered merely in his quality of Beau, Beau Douro was
of course never a match for his great contemporary Beau
Brummel, the King of the Dandies; but his concern for his
toilet and his apparel was very marked, and despite the fact
that when in the field he was overwhelmed with business he
liked to shave twice a day, and always performed the operation
himself. It was his invariable habit to rise very early — at the
latest about four o'clock; and once the business of dressing was
safely out of the way he sat down to his writing-table to deal
with a correspondence which for volume can have had but few
equals. There are even a number of autograph letters from him
written on the early morning of the day of Waterloo. During
the years in Spain he was always labouring under a deluge of
urgent military, administrative, political, financial and other
problems which poured in on him from all quarters, and the
unfailing conscientiousness with which he attended to his correspondence is truly admirable. Of his characteristic qualities
as a letter-writer no one — not least himself — had much idea,
until in later years a Lieutenant-Colonel Gurwood began the
publication of his collected Dispatches, Memoranda and
Letters: in all thirty-four volumes were published covering the
years down to 1832. Wellington, on reading over his writings
from the Indian years, was himself agreeably surprised, and
took pleasure in the clarity and vigour of expression which

were already to be found in them. With the help of the numerous quotations from his correspondence to be found in various books about him, it is possible to form an approximate idea of his epistolary style in different moods and differing circumstances. Here is one from 1809, to a Spanish general by the name of Eguia, Cuesta's successor, who had been pleased to doubt Wellington's veracity: the necessary politeness is there, but also a notable clarity and vigour:

> I have had the honour of receiving your Excellency's letter of this day's date, and I feel much concerned that any thing should have occurred to induce your Excellency to express a doubt of the truth of what I have written to you. As, however, your Excellency entertains that doubt, any further correspondence between us appears unnecessary; and accordingly, this is the last letter which I shall have the honour of addressing to you.

The most famous, and the shortest, of all his letters comes from his later years: an answer to a somewhat naive old flame who had informed him that she would find herself compelled to sell, for purposes of publication, a bundle of piquant letters from him, unless he assisted her with a good round sum:

> Dear Fanny, publish and be damned.

In a letter to General Beresford of 2 July 1815, concerning Portuguese decorations and Albuera medals for his officers and men, he devotes a dozen lines to an account of the newly-won battle of Waterloo:

> You will have heard of our battle of the 18th. Never did I see such a pounding match. Both were what the boxers call gluttons. Napoleon did not manoeuvre at all. He moved forward in the old style, in columns, and was driven off in the old style. The only difference was, that he mixed cavalry with his infantry, and supported both with an enormous quantity of artillery.
>
> I had the infantry for some time in squares, and we had the French cavalry walking about us as if they had been our own. I never saw the British infantry behave so well.
>
> Boney is now off, I believe, to Rochefort, to go to America.

And here is a letter which bears witness to his good humour,
written in 1811 in the thick of all his troubles with Marmont,
in reply to a request from a friend in England to have a certain Major sent home as soon as possible, since a young lady
was dying of love for him:

> It is impossible not to feel compassion for the condition of the
> young lady, so eloquently described by you; but it is not so easy to
> apply the remedy as you appear to think.
>
> It appears to me that I should be guilty of a breach of discretion
> if I were to send for the fortunate object of this young lady's affections,
> and to apprise him of the pressing necessity for his early return to
> England: the application for permission ought to come from himself;
> and, at all events, the offer ought not to be made by me, and par-
> ticularly not founded on the secret of this interesting young lady.
>
> But this fortunate Major now commands his battalion, and I am
> very apprehensive that he could not with propriety quit it at present,
> even though the life of this female should depend upon it; and, there-
> fore, I think that he will not ask for leave.
>
> We read, occasionally, of desperate cases of this description, but I
> cannot say that I have ever yet known of a young lady's dying of love.
> They contrive, in some manner, to live, and look tolerably well, not-
> withstanding their despair and the continued absence of their lover;
> and some even have been known to recover so far as to be inclined
> to take another lover, if the absence of the first has lasted too long.
> I don't suppose that your *protegée* can ever recover so far, but I do
> hope that she will survive the continued necessary absence of the Ma-
> jor, and enjoy with him hereafter many happy days.

The pleasant sojourn in Madrid was not of long duration,
and the latter half of 1812 was a black time for Wellington.
The French began to be impudent again, the Spanish generals
proved if possible worse than usual, an attempt against the
fortress of Burgos failed after vain waste of lives. It seems
likely that Wellington at this time was suffering from strain,
though the only sign of anything of the sort was a certain
access of irritability. He had not had a day's leave since he
set foot on Portuguese soil; his wiry constitution did indeed
seem capable of standing up to anything, but its powers of

resistance were certainly very severely taxed. The year's campaign ended with a somewhat ignominious and extraordinarily arduous retreat upon Portugal, in the course of which many died of hunger, since the Quartermaster-General (the Duke of York's friend) found it good to send the stores by another road from that followed by the troops, so that no rations could be issued for four days. It was clearly impossible to shoot this individual, but Wellington at least succeeded in getting rid of him before the opening of the next campaigning season — at which the army must have fetched an audible sigh of relief.

Napoleon's disaster in Russia was by this time common knowledge; but the idea that he would now be forced to make perceptible reductions in his forces in Spain turned out to be unfounded. Wellington sent a laconic message to the Emperor of Austria, who was still Napoleon's nominal ally, to the effect that he undertook in 1813 to keep at least 200 000 Frenchmen fully occupied in Spain; and as soon as the grass began to shoot he broke up with a united force of 80 000 men, to implement his promise. As they crossed the frontier he waved his hat, and cried "Farewell, Portugal!" — an unusual outburst of rhetoric for him; and thereafter continued his march, with the army divided into three parallel columns (of which the strongest and most northerly long remained absolutely unperceived by the French) — up along the Rio Seco, and on by long marches through Old Castile, moving steadily north-eastwards, and outflanking the French all the time. Jourdan was now Commander-in-Chief on the French side; he was a man who had won a great reputation before anybody had heard of Bonaparte, and despite his age he was still not lacking in ideas; but his scattered subordinates had become too used to being commanded from Paris, or to acting according to their own taste and fancy. On the morning of 13 June, when Wellington, advancing along the Pisuerga, had come to within a few miles of Burgos — the fortress which had so recently repulsed him — the ground quivered to a gigantic explosion: the French had blown up the fortress. In later years he narrated how, when he heard the rumble of the explosion, he at once realized that the game was in his hands, and decided on the spot to press on with all speed to the Ebro, cross that river without delay, and thereby either cut off the French from their native country or drive them in on the Pyrenees.

On this long summer march the troops were in superlative condition, and sang the whole day "even on the last mile"; and as they passed through the little towns of Castile even the nuns became slightly unbalanced, and might on occasion be seen rushing with roses and other objects to welcome them: heretical and godless they might be, and no doubt were; but just at present they were simply the much-loved English. The soldiers were soon to have entertainment considerably more hilarious, for one evening at all events; but it would not be with Wellington's approval.

On 15 June they passed the upper Ebro; and soon their course bent east and south-east upon Vittoria, where Jourdan and King Joseph had resolved to concentrate their forces and offer battle. They had managed to collect barely 60 000 men, when on 21 June Wellington was upon them. From the start Jourdan was half-surrounded. Sir Thomas Picton led his division to the attack, characteristically adjuring it, in a voice which could be heard above twenty trumpets, to "Come on, ye rascals! Come on, ye fighting villains!" By the late afternoon Jourdan's army had been transformed into a collection of scattered fugitives, the whole of the French artillery had been captured, King Joseph was in flight with the rest, and the French power in Spain was at an end, except in Aragon and Catalonia.

It was now that Wellington's soldiers, who ought to have been pursuing the fleeing foe, but had discovered more alluring possibilities, had the time of their lives. For, parked in the rear of the beaten army, was all the baggage of King Joseph, piled up in one gigantic medley; and it was a baggage-

train which repaid inspection. All the plunder which French
officers and officials had accumulated in the course of years —
among it King Joseph's own collections of one sort or another
— padlocked pack-waggons full of coin, table-silver, church
plate, valuable paintings, and much else, and to crown all five
million francs in silver, which had just arrived from France to
pay the troops, were here for enterprising men to rummage
in at pleasure, without any other interruption (to begin with,
at all events) than the shrieks of a crowd of French officers'
ladies, who were stuck fast in their travelling coaches, and
could not get away. Professor Oman, an author not prone to
lyrical exaggeration, considers it probable that this was the
richest booty offered to any army since the Persian camp was
plundered after the battle of Issus. At all events, this was one
authentic case where money was measured out by hatfuls — a
thing which is otherwise told only of the age of the great buc-
caneers, and even then without the citing of precise instances.
Wellington wished to round up the fleeing French along the
Pamplona road, but not even the anger of Wellington could
shift his men at that moment. For himself he reserved Jourdan's
marshal's baton, and in addition a number of pictures by Velas-
quez (a painter not then appreciated at his true worth) which
had been found in one of King Joseph's waggons. He would
much have preferred the five million francs, for which there
was plenty of space in the army's somewhat empty pay-chests,
but only an insignificant part of this sum escaped the attentions
of private enterprise.

Jourdan's baton was sent home to the Prince Regent, who in
an ecstasy of pleasure wrote a letter of thanks to Wellington in
which he informed him that the baton of an English Field-
Marshal should be sent to him in its place. This induced head-
aches in the military authorities at home, since hitherto there
had been no such thing in England; and we may perhaps hope
that the Duke of York found himself compelled to take some
part in the designing of the first English baton. The pictures

were sent to England too, with the idea of restoring them to their proper owners when times were quieter; but when the time came King Ferdinand courteously refused to accept them, and asked Wellington to keep them for himself.

But the most important thing which Wellington sent home was really the dispatch announcing his victory. The government lost no time in having it printed in a number of European languages, and disseminated it all over the Continent. The immediate result was that Austria, which hitherto had remained neutral — the more so since Napoleon had recently won victories at Lützen and Bautzen — at the news of Vittoria cast aside her hesitation and joined the coalition.

Napoleon dismissed Jourdan, relegated brother Joseph to a French country estate, gave Soult the Spanish command, and on at least one occasion devoted himself (despite the mass of urgent business from other quarters) to drawing up, literally with his own hand, a lying report of Soult's victories. During the battles in the Pyrenees Soult at first acted with resolution; but Wellington's advance into France was deferred less perhaps by any exertion of his than by a number of delicate political considerations, involving (among other things) the question of what sort of régime was to be put in Napoleon's place. Wellington held that a state of chaos in France was to be avoided at all costs: the civil population was to be treated with the greatest consideration; starving and vengeful Spaniards in the invading army were if need be to be sent home; French mayors and other prominent citizens were to be invited to dinner, and their wives were to be danced with; and all the army's requirements were to be paid for in cash.

This last proved in practice more difficult to carry out than might have been expected. The British government did what it could, despite a severe shortage of metal, to keep him provided with what he required; among other measures they melted down Indian mohurs in order to coin, for his exclusive use, the last guineas ever to be issued: among modern numismatists the

coin is known as "the military guinea". In addition, he was provided with dollars (5/-pieces). But the French peasants would
have nothing to do with these unfamiliar coins, and although
Wellington proclaimed very reasonable rates of exchange, they
persistently refused to accept payment in anything but the 5-
franc pieces to which they were accustomed. But not even a
difficulty such as this could baffle the resource of the man of
common-sense. The five millions of French silver would have
been useful now, but most of it had been appropriated at Vittoria by the "scum of the earth". The scum of the earth...
silver coin... but the thing was obvious! He caused to be issued
from his Headquarters at St Jean de Luz a confidential circular
to his Colonels of foot, in which he promised that all former
counterfeiters in the ranks should be given good pay and in-
demnity for the past, if they would report for special duty at
an appointed spot near Headquarters. Between 40 and 50
former practitioners of the art came forward, happy, no doubt,
to have a chance to get their hand in again, and the English
silver in the pay-chests was recoined into irreproachable Napoleonic 5-franc pieces. The work was done under strict super-
vision, so that the artists engaged upon it should not play any
of their old tricks with lead, or similar materials. Every coin was
provided with a little secret mark, so that it might be withdrawn
from circulation later, if that should be found necessary; and
Wellington was so anxious for complete success in his unexpected role of mint-master, that the coins struck bore, not the
actual date, but a date some years previously. The confidential
circular was not included in his printed Correspondence; but
Wellington liked to tell the story in after years. And the conviction, to which he always recurred after momentary irritation
had evaporated, that no troops in the world could compare with
British infantry "of the old stamp", gains special confirmation
from an episode of this nature.

The final cycle of battles, during which Soult was pressed
back to the north and east, was marked throughout by great

violence, and losses on both sides were severe. But in the intervals of calm between the actions relations between French and British were entirely free from bitterness. Outposts fraternized pleasantly with each other, and a system of signals was devised, whereby one side warned the other in good time of an impending attack. At this time a little river, spanned by a bridge, formed the dividing line between the two armies; and at either end of the bridge was a British and a French soldier on guard. One day when a British lieutenant arrived on his tour of inspection, he saw his man — an Irishman — coolly marching up and down with his own musket on one shoulder, and his French colleague's on the other, guarding the bridge by himself on behalf of both armies. The Irishman explained that the Frenchman had gone to buy brandy for both of them; and since he had taken the Irishman's last piece of silver, he had retained the musket as a pledge. At this point there appeared on the French side a lieutenant, also doing his rounds, and announced that he had found his man far to the rear, without his arms, but with two bottles. The two lieutenants debated the case; and after agreeing that both men might expect a court-martial and a firing-squad if the incident were reported to their colonels, they decided to say no more about it.

In cases where no important issue was at stake, Wellington never took action against fraternization; and his attitude to Soult's spies, who were to be found in his camp in considerable numbers — and even, in a few superior instances, at his own dinner-table — is also characteristic:

Why should I bother about them? It was a matter of indifference to me what they saw or heard. I got from them pieces of information which were useful to me, and the information they could carry back to Soult gave me no cause for uneasiness ... There are spies in every army. I knew there were many in mine; but it never occurred to me to hang them. If I could not arrange matters so that their tale-bearing did the enemy no good, I should have been a bad commander.

From the point of view of Wellington's staff-officers and casual guests there was no great enjoyment to be extracted from eating at his table while in the field — at least as regarded the food, which was decidedly spartan. He was one of those men who eat to satisfy their hunger, but for the rest are indifferent to what is put before them, provided it is nourishing and sufficient. On one occasion some years later he was invited to dine with Cambacérès, the former second consul, who was mainly known in later life as a gourmet of the most refined taste (only surpassed, perhaps, in the Paris of his day, by Talleyrand, who had the incomparable Antoine Carême for cook); and when the host asked what he thought of some important gastronomic novelty which had just been handed round, Wellington answered that he had not noticed it particularly: at which Cambacérès raised his hands to heaven in despair and cried "My God, what did you come here for?" But though his indifference to food remained unchanged, his table underwent a considerable alteration after he became a Field Marshal. Somebody, maybe, gave him a hint that an improvement in this respect was now essential; and with his usual wisdom Wellington hastily put things on the best basis he could contrive by giving himself an establishment of three cooks, one Englishman, one Spaniard, and one Frenchman, who each commanded in the kitchen for one day at a time and sought to excel the others.

For the rest, the atmosphere at Wellington's dinner-table seems in general to have been good. He had about him his personal staff, composed of young men of good family whom he had chosen himself, and with whom he got on well; and their loquaciousness and easy habits do not seem to have suffered much check in his presence. He called this staff of his "my military family", and was grieved to lose several of them at Waterloo; those that survived proved in many cases to be as long-lived as himself; but there seems to have been no budding military genius among them — for Lord Fitzroy Somerset, his constant companion and confidential friend, who was one day to command in the Crimea under the name of Lord Raglan, can hardly be included among the great commanders. Among his adjutants was a young Spanish general named Alava, of whom Wellington thought highly — the only man, it is said, who could later boast of having been present at both Trafalgar and Waterloo; and William of Orange, the rightful Crown Prince of the Netherlands, who in the unconstrained atmosphere of the staff meekly bore the nickname of Slender Billy.

Wellington's last great fight with Soult, the battle of Toulouse, took place after Napoleon's abdication, for the news of it had not yet reached them; and on 12 April Wellington rode into the town, where the enthusiasm was tremendous, and the cheering for Louis XVIII universal. With the cheers Wellington refused to associate himself officially, so long as the question remained open as to whether the allies might not conclude a negotiated peace with Napoleon. The only member of the house of Bourbon with whom he was personally acquainted — the Duke of Angoulême — was a faintly grotesque figure, and seems by no means to have produced in Wellington a disposition to premature hurrahing for the Bourbons.

On the same day a dinner to Wellington and his personal staff was organized; and at this dinner a number of French royalists were present. During the dinner, or immediately before it, came the official news of Napoleon's abdication, with all the attendant circumstances. Wellington's reserve in regard to the Bourbons thus became unnecessary; and at the end of the meal he rose, told the company the news, and gave the toast of Louis XVIII. It was drunk with proper enthusiasm; but this was only a modest beginning. For no sooner had Wellington sat down again, and order had been restored, than Alava, his Spanish adjutant, leaped upon a chair, raised his glass and cried: *El Libertador de España!* Others clambered on their chairs, glass in hand, and a great clamour arose: *Liberador de Portugal! Le Libérateur de la France! Le Libérateur de l'Europe!* There followed a tremendous outburst of cheering, which drowned all attempts at a regular toast, and continued a long while.

And then, it is said, Wellington rose; bowed to the company; looked around him with eyes filled with tears; was unable to say a word in reply; ordered in the coffee, and resumed his seat.

It was probably the most glorious moment in his long career. It was at all events, as far as we know, the only occasion upon which he found himself overwhelmed.

And with that we have reached the end of this very little essay upon a very great man. For at this point ends also the source which by itself is worth more than all the rest — Sir Charles Oman's great work *The Peninsular War*. Waterloo is a separate study, not susceptible of summary treatment; and in any case I have no adequate sources for it available. And his long life thereafter, for a time in the tangle of politics, and at last in the well-earned glory of a peaceful old age — this is a world in itself.

Translated by Michael Roberts

STONEWALL JACKSON

$\mathcal{N}$OBODY, as far as I am aware, has ever been able to point to two blades of grass growing where one grew before, and claim it as the result of his achievement. Like the lily of the field, he toiled not, neither did he spin, contributing nothing to the welfare of mankind; and any glory which may nevertheless attend him, is derived exclusively from the circumstance that he was a unique personality and a great general. It is still less than ninety years since he was alive, and it is perhaps not so very many years since the last of his veterans followed him. Yet a figure such as Jackson's seems now as remote from us as if he had lived in a distant epoch and belonged to a race long since extinct. "O Napoleon!," burst out Paoli to a morose young lieutenant of artillery, "in you there is nothing modern; you are taken bodily from Plutarch!" This remark turned out subsequently to have been an exaggeration; but such a thing might well be said of a man such as Jackson. His philosophy, his creed, the ideas for which he strove and fought — all have long since been relegated to the lumber-room for battered antiques. It is difficult for us to imagine that his type of religiosity, strikingly old-fashioned even in his own age and society, could now be associated with any man of real consequence. His views upon the justification of negro slavery and the sovereignty of the separate states of the Union are certainly no longer taken seriously by anyone, not even in his own State.

But he has his compensations. He easily retains his place as the most individual general of the American Civil War, as the figure most sharply defined against its background;

though it was by no means a war that was poor in such characters. His career was short, but from beginning to end it was highly remarkable; and it was drawn by Fate with a fine artistry — from the hour when, as an obscure pedagogue he trod the first battlefield of the war at Bull Run and with his brigade decided the issue, to that day, scarcely two years later, when, with a reputation already world-wide, he rode into his own firing-line at Chancellorsville and was borne dying from the scene of his greatest achievement. To him was reserved the advantage of perishing unconquered at the moment of his most brilliant victory — as Gaston de Foix fell at Ravenna, Desaix at Marengo, Claverhouse at Killiecrankie, and Wolfe on the Heights of Abraham.

Men of superior ability are often said to be aided by a marked turn of good luck; and if, in that first battle of the war, it was Jackson's ability that obtained the victory, it was none the less his good fortune which contrived that he should then acquire his celebrated *nom de guerre,* which henceforward, for friend and foe alike, cast a peculiar nimbus about him. One bright July day in 1861, the Federal General McDowell moved forward to the little stream called Bull Run, some way to the south of Washington, dispatched by Lincoln with a beautiful brand-new army, and borne on his way by the battle-cry "Forward to Richmond!" resounding powerfully behind him from all the impatient North. The road to Richmond was no great distance on the map, and the Confederate Generals' talents for bestrewing it with thorns still awaited discovery. It was a Sunday, and a number of Senators and Congress leaders had taken advantage of the holiday and driven out from Washington with their parasolled ladies to view the war. On the other side of the river lay the Confederates under Beauregard; his force was not large, but his colleague Joseph Johnston had come up by forced marches, and was on the point of effecting a junction with him. The junction took place unostentatiously, with the idea of preparing a little surprise for

McDowell and the binoculared statesmen on the northern bank, who were under the impression that Johnston was still busy with the Federal General Patterson, several days' march to the west. McDowell, who even after the junction had still the advantage of numbers, took the offensive, forced his right wing over a bridge, and soon stood with a strong detachment on the flank of the rebels. Johnston's newly-arrived brigades were then sent forward to meet him there. Two of them — Bee's and Bartow's — were led by men whose fate it was to be to fall on this field; but the commander of the third, Professor Jackson of Lexington, Va., — a loose-limbed, brown-bearded man in the flower of manhood, pedagogically thoughtful in mien and action, with friendly eyes and a quiet voice, taciturn and reserved in manner, and in respect of eccentricities fully comparable with any of his profession — Jackson was this day to escape with a scratch, and was to achieve a good deal, of one sort or another, before the close of his career. Bee's brigade, which came up first, was overwhelmed, and presently streamed back in disorder; Bee met Jackson, who was moving forward. "General, they are driving us back!," said he. "Well, Sir," answered Jackson, "then we will give them the bayonet"; whereupon he took up a strong position along a small height, and there resolutely faced the oncoming Federals. Bee galloped sword in hand among his troops to rally them. "Look," he cried, "there is Jackson standing like a stone wall! Rally behind his Virginians!" After a short time the panic was checked; Bee fell, but reinforcements came up; at the right moment Jackson launched a counter-attack which smashed the enemy's flanking force; general disorder spread among the Unionists; and towards evening what had once been their army rolled back along the Washington road in hopeless confusion, while stray Confederate bullets whistled impertinently around the ears of retiring Senators and Congressmen. Jackson declared himself to be in a condition to advance forthwith upon Washington on the heels of the panic-stricken foe; but President

Jefferson Davis, supreme commander of the South, prevented any serious pursuit, and the senior Generals agreed with him in thinking that the troops were too drunk with victory and too deficient in training for any forward thrust. Dispirited by such timidity and indolence, Jackson had to content himself with camping on the battlefield; but for his own part he could be well content, for this day had made his name in more senses than one. In future he was to be "Stonewall", despite his constant insistence that the appellation ought really to have been given not to himself but to his brigade.

His real Christian names — which henceforward were increasingly forgotten — were Thomas Jonathan; and with these he had been endowed some thirty-seven years previously, in a pioneer home in West Virginia. Of Scotch-Irish extraction, he had grown up in humble circumstances in the house of a relative, for his parents had died young. At the age of twenty he gained admission to the Military Academy at West Point, inadequately equipped in point of physique, but possessed of unbounded energy; and here his oddities (which were already apparent), his rustic manners and his quiet and retiring habits, exposed him at first to the humorous attentions of his fellow-students, the more so because for some time he was one of the weakest cadets at the Academy. Gradually he worked his way up; and he finished the four-year course seventeenth out of a class of some sixty: another future General, G. B. McClellan, later to win a tragi-comic celebrity as the "young Napoleon of the North", passed out number one in the same year. Jackson was lucky enough to be examined just in time to serve as a second-lieutenant of artillery in the Mexican war of 1849—50 — an episode now mostly forgotten, which Grant (who also took part in it) elevated in his *Memoirs* to the dizzy eminence of being perhaps the most unrighteous war ever started by a strong state against a weak one. Jackson served with credit, and returned home a Major; but tiring soon of the dull routine of military service in peace-time, applied for and obtained a post at the Virginia Military Institute at Lexington, where he worked quietly until the outbreak of war as Professor of Optics, Astronomy and Artillery-tactics.

The eccentric tendencies in his nature were now given a chance to come to full flower; and in course of time his resemblance to resurrected seventeenth-century Puritan became ever more exact. The heavy demands he made upon his pupils, and the dryness of his manner, prevented his ever gaining much of their affection; a real enthusiasm for their Professor was reserved to that later time when they were to follow his standard. In his leisure-hours he studied military history, especially the campaigns of Napoleon, and for the rest devoted himself to domestic felicity, and to the practice of religion. A pious general of division had in the course of the Mexican campaign aroused his interest in spiritual things, and it was an interest which grew deeper with the passage of time. He was a man who disliked half-measures, in religion as in everything else; after ripe deliberation he joined the Presbyterians, and thereafter regulated his life in every detail in accordance with the austere demands of their creed. The Bible he studied daily, with commentaries and pencil in hand; a tenth of his income he devoted to almsgiving; the day of rest he observed with the rigour of the Old Testament. He never opened a letter on a Sunday, and in his view the state was guilty of a gross impropriety in forwarding the mails on the Sabbath, and thus leading weak spirits into temptation. Indeed, this question of the Lord's Day vexed him all his life: difficult as it was in peace-time, in war it became sometimes almost more than he could bear; his official reports and his letters to Mrs. Jackson take on a tone of anguish when he sees himself obliged to march or fight upon the Sabbath. During his famous campaign in the Shenandoah Valley, in particular, at a time when he had as a rule three superior hostile armies around him, and every moment was precious, he was often obliged to swallow his scruples; but he sought to minimize these horrors by utilizing the first pause in the campaign to keep Sunday for himself and his soldiers for three successive days, thus squaring the account. In his speeches — which were never loud and never long — he loved to employ Biblical phraseology: his favourite expression was "by the blessing of Providence", a phrase which in more peaceful days he had often been heard to murmur piously in the course of ecclesiastical discussions in the congregration where he served as deacon, or in confidential converse with Mrs. Jackson upon the welfare of that negro Sunday-school which together they founded and conducted; and later during the war it was frequently overheard by his staff, uttered in the same tone of pious importunacy, when some particularly ingenious snare was being set for Banks or Frémont, or some desperate bayonet attack was let loose on McClellan, Pope, or "Fighting Joe" Hooker.

Religiosity of this kind may now appear sufficiently curious: the detached observer easily falls into an attitude of pitying superiority, and is tempted to presume that it must be associated with intellectual endowments of a somewhat meagre order. But Jackson was perfectly happy in his religion, which was certainly not assumed for theatrical effect, and oddly enough there was nothing whatever the matter with his intelligence. For him, in the course which Fate marked out for him, his religion was of invaluable practical aid. In his rocklike conviction that he lived under the immediate hand of God he was always equipped to take upon himself responsibility of any kind and any magnitude, with the most complete composure; he never hesitated, never despaired, never for a moment doubted that an enterprise which had been planned could be carried out, however desperate the situation might appear, and rode among whistling bullets and bursting shells as calmly as in former days he had walked to his lectures. In the field he carried with him three books, which he constantly consulted: the Bible; Noah Webster's Dictionary — this because he often felt himself somewhat shaky in his spelling — and Napoleon's

maxims on war. As he lay dying at Guiney's Station, he spoke
to one of the members of his staff who was in attendance at
his bedside of the value of the Bible to a military commander,
and among other things asked him if he could tell him where
in the Bible a man could learn the right way to write a report
of a battle. When the young lieutenant answered that it had
never occurred to him to look there for information of that
kind, Jackson pointed out gravely that the unsurpassable models
for such cases were to be found in the Book of Joshua — short,
clear and factual information, free from self-glorification and
empty verbiage, and with due honour given to God.

Life at Lexington moved smoothly on, regular as clockwork,
and year succeeded year without any noteworthy interruption.
One summer he paid a visit to Europe, where he inspected
English cathedrals (which delighted him extremely), viewed
the topography of Waterloo, and perambulated the galleries of
Florence; but this was an isolated outbreak of wanderlust. The
hours of religious meditation at home retained their charm for
him undiminished, family life continued unbrokenly happy;
and through his studies of Napoleon's teaching, steadily pursued, the thoughtful professor's insight into the esoteric art of
winning battles grew ever more profound. Nothing seemed less likely than that he should ever come to translate his
military lore into practice. In all human probability he had
every prospect of departing this life in peace, surrounded only
by that lustre which attends the conscientious discharge of
teaching duties and the zealous activity of a deacon. In Washington, indeed, noisy strife between the slave-owning states and
the "free" states had become a normal feature of political life;
but it had been going on now for many years, and intelligent
men did not take seriously the possibility that this traditional
squabble should ever come to a violent issue. Should the cham-
pions of the negroes in the North press the question too hard,
it was considered in the South that it was always open to them
to meet the situation by simply announcing their secession

from the Union; it was a step clearly permitted by the constitution, and consequently a solution which ought not to give rise to any trouble. Personally, Jackson considered negro slavery as an onerous institution, entailing high responsibilities, though for the moment, nevertheless, it probably constituted the most suitable form of social organization for the negroes, and was in any case unambiguously approved by the Bible. It is hardly likely that he would have taken the field with any great enthusiasm merely on the issue of slavery: it was rather the question of secession, as it affected his own state, which weighed most heavily with him. When Lincoln, against all expectations, was elected President, panic broke out in the South, where Lincoln enjoyed the reputation of being a particularly violent emancipist: the states along the south coast at once notified their intention of withdrawing from the Union, while Virginia assumed a waiting attitude. Lincoln, however, soon showed himself disposed to contest the right of any state in any circumstances to secede from the Union, and began to make powerful preparations to compel the recalcitrants to return. At this infringement of a right which the South considered sacred, still other states seceded, and among them Virginia: the South stood united as one man against every attempt to infringe the principle of state sovereignty. In these circumstances the call was clear for every son of Virginia: Jackson put by his text-books of optics and astronomy and offered his sword to the new-born Confederation. The full import of the offer could hardly at that time be realized by Jefferson Davis and the men who surrounded him; but those who knew Jackson personally had at all events no doubt of his reliability and his doggedness. "Who is Jackson?" asked someone in the President's entourage, when the question of giving him a command was discussed. "Jackson," replied one who knew him, "is the kind of man who if he is given a position with orders to hold it will not retreat while he has a single man and a single rifle that can shoot."

Soon after Bull Run Jackson was sent out westwards with

a few thousand men to an independent command in the Shenandoah Valley. The autumn and winter passed quietly everywhere: both sides were busy training recruits. McClellan, nominated by Lincoln to the command in chief, rendered important service by organizing this training for the North, and thereby acquired a great reputation. At last his preparations were complete and his plans ready, and he set his troops in motion on all fronts. When in the early spring of 1862 Lincoln and his Secretary of War, Mr. Stanton, surveyed the situation as a whole, they could not but feel well satisfied with everything. In the "peninsula of Virginia", a little way below Richmond, the Confederate capital, lay the main army under McClellan, 100 000 strong, which had been moved there by sea so that it might strike as directly as possible at Richmond, which was defended by a force scarcely half as numerous under Joseph Johnston. Lee remained in Richmond as President Davis' adviser. Near Washington was a strong corps under McDowall, which was intended to unite with McClellan's and render his superiority still more crushing. Somewhat to the west, in the country around the Shenandoah Valley (also called "the Valley of Virginia", or simply "the Valley") two splendid corps under Banks and Frémont kicked their heels in idleness; and away in the far west, on the Mississippi, a dubious personage from Galena, Ill., by the name of Ulysses S. Grant — regarded with ill-concealed distrust by all his superiors on account of a well-established reputation for inebriety — had just begun to make himself felt in an unexpectedly gratifying manner. It all looked as promising as possible: the downfall of the South appeared, taking it all round, to be imminent; the fate of Richmond, at all events, seemed sealed; McClellan was only waiting for the last reinforcements. But at this point curious things suddenly began to happen in the Valley.

The Valley is a long narrow dale running in a north-south direction between the Alleghanies on the west and the Blue Ridge on the east; to the north it opens on the Potomac, which forms the boundary between Virginia and Maryland — at that time also the boundary between North and South. The Massanutten Mountains, an independent and inaccessible group, lie somewhat to the south, set in the Valley like an eye in a needle; streams and roads run on either side of them, and, incidentally, cross and re-cross one another throughout the entire length of the Valley. All this was now to serve as a highly remarkable strategic dancing-floor, on which Jackson executed sundry *pas de seul* in the centre, to a confused accompaniment of opponents on the periphery. His winter quarters he fixed at Winchester, near the Valley's northern end, and his force numbered 5 000 men; Banks lay on the Potomac with 30 000. Banks was a pompous and rhetorical person, by profession a politician, to whom Lincoln had been forced to give a command in order to keep him in a good humour; he had been turned loose in the Valley, since humanly speaking nothing could happen to him there. For Jackson the situation looked as black as possible: no reinforcements were to be had; Banks began to move forward; and to crown all Jackson had trouble with his own men and with the Secretary of War in Richmond, Mr. Benjamin, whom many of his officers asserted in all seriousness to be completely out of his mind. At last he evacuated Winchester and withdrew southwards; but when he had gone but a short distance he suddenly faced about and hurled himself upon Shields, one of Banks's lieutenants, who with 12 000 men had ventured within striking distance. Throughout one starry evening they fought long and fiercely among the wintry woods around Kernstown, until at last Jackson's thin lines, after taking severe punishment, were pressed back. Frowning but by no means dispirited he drew off slowly from the battlefield, leaving a couple of useless guns behind him; and the enemy did not venture to pursue. It was a Federal victory; but none the less the action caused the greatest disquiet in Washington. Lincoln, with all his impassivity in other things, was as sensitive with reference to the safety of his capital as the princess was to the pea. What

was really afoot down there? How could Jackson venture to
take the offensive so far to the north? He must have received
reinforcements: the action was a clear foreshadowing of an impending advance upon Washington. Lincoln came hastily to
the conclusion that no more troops could be spared for McClellan, since they would all be needed to protect the capital.
McClellan conjured and implored, but to no purpose: the President and his Secretary of War declared that the Valley must
first be cleared and the back door to Washington effectively
shut; and in any event McClellan ought to be in a position to
effect something with the forces already at his disposal. There
the matter rested; and McClellan was left to stifle his lamentations and begin his task of working his way forward towards
Richmond, through marshes and trackless forests, without any
assistance from McDowell's corps. Some of these were sent to
the Valley instead; and upon the numerous generals in this
area there now fell a steady rain of orders from Mr. Stanton:
they were to isolate Jackson's corps without delay... they were
to harry Jackson relentlessly... to drive Jackson and his men
out of the Valley...

This turned out to be unexpectedly difficult; for while the
Federal generals endeavoured to execute their orders to the best
of their ability, it was Jackson who isolated *them*, harassed
them, and herded whole flocks of Federal strategists in the
Valley. His feints, his forced marches, above all his capacity
for constantly turning up in places where he could not by any
rational calculation be expected to be, induced in his opponents
first pensiveness, and later panic. Frémont, who came marching
in from the west suspecting no evil, was surprised far from all
reported danger-zones at Sittlington Hill, and driven back badly
mauled upon the Alleghanies. Jackson thereupon executed an
involved series of manoeuvres, which neither his own men nor
the enemy could fathom; and having thus created sufficient
confusion (under cover of which he succeeded in collecting unobserved some recently-arrived reinforcements) he fell suddenly

like a thunderbolt upon Banks from the most unexpected quarter. Banks, flustered by the surprise, made what stand he could, but was quickly routed, lost his baggage-train and artillery, was hunted down the Valley, driven through Winchester streets at the point of the bayonet, and finally hurled over the Potomac in utter dissolution. Praising God for the victory (though the mistake of a cavalry commander had robbed him of its full effects, and thus lost him the chance of finishing with Banks for good) Jackson camped for a few days on the banks of the Potomac, occupied with providing for his starving and ragged troops from the captured stores, and by his presence brought the confusion reigning in Washington to the highest pitch.

But his own position was extremely precarious, and it was not long before he received grave news. A good way to the south, Shields — who was now under McDowell's command — and Frémont, who had rallied his forces, were advancing from different directions to cut off Jackson's only line of retreat; their distance from the intended rendezvous was less than half his own. The utmost speed was required, and Jackson wasted no time in reorganizing. Taking with him prisoners and stores, he at once faced about. His battle-worn scarecrows, interrupted in their ransacking of Banks' scattered effects, fell in at once to the sound of the bugle, filed once more through the streets of Winchester, settled again to their usual quick-march tempo, and swept swiftly southwards along the turnpike road which follows the course of the Shenandoah — a road which was the scene of many of those prodigies of rapid movement which earned them the name of Jackson's foot-cavalry. Jackson had now succeeded in gaining the unquestioning trust of his men: at his command they were always willing to attempt the impossible. They bore without complaint the most extraordinary hardships. "Three fights a day and one meal a week" — such, according to the later testimony of his veterans, was the ordinary routine in the Valley. They had their own jokes about the forced marches. "Moses," they said, "took forty years to cross the desert; but if Stonewall had been in command he would have drummed the people through in three days, at the double and on half-rations." His great secretiveness, which led him never to betray a hint of his plans even to his nearest subordinates, was now accepted without complaint: when asked by an outsider "Where are you going, boys?" they would answer cheerfully: "We don't know, but Old Jack does."

On this march to the south they were now to be taxed to the uttermost. The situation during the race with the two generals who were trying to effect their junction in front of Jackson was not unlike a sort of musical chairs, and for Jackson all was upon the hazard. At the last possible moment he succeeded in slipping between his two adversaries, who had been seized with caution as they approached his line of march; and he continued southward with undiminished speed past the Massanutten Mountains, while one pursuer followed on either side of them. When he had reached a spot below the southern point of the *massif* he halted in a strong position on a river, received Frémont's attack at Cross Keys and drove him off, recrossed the river under cover of darkness, met Shields at Port Republic the following morning, and inflicted upon him a crushing defeat. After which Jackson vanished, suddenly and without trace, as though he had dissolved into thin air.

If Jackson's opponents found their encounters with him somewhat trying to the nerves, they found his disappearance even more so. With infinite caution they began once again to put out a tentative feeler here and there, with rumour constantly buzzing around them, fearful every moment of treading in some snare set for them by the terrible Professor. But he continued invisible. While Shields and Frémont sought to recover their breath after their last encounter, he lay in bivouac somewhat to the southward, in the woods around Mount Solon, holding prayer-meetings and shoeing his horses; and by the time that they felt themselves ready to play hide-and-seek with him again around the Massanutten Mountains his columns had already wound their way eastward unobserved, and were deep in the passes of the Blue Ridge. McClellan, who in his positions before Richmond was kept informed of the course of events in the Valley, became anxious for his colleagues. "I do not like Jackson's disappearance," he informed the Ministry of War in a telegram. "He is liable to turn up shortly where he is least expected." And in this McClellan was perfectly correct; for immediately afterwards Jackson once more made his presence felt by driving in McClellan's own outposts at Mechanicsville. He had crossed Virginia by forced marches and linked up with the main army outside Richmond. The so-called Seven Days' Battle now began, with the crushing of one wing of McClellan's army at Gaines' Mill, mainly by Jackson's troops, after which McClellan in extraordinarily heavy and bitter fighting was slowly driven back through the marshes of the Chickahominy by the united Confederate army, led now by Lee, and averted only with difficulty complete annihilation by standing to the last at Malvern. Soon afterwards McClellan took ship, broken in courage and with a shattered army, and returned to Washington, there to be relieved of his command.

And with that the great attempt upon Richmond had ended in a gigantic fiasco, mainly owing to the activities of Jackson. With a force that at no time exceeded 15 000 men, and was at first far less than that, he had operated against enemies five times as numerous, beaten all his adversaries one after the other, contained a strong corps at Washington, and finally put in an appearance at the decisive moment before Richmond. No wonder that already his name flew around the South on wings of enthusiasm, while the North pronounced it with a gloomy respect; and his Bible-thumping ragged corps, optimistically interpreting a remark of King Solomon, could sing with perfect justice in one of its marching-songs:

> The race is not to those who have got
> The longest legs to run;
> The battle to those people not
> Who shoot the biggest gun.

Richmond bedecked itself with flags and arranged days of thanksgiving after the liberation from McClellan's threat, but Lee and Jackson had little time for such diversions: they and their soldiers, who were in poor condition after the campaign in the marshes, marched off immediately to recuperate in the higher and healthier air of new battlefields. In north Virginia was already another Federal army, formed of the now united and strengthened divisions which Jackson had fought in the Valley. The command of this army had been given to Pope, a general who had been recalled from the West to teach less successful troops how war was waged on the Mississippi. Pope took over the command in a proclamation in which he laid emphasis on his offensive spirit, and promised speedy victories. He forbade all nervous speculation about his own lines of retreat, and recommended instead the idea of seeking out the lines of retreat of the enemy, and severing them without delay; he made pitiless mock of McClellan's caution and sluggishness; and clinched matters by urging severer treatment of the civil population within the occupied territories. This famous proclamation was studied with different feelings in different places — by the population of the North with joy and confidence, by Pope's own army somewhat pensively, by McClellan's men — who adored their general, though no one quite knows why — with mocking laughter, and by the population of the South with the extremity of fury. Lee and Jackson, cool as ever, took careful note of it, being desirous of getting some idea of the psychology of their new opponent and regulating their treatment of him accordingly. "This new general has claims upon your particular attention," said someone to Jackson. "And, please God," replied Jackson thoughtfully, "he shall have it."

Henceforward Jackson served with "the Army of Northern Virginia", as Lee's second-in-command, though for the purpose of executing large-scale and difficult combinations he often operated apart from the main army; and on these occasions he did not allow the laurels plucked in the Valley to wither. Lee and Jackson, both noble men and superb generals, had the warmest regard for one another, and cooperated with rare harmony. Lee was urbane and far-seeing, wise and lucid, the perfect aristocratic type, whose countenance mirrored his noble and humane spirit; and in the angular pedagogue from Lexington, that strange thunderbolt of war, with his unimpressive exterior, his laconic speech, his quiet voice, his pious asides, his friendly melancholy eyes which looked as though they had tired themselves out by overmuch brooding on close-printed biblical commentaries or overmuch peering through the smoke of battle, he found a complement which made them, as a combination, a force of perfect efficiency in the field. They understood the game of war to the very bottom. They shaped events, moulded situations, sovereign masters of their art for so long as their resources at all permitted them. Through the fog and confusion of war they passed with a clarity of vision which was vouchsafed to them alone. However the situation might appear, with whatever odds they had to contend, one thing remained constant: it was always they who stood at the centre, always they who were able to trace the thread of Ariadne. Their opponents — with stronger battalions but weaker characters, and much less able to make an accurate estimate of the factors in any given situation — were always relegated to dwell in an outer darkness (where indeed, very often, there was wailing and gnashing of teeth), always fumbling and unprepared, always waiting for something, or exasperated about something which would not go as it ought, always framing in their minds and on their lips the same question, in uncertainty of purpose and heart-rending concentration: "what is happening? what is really going on?" In comparison with their adversaries, Lee and Jackson are as spirit to dull matter. Within a brief space these two account for a whole series of Lincoln's generals: McDowell, McClellan, Pope, Burnside, Hooker, Meade — generals who, after starting with what appears to be the most justified hope of exploiting within a short time the numerical superiority of the North, soon retire from the command, after having seen, in every case save the last, their armies smashed to atoms and themselves transformed into failures. In many cases these generals of the North have achieved the renown which attends the classic bungler; but this is certainly largely attributable to the accident which pitted them against two such rare experts. When at last Grant arrived from the west and began his long-drawn hammering, Lee was forced to fight with dwindling resources and without Jackson's aid. As an old regimental chaplain expressed it at the unveiling of a statue in New Orleans long after the war: "When God in His inscrutable wisdom decreed that the Confederation should not stand, He found it necessary first to take away from us His servant, Stonewall Jackson."

It was now the turn of Pope, and his short appearance as guest-artist in Virginia ran on notably epic lines. The campaign against him began when Jackson surprised at Cedar Mountain the commander of his advance-guard, none other than his old acquaintance Banks — Mr. Commissary Banks, as Jackson's soldiers used to call him, because of the rich booty he invariably afforded — and dealt not less hardly with him than before. This was for Jackson's men a sensational battle, in that on one occasion, when a portion of his infantry was thrown into disorder by a counter-attack, they were for the first time afforded the spectacle of their general appearing with his sword drawn, as he rode into the confusion to restore order. Shortly afterwards Pope's and Lee's united armies settled themselves on either side of the Rappahannock river, Pope on the north bank, Lee on the south. The guns exchanged occasional cannonades across the stream, the cavalry skirmished a little, but otherwise all was quiet. Pope, already superior in numbers, was in good heart, since he was expecting further reinforcements very shortly, as the troops which McClellan had shipped home were gradually drafted to the front. For Lee, on the other hand, the situation looked critical, since no reinforcements were to be hoped for. A couple of preliminary attempts to compass Pope's destruction had been unsuccessful, and the best that could be expected, it seemed, was a slow withdrawal upon Richmond. But Lee and Jackson, who were not to be daunted by relative numbers, met one day in the open for a confidential talk. The Senior Medical Officer in Jackson's corps, Dr. McGuire, who happened to be passing, was amazed to see the undemonstrative Jackson gesticulating and even drawing lines in the sand with his boot. And then Lee was seen to nod assent, and the doctor understood at once that something very out of the ordinary was in the wind. The same evening Jackson began his preparations for his most famous march.

In the early dawn of the following day (his soldiers used to say that Stonewall always began his marches at dawn, except when he began them the previous night) he broke camp with the whole of his corps for a destination known only to himself and Lee. He had with him nearly half Lee's force — something like 20 000 men — and he steered his course westward, marching parallel to the river by concealed roads, with his friend J. E. B. Stuart's cavalry for screen. Lee spread his remaining forces over the resulting gap in his line, and calmly continued to amuse Pope with his gunfire. Jackson had ordered that all baggage should be left behind; a herd of oxen was driven along with them to serve at rations; and for the rest they had to live on unripe corn and green apples, picked up along the route. The only food which many of his officers took in their saddlebags was a handful of crusts and a screw of salt. All that the soldiers had to carry, besides their packs and their arms, was a billycan here and there and a limited number of frying-pans per regiment — each with its handle stuck down the muzzle of a rifle. No one had any idea where they were heading — perhaps to the Valley, perhaps to Washington — but the spirit of all was high, for it was clear that this was to be an effort in Jackson's best manner. Jackson, as usual, rode in silence, slumped in his saddle with his cap pulled down over his eyes, sunk in meditation. The column forced the upper Rappahannock,

pressed on through the villages of Orleans and Salem, continued northwards far into the night, and were at last permitted
to halt in the region of White Plains. The weary soldiers slept
where they stood; but after a few hours they were woken, while
the dawn was still grey, and, half-sleeping, were once again put
in motion. Their course now bent to the east, wound up the
Bull Run Mountains and through the pass called Thoroughfare
Gap. When at noon Jackson's men looked down from these
heights over the peaceful August landscape before them, every
man grasped what was afoot: they were now some considerable
distance behind Pope's right flank, and the road immediately
ahead of them cut the communications of that celebrated author
of proclamations and severed him from Washington. All weariness was forgotten in a moment: throughout the long summer
day they pushed indomitably forward, burnt by the fierce sunshine, and wrapped in a continuous cloud of dust. Towards
evening Jackson rode to the head of the column, watched the
troops pass by, and complimented his officers on the good
condition of the men and the steadiness of their march-disci-
pline. One by one as the divisions came up — first Ewell's, then
Jackson's own (now led by Taliaferro), then A. P. Hill's — and
the men caught sight of the wellknown figure at the roadside,
they prepared to greet him with the usual shouts and cheering;
but Jackson stopped them with a gesture, and backward along
the ranks the word was passed, "No noise, boys; the Yankees
can hear us!", and the men contented themselves with waving
their hats in silent salute. Jackson could feel well satisfied: so
far, at least, all had gone admirably, and there was no sign that
Pope had noticed anything. But the position was as fluid and
chancy as possible: Pope now lay between Lee and Jackson,
numerically superior many times over to each of them.

Late that evening Stuart with his cavalry and Stonewall's old
brigade reached Manassas Junction, which was Pope's supply-
depot, and after a short fight occupied it. The following
morning Jackson came up with the main body:

And to the bugle's din,
Sweating beneath their haversacks,
With rifles bristling on their backs,
The dusty men trooped in.

One handsome preliminary result of two days' forced marches
was now obvious to all. Manassas Junction, lying close to
Washington under the shadow of Pope's wing, was humanly
speaking the very safest place that could have been selected as
a depot for Pope's stores. Enormous quantities of everything
which the opulent North could think of for the maintenance of
a great army was here displayed to the astonished gaze of Jackson's men: sybaritic things which these hard-living soldiers had
scarcely dreamed of: field-kitchens, field-bakeries, goods-trains
full of preserved foods, mountains of meal sacks, kegs of whisky
in massive piles, magazine on magazine stuffed full of shoes
and clothing. After Jackson had sent out patrols, held prayers,
and put the whisky on ration under a guard with fixed bayonets, he let loose his men for a couple of hours' free plundering;
and there followed an unwonted festivity, pleasantly enshrined
in the memories of those who took part in it.

At this point Pope had begun to have some dawning inkling
of what was happening, and at first a feeling of unutterable
woe possessed him. But he soon got a grip on himself, and
resolved to crush Jackson before he could reunite with Lee. To
this end he put all his troops to the right-about, and moved
them on a broad front to converge on Manassas, where, as he
said, he would "bag the whole crowd". He himself arrived near
the scene late in the evening; the horizon was by this time gaily
illuminated by the flames from his burning stores, and violent
detonations from exploding ammunition-dumps greeted him,
like the din from a great battle. Jackson had vanished without
trace. Pope tore his hair and issued orders and counter-orders
throughout the whole night. Next day the corps which formed
his westerly wing was suddenly attacked at Groveton; in his
relief at this intelligence he directed his whole army thither and

despatched a telegram to Lincoln informing him that he had
Jackson cornered, and that henceforward everything would go
swimmingly. For the next two days Pope made vain attempts
to batter down Jackson, who had taken a strong position along
a railway embankment; but by the afternoon of the second day,
when Pope was still straining every nerve, Lee had reached
the scene of action. Under cover of belts of woodland he drew
up Longstreet's corps in battle order, to launch them in a concentrated flank-attack which swept Pope from the field and
drove his beaten army reeling into the outer defences of
Washington. And with that Pope's career as a commander came
to an end, and one of the most brilliant victories of the war
— the so-called Second Manassas — was inscribed upon the
roll of the Confederates' brief but glorious history.

Lee now crossed the Potomac and invaded Maryland with
an army, small indeed, and ill-equipped, but high in spirit and
habituated to victory; Jackson opened his account by compelling 12 000 Unionists to capitulate at Harper's Ferry. For want
of anyone better, McClellan was now taken once more into
favour by Lincoln, and moved slowly to meet Lee. An unusually bloody battle (called by the North after the river Antietam,
by the South, Sharpsburg) was now fought out on the northern
bank of the Potomac, when McClellan, dilatory as usual, but
more than twice as numerous, went in to the attack against
Lee's 40 000. The main thrust was against Jackson's wing, but
after violent vicissitudes it was finally beaten off. Lee remained
all the next day on the battlefield, considering the possibility
of outflanking McClellan, and subsequently retired unmolested
behind the river, Jackson covering his withdrawal. After a
pause for rest McClellan once more began to manoeuvre himself forward against Lee, but in so extraordinarily torpid and
melancholy a fashion that he excited general displeasure in
Washington. When at last Lee's celebrated cavalry general,
Stuart, undertook a great ride right round the entire Federal
army, producing a state of panic among McClellan's horse,

without himself sustaining the least damage, Lincoln felt that men were laughing overmuch at his general, and McClellan was again relieved of his command, this time for ever. Not long afterwards Jackson suddenly appeared in the Valley, advanced northward and occupied Winchester, close by the Potomac. In the North the terror of his name was now such, that the correspondent of *The Times* in Washington, describing the panic which now broke out, reported that it was the firm conviction of every man in the capital that "Stonewall Jackson stands ready to pounce upon Washington from the Shenandoah, and to capture President, Secretaries and all". But before any further development could take place, Jackson was called away eastward to Lee, to meet a great thrust against Richmond by Lincoln's newly-appointed general, Burnside. Burnside's attack on Fredericksburg earned him an unenviable notoriety, and ended in total collapse; and he was afterwards replaced by Joseph Hooker, Lincoln's last resource for the time being. Hooker had as general of division acquired the nickname "Fighting Joe", and he lived up to it; in addition there were to be detected in him (or so the men of the North believed) certain higher intellectual endowments, not unapt for a commander; and hence his forthcoming encounter with Lee and Jackson, backed as he was by 120000 men, was considered to promise interesting developments. But the autumn was now far advanced, and for the time being both sides were content to go into winter quarters along the banks of the Rappahannock.

This period in winter quarters is the only idyllic interlude in Jackson's meteoric military career. He had taken part, without any interval for repose, in every military incident of the eventful year which was now closing. His feats of endurance did not seem to tell on him, in spite of the fact that he always spoke of his health in accents of quiet melancholy; but for his men a spell of inactivity might well be needful. The Stonewall Brigade, which at Bull Run had numbered 3000 men, had thereafter been constantly under his command, and had usually

been placed in the most perilous positions, had now been re-
duced to a venerable remnant, which in a strength-return after
the battle at Sharpsburg appeared as 246 rifles in all. Now they
were to have a chance to draw breath and to minister as best
they might to the comfort of an existence which had thus far
so miraculously been preserved. Sometimes they were even
given a little to eat, to their great joy and surprise; the Confederate armies having long since ceased to cherish any illusions
about their luckless overworked commissariat. Depression never
seems to have affected Jackson's corps, despite all they had to
undergo: they found no mean antidote against it, perhaps, in
the sense of glory and the assurance of victory. Besides, they
had other diversions: a private retail-trade flourished between
the hostile armies on either side of the river; the rebels exchanged their most valuable commodity — roll-tobacco — for
any surplus of coffee and shoes which the Yankees might have
at their disposal. Presumably it was while such a market was in
progress that Jackson on one occasion came riding along the
river to inspect his outposts: his soldiers, who were on the bank
in considerable numbers, sprang up and formed cheering lines
along his route, so that some inquisitive persons on the northern
shore called across the river to find out what all the excitement
was about: when they were told that the cheering was for General Stonewall Jackson, many of the Federal soldiers hurried
forward along their bank and cheered enthusiastically with the
rest.

Jackson's popularity among his people had now exceeded all
bounds, and this although he made as few concessions to his
men in point of discipline as in any other respect. His punishments were known as the severest in the whole army. He was
not, indeed, any such bluff and brutal a figure as Whittier, the
poet of the North, represents him to be in "Barbara Fritchie";
on the contrary, he was gentle and compassionate, extremely
chivalrous to non-combatants, and so fond of children that on
one occasion in the presence of his adjutant he was unable to

restrain his tears at the news that the daughter of the house in which he had his quarters — a six-year-old girl who sometimes came in to play with the general — had died unexpectedly; but he tolerated no paltering with discipline. Other generals — and Lee among them — applied psychological criteria to such soldiers as these, who had little notion of the laws of war, and tempered justice with mercy; but in all serious cases Jackson was immovable. Men who defied their superiors, or refused to obey orders, soldiers who committed theft or violence against civilians, deserters who were caught, and other such persons, found themselves without exception (if they belonged to his corps) in front of a firing-squad. He even as a rule rejected those appeals for mercy in which the delinquent pleaded to be placed in the foremost rank, so that he might meet his death in the next battle: to fight and fall for the freedom of the South was in his view an occupation exclusively reserved to decent folk. Despite all this, his soldiers adored him. In part, no doubt, this was because his oddities made it easy for the ordinary soldier to conceal his idolatry under a friendly mockery. They never wearied of telling anecdotes of their general, were always inventing new stories about him; as for instance this one: "Stonewall died, and was to go to Heaven, and two angels were sent to fetch him. They looked for him in his tent, but he wasn't there. They looked for him at the prayer-meeting, but he wasn't there. They looked for him at the outposts, but he wasn't there either. Then they went back to report that he had vanished; but when they reached home, they found that Stonewall had made a flank-march and got to Heaven before them." When Jackson rode between the tents in his camp, such an uproar always broke out among his men that listeners at a distance used to say, "That's either Stonewall or a rabbit" — these being the only two phenomena capable of exciting such transports.

This autumn he was promoted Lieutenant-General; and a few days afterwards he wrote home to Mrs. Jackson that he would much have preferred to be a parson: the rank of a preacher of the Word appeared to him as the most enviable distinction of all. He was a man who always meant exactly what he said; yet it is clear that another side of his nature drew him to war and everything connected with it, despite all the attractions of the religious life. The Confederates had a special war-cry which they used in bayonet-charges — a shrill, long-drawn, wavering affair, possibly of Indian origin; and sometimes to amuse themselves this famous "rebel yell" would be raised in one tent, taken up by those that lay nearest, and carried with ever-increasing volume from one end of the camp to the other. Jackson loved to listen to this sound, which reminded him of some of his greatest hours. An adjutant has preserved a story of how one evening, when Jackson was occupied in his tent with administrative business, this war-cry suddenly broke out in one of his brigades, and spread until the whole area resounded with it; Jackson came out bareheaded at top speed and stood to listen, "with his elbows on a post, as a countryman listens to the nightingale", silently savouring the rise and culmination of the swelling waves of sound, until, as they died away at last in an echo among the mountains, he inclined his head to catch the last faint vibrations; after which he went in again, muttering to himself with the air of a connoisseur, "The finest music I ever heard".

With the coming of April Hooker began to roll up his sleeves and lay his plans for a spring campaign. Swiftly and efficiently he moved his army a little to the westward, and crossed the Rappahannock at Chancellorsville, where, in difficult wooded country, he took up a strong position with his back to the river-crossing. Lee and Jackson hastened after him. Hooker had by this time already succeeded in establishing himself on a broad arc, his wings resting on the river, his front protected along its entire length by strong field-works constructed of fallen trees; and he was, moreover, nearly twice as strong as Lee, who for the moment had at his disposal only Jackson's corps and two of Longstreet's divisions. It would have been hopeless in such circumstances to batter their heads against Hooker's breast-works; but on the other hand the Confederates could not afford to sit down quietly in front of his position and await his attack, for as the result of secondary operations by one of Hooker's subordinates some way down stream the situation did not admit of any delay. The only bright feature in the prospect was that the greater part of Hooker's cavalry had been lured away to the west on a hunt after a couple of Stuart's brigades; Lee was therefore superior in this arm and could reconnoitre at will. The intelligence which came in was at first sufficiently depressing; everything about Hooker looked disconcertingly strong and solid. At last, however, it was discovered that his right wing did not extend right back to the river, but rested only on a wood, called The Wilderness, which was considered to be absolutely inaccessible. Jackson at once conceived a lively interest in this wing and this wood. After most careful investigation had been made, he discussed the situation with Lee, and the two quickly came to a decision. Lee calmly agreed to divide his greatly inferior forces: a plan analogous to that against Pope, but this time on the plane of tactics, was once again to be initiated by Jackson. The battle of Chancellorsville, which is marked by a rare elegance, turned out to be something similar to Banér's dispositions at Wittstock, with Jackson in the role of King and Stålhandske; though Jackson's part was a more immediately effective one than theirs. Lee was to keep Hooker busy to his front, while Jackson with the whole of his corps was to make a concealed flank-march and fall upon him from The Wilderness.

At an early hour on the morning of 2 May 1863, Jackson said farewell to Lee, and, with 26 000 men, disappeared along winding forest paths to the west. The march-orders he had issued sufficiently evinced the importance of the enterprise: they enjoined, among other things, that the march was not in any circumstances to be interrupted, that no attention was to be paid to any cavalry skirmishes which might occur, and that stragglers were to be despatched with the bayonet. Despite every precaution the movement across Hooker's front was at one place observed by the enemy, and Hooker sent forward one of his corps to harass what he imagined to be retreating troops. Jackson detached a brigade from the rearguard to occupy this corps, and pushed on unmolested, silently and with compressed lips, only muttering now and then, "Press on!" The march continued throughout the entire day, in much heat, and with few rests; but the men in the ranks had an idea of what was in preparation, and every soldier did his best. One of Jackson's staff officers, who was riding on in a hurry through the press of troops to reach the group where Jackson was, found the men in high spirits, and was everywhere greeted with cheery cries of "Here's one of Jack's kids; let him pass, boys... Did you have a nice breakfast this morning, sonny... Better hurry up, or you'll catch it for coming too late... Tell Old Jack that we are all coming, and don't let him begin the fuss till we get there!"

Unruffled calm and confidence still dwelt in the bosoms of General Hooker and his troops on the afternoon of this day. The corps which had been sent southward under Sickles was considered to be occupied with collecting prisoners and booty at leisure from among the rebels who had been observed withdrawing, and no reports of disquieting symptoms had come in from any quarter. In General Howard's corps, on Hooker's right wing, nearest to The Wilderness, they had piled arms behind the southward-facing breastwork, and the men were busy cooking or playing cards. Some patrols reported that they had seen rebels in the wood, but no one bothered to attach any importance to this: obviously it was a question only of a few isolated marauders.

At this moment Jackson's troops were engaged, after their ten hours' march, in getting as best they might into battle-formation, about one kilometre in from the edge of the wood. At the side of a road which ran through the wood and thence directly

into Howard's flank, Jackson sat his war-horse, "Little Sorrel",
watch in hand. His face was a little flushed; from time to time
his lips moved noiselessly; probably he was holding converse
with the God of Battles. He had just sent off his last report to
Lee, informing him that he intended to attack almost at once,
and that it looked as though an ever-gracious Providence would
vouchsafe them a great victory. His divisions under Rodes,
Colston and A. P. Hill, were drawn up in three lines at a
couple of hundred metres' interval, accurately placed at right-
angles to the road, on both sides of which their weapons
gleamed in the evening sunshine, under the high vault of
greenery, to lose themselves on either hand among the dense
undergrowth. A mounted battery had driven forward to the
front, and stood on the road near Jackson: the horses tossed
their heads and reared with excitement. To the rear, against
the sinking sun, Hill's last brigades were just coming up. Rodes,
in command of the first line, stood by Jackson; obliquely to
their front, and far away, could be heard sporadic gunfire from
Lee's wing. Jackson looked at his watch; it was nearly six
o'clock. "Are you ready, General Rodes?" "Yes, General; everything is in order." Jackson nodded and put the watch in his
pocket. "You can go forward, Sir." The sound of a trumpet
shattered the expectant silence under the overarching boughs;
there came a great crashing and rustling, as the lines pressed
forward through the thickets; and the next moment the "rebel
yell" burst from twenty-six thousand throats, to fall more ter-
rifically than ever before upon the ears of their confounded
adversaries.

Officers and men on the Federal side, who turned their gaze
towards the edge of the wood, now of a sudden become so
menacing, saw running out of it first their own outposts, then
a number of startled hares and roe-deer, finally long grey lines
at the double, with gleaming bayonets. Destruction now came
rushing upon the whole of Howard's corps with extreme speed.
That body appears to have put itself in such posture of defence

as the circumstances permitted, but in less than half an hour it had been driven in and annihilated — killed, captured, or in uncontrollable flight in the direction of Hooker's headquarters in the centre. Hooker was sitting with some members of his staff taking coffee on an open verandah at Chancellorsville Farm, talking of Sickles's probable successes to the south, when suddenly a sharp burst of gunfire was heard close at hand, immediately to westward. "My God, here they come!" burst out an officer who had gone down to the road below the verandah to see what it was all about. The next moment a wild medley of baggage, commissariat waggons, gun-teams, maddened animals and shrieking fugitives poured along the road before the eyes of the Commander-in-Chief: it was all that remained of Howard's corps.

> Our leader is Joe Hooker,
> He takes his whisky strong,

ran a popular song in Hooker's army; and in the North an attempt was afterwards made to provide at least a partial explanation of the disaster at Chancellorsville with the aid of the hypothesis that the Commander-in-Chief was drunk at the time of the battle — as malicious tongues also asserted of Grant at Shiloh. Hooker and his intimates vehemently denied it; but it does appear probable that during the subsequent course of the battle he never succeeded in recovering his poise after that unexpected vision of the streaming remnants of Howard's men: proud and confident until that moment, he became at a stroke completely confused, and lost all faith in himself.

In the gathering darkness, filled with the cries of men and the rattle of musketry, and lighted ever more luridly by the flashes from the many guns and the flames from woods that had been set alight by artillery fire, Jackson pressed irresistibly on, forward towards Hooker's centre, like the dark shadow of total annihilation falling suddenly athwart the army of the Potomac; and brigades from Rode's and Colston's lines, intermingled after many bayonet charges against breastworks and redoubts, had by ten o'clock come close to the two dominating heights of Fairview and Hazelgrove, whence Hooker's only line of retreat across the river could be commanded by artillery. It was Jackson's intention to straddle this road with his entire corps, and thus force Hooker and his army, wedged between himself and Lee, to choose between capitulation and extinction. But it was now that the disaster occurred — a stroke of chance which possibly decided the whole war.

About ten o'clock Jackson called a halt in order to re-form his ranks for the final night attack which was now imminent, and himself rode with his staff forward through his front along the road to reconnoitre. When he returned his troop of horse-men were mistaken in the darkness for Federal cavalry, and a salvo was fired from a North Carolina regiment of Hill's di-vision, which was just taking its place in the front line. Horses and riders fell in heaps by the roadside; Jackson received two bullets through his left arm, and one in his left hand; his horse turned and shied off towards the enemy's lines, but was stopped at the last moment, and Jackson fell into the arms of one of his aides. "All my wounds are from my own men," he said faintly, before he lost consciousness. An artery was severed, and there was danger that he might bleed to death; with great difficulty he was got to an ambulance as quickly as possible. The stretcher came under artillery fire, and one of the bearers was hit; Jackson fell heavily to the ground, sustaining internal in-juries. When his arm had been amputated, and he recovered consciousness after the chloroform, an adjutant came from the front with reports, and a request for further orders from Gen-eral Stuart, who had been summoned to the spot and had as-sumed the command. With quick, decided questions Jackson informed himself of the details of the position, his eyes lighted up as of old, and with a powerful effort he attempted to force his enfeebled consciousness to grasp the situation, that he might render one last service to his cause; but after a moment he sank back sadly: "I do not know... General Stuart must do what he thinks best."

The battle ended with Hooker's being driven back across the river, totally demoralized; complete catastrophe he succeeded in escaping, thanks to Jackson's fall. This victory marked the culmination of the fortunes of the South. The triumph was great at the fabulous success, but it was clouded by the thought of the hero who had been the chief architect of victory, and who now lay fighting for life at Guiney's Station. "General Jackson has lost his left arm, but in him the army has lost its right," said Lee, and it was the thought of all. For a few days his condition seemed encouraging, but pneumonia set in — the effect, it was thought, of his injuries from the fall from the stretcher; and on a Sunday, fourteen days after the battle, it became clear that he had but a few hours to live. He learned with pleasure that the whole army was holding a service of prayer for him; when his wife threw herself weeping upon the bed and told him that their separation was very near, he answered with his usual stoicism, "Very good; it is all right". Soon afterwards his mind became clouded; as in his delirium he ranged his hosts for battle for the last time his voice took on the loud accents of command: "Order A. P. Hill to prepare for action! Pass the infantry to the front! Tell Major Hawks..." He broke off in the middle of the sentence. For a little while he remained silent; and then said quietly: "Let us go over the river, and rest in the shadow on the other side", and a moment after the great soldier had entered into eternity.

Six weeks later, away up in Pennsylvania, Lee fought out the battle of Gettysburg, the first battle in which he had not Jackson to assist him. Jackson's corps, which began the engagement, was now led by Ewell, a respectable mediocrity. The Confederate General J. B. Gordon — an able writer and a highly esteemed soldier — was at this time commanding a brigade under Ewell, and two years later was to lead the surviving remnant of Jackson's corps at Appomattox, where he ca-

pitulated; and in the Memoirs which in his old age he committed to paper he writes of his feelings at that moment during
the first day of the battle when he was forced to stand by and
see the victory which was already in the Confederates' grasp
slip through their fingers because of Ewell's anxious pedantry
and unintelligent obedience to the letter of his orders; and of
how he was filled with a desperate longing for "half an hour
of Jackson". It is narrated of Lee himself — a man little given
to loose statements — that a few years after the war, when he
was Principal of the Lexington High School, he received a
letter containing questions from some historian concerning details of the battle of Gettysburg. With an emotion such as he
displayed but rarely, he banged his fist on the table so that pens
and inkpots danced, and turning to a clergyman who was
present declared that if he had had Jackson at Gettysburg, that
battle would have ended in a great victory: Baltimore and
Washington would have fallen, and the liberty of the Confederation would have been assured. It is a possibility: in the
nature of things it can hardly be more than that; but in any
case this pronouncement, by one of the two greatest soldiers
America has produced, is a noble tribute to the other.

Translated by Michael Roberts

ROBERT MONRO

*S*OME time in the 1630's the Scottish mercenary Colonel, Robert Monro, sat down to compose a narrative — "to the use of all worthie Cavaliers favouring the laudable profession of Armes" — of the services in Germany of himself and his regiment, "the honourable Scotch regiment, call'd McKeyes" — "first under the magnanimous King of *Denmark,* during his warres against the Emperour; afterward, under the Invincible King of *Sweden,* during his Majesties life time; and since, under the Directour Generall, the Rex-chancellor *Oxensterne* and his Generalls." Monro had returned to his fatherland in 1633, with Oxenstierna's commission to levy troops in order to bring his depleted regiment up to full strength. It was presumably the disaster at Nördlingen that intervened to prevent his return: Swedish shares, we may suppose, no longer stood very high on the mercenary market in the months that followed, and in that fatal battle his regiment had been as good as wiped out. For lack of any better occupation this unemployed Colonel now took to the pen, and proceeded, in a narrative whose particularity does not make it the less moving, to reduce to words the epic experiences of seven years, adding by way of adornment such quotations, applications of military lore, pious reflections and tangled pedantries of style as might reasonably be expected of a right-thinking cavalier with some pretensions to education, some hazy recollection of his youthful studies in the Latin tongue, and a clear eye for the inherent majesty of his subject. His book appeared in London in 1637; its title, long as a preface, is well-known to readers of *A Legend of Montrose,* where

Scott inserts it into his Introduction. It is usually referred to simply as *Monro his Expedition*.

Colonel Monro himself is not wholly unknown to those who remember their Scott; for it was he who provided a good deal of the material for the immortal Dugald Dalgetty — "Ritt-master Dugald Dalgetty of Drumthwacket", the valorous soldier of fortune and military theorist, who returned to Scotland just in time to take part in Montrose's campaigns, and to edify his brothers-in-arms with endless reminiscences of the time when he followed "the invincible Gustavus Adolphus, the Lion of the North, and the Bulwark of the Protestant Faith". Dalgetty is of course by no means a mere copy of our Colonel: Scott has in great measure stylised him. As a rhetorician he has been made better than his model, and can at any moment produce well-turned periods of preposterous phraseology, to the frequent imperilment of the gravity of his audience; while Monro keeps to a more modest level and achieves the sublimely comic only by way of exception. On the other hand Scott's hero, for artistic reasons, has been made of coarser moral fibre than his original. Dalgetty is a pure mercenary without ideals of any sort, push-ing, valiant, and jealous of his honour; proud of his profession, and imbued with the most minute interest for its etiquette and technique, but completely devoid of any idea that the trade of war may have a more ideal side. He fights as cheerfully for Papists, Arminians and Anabaptists as for Protestants — pro-vided only that his wages be honestly paid, or at least that he be given now and then a decent chance of plunder; for a mo-ment he has even contemplated entering the Turkish service; the religious element in him is limited to the Biblical phraseo-logy of his descriptions of Gustavus Adolphus. Monro, on the other hand, takes a personal interest in the success of the Pro-testant Cause, and is in general very ready to speak of religion; he could never have reconciled himself to serving with Tilly or Wallenstein; he notes with satisfaction that English and Scottish soldiers of fortune prefer to follow the Swedish stan-

dard. On the battlefield of Breitenfeld, where Monro had intervened effectively in the hand-to-hand struggle which brought
Tilly's great infantry attack to a standstill, he applied to the
King after the victory was won for permission to reinforce his
depleted regiment by incorporating all prisoners of British na-
tionality. He obtained leave to do so, and applied to Banér, who
had charge of the sorting-out of the prisoners. And when,
among all the thousands of prisoners available, the two of them
succeeded in dredging up only three Irishmen — then Monro
was indeed somewhat downcast at a recruitment so poor from
the point of view of the service, but derived none the less a
certain moral satisfaction from telling the King of his ill-success,
as being proof that the British Isles produced in the main men
who fought for the cause of righteousness.

The sword and the half-pike were instruments whose use
Monro understood down to the smallest particular; with the
pen he felt himself less at ease, and his manoeuvres to get to
grips with what he wishes to say can often become somewhat
tedious. His subject is akin to Xenophon's, his enthusiasm for
Gustavus Adolphus is reminiscent of Joinville's for St Louis;
but while the lucidity of the Athenian and the easy conversa-
tional style of the Sénéchal of Champagne have put their military memoirs among the fixed stars in the literary firmament,
Monro has not succeeded in making his narrative of the campaigns in which he took part much more than a forgotten curiosity of literature. No subject is great enough and interesting
enough in itself to make a book readable. It may be treated as
seriously and conscientiously as you please; but a certain
literary instinct — often almost impossible to detect, but still
decisive for the reader — must have been operative at the moment when events were clothed in words, if any such narrative
is to escape the fate of becoming no more than a source for the
historian. Few men have been less affected with literary *arrière-
pensée* than a man such as Joinville when he dictated his book
on King Louis; in so far as he troubled himself about the ar-

rangement of his material at all, he usually succeeded in putting the cart before the horse, and in his narrative he chattered away, just as things occurred to him, with supreme disregard of other considerations. Nevertheless his book emerged as great literature, partly perhaps because he had in comparison with a writer such as Monro one great advantage: as became a *gentilhomme* in his day, he could neither read nor write. He spoke to his secretary in the tone of a man of the world, easily and with a charming lightness, entirely fascinated by his subject, and the result was readable from start to finish. But Monro, full of Latin quotations, and with Frontinus and Quintus Curtius at his finger-ends, saw (thanks to his studies) the portals of the land of pedantry open wide before him; and with much painful care he has succeeded in rendering his book largely unreadable, unless the reader bring considerable patience to the task. Parallel to every narrative chapter in his book runs a chapter of *Observations,* highly repetitious and packed with didactic verbiage; but containing nevertheless matter which makes it impossible simply to skip them in the reading. Thus Monro spreads over the events he describes a veil of heaviest baroque ornamentation, obscuring them from the eye of the reader; and it is only rarely that he permits a more or less clear image to slip through.

Nevertheless Monro is a writer worthy of all respect — a barbarized Xenophon from an age when literary products blossomed only with extreme rarity in the tented field. In bibliographies of the Thirty Years' War his book occupies an almost unique place: memoir-writing by active participants — whether in war or politics — seems to have been almost exclusively confined to France. He stands therefore as a virtually unique spokesman for a great confraternity: many inarticulate spirits, many simple-minded men of the sword in him find a voice, and the uncomplicated philosophy and ethics of the honourable craft of arms is given clear expression in his reflections and commentaries.

The regiment whose fortunes Monro relates (he commanded one half of it throughout the period of its Swedish service) was levied by Lord Reay, and was originally intended to be used as reinforcement for Count Mansfeld, at that time Protestantism's one remaining champion in Germany. But by the time it was brought up to full strength and embarked at Cromarty — in the autumm of 1626 — Mansfeld's restless life had already closed, and instead they steered their course to Christian IV of Denmark, then busily engaged in raising men for his German war. Monro began his career as Lieutenant under "the worthie and well-born Captaine, Thomas McKenzie of Kildon"; but his own merits — assisted by sword and pestilence — brought him quick promotion, and after little more than a year he became Lieutenant-Colonel, and commanded the regiment in Lord Reay's absence. Lord Reay tended to be mainly absent. Men of rank such as himself raised regiments and lent them the lustre of their name, and arranged the details of high finance with any Kings who might be interested; but for routine service on the battlefield or at the head of the storming columns they rarely had the time to spare: such things fell to the lot of simpler folk such as Monro. The clan of Monro was numerously represented in the regiment: the subalterns, N.C.O.'s and privates of that name, whom the conscientious Colonel notes down in the course of his narrative as dead, are as the sands of the sea in number. The regiment included no less than three members of the family who afterwards became Colonels under Gustavus Adolphus: Robert Monro the Lord of Fowles, head of the house, called "the Black Baron", who had been compelled by financial difficulties to mortgage his estate and enlist as a soldier, and who died of wounds at Ulm; John Monro of Obstell, who fell at Wetterau on the Rhine; and the author himself, longer-lived than most of the others — though he was rarely out of the way when an important action was to be fought.

During the Danish period of the war the regiment's experiences in the field were certainly extremely arduous, but on the whole they were satisfactory to Monro, who looked at them wholly from the regiment's point of view. The campaign itself was as unfortunate as possible; but the regiment covered itself with glory at the storm of sundry places and in a number of rearguard actions. The Scots soon won the reputation of a picked regiment; and the Danish command relied largely upon them in moments of difficulty, gave them the posts of danger, and allowed them to bear the brunt of the fighting without reinforcement for much longer periods than in the case of other troops. All of which is no doubt very honourable for a regiment, and redounds to the glory of Scotland too; but even Scots have limits to their endurance and their taste for fighting, and once or twice in Oldenburg Monro seems to have felt that here was too much of a good thing. When Tilly advanced into Holstein the regiment sustained a serious disaster. Three of its companies were defending Bredenberg, a fortified castle in those parts; after a summons to capitulate had been rejected, the Imperialists stormed the castle and put to death every man, woman and child inside it; only one ensign escaped to carry a report to the regiment. What particularly irritated the Scots about this was that their regimental chaplain had been slain with the rest, although he had been found on his knees, praying for his life with uplifted hands. Shortly after this Monro in his turn stormed a place in Holstein garrisoned by the Imperialists (disguised in his narrative under the name of Aickilfourd); the Scots now, by way of *quid pro quo,* refused to give quarter; the Imperialists at last barricaded themselves in a church; and Monro, after a short struggle with his conscience, caused the door to be broken open with battering-rams: no place, he felt, could be sufficiently sacred to afford sanctuary to people who killed regimental chaplains. These two episodes provided a sort of prelude in miniature to the similar incidents at Neu-Brandenburg and Frankfurt on the Oder in which the regiment was to play a part a few years later.

With the King of Denmark Monro was well-pleased; he was not, perhaps, much of a commander, but wages were punctually paid, and he took pains to arrange for good quartering. His standing epithet with Monro is "the Magnanimous"; his appearance was truly regal; his wisdom, carefulness and tenacity win Monro's commendation. He was, besides, in his dealings with honourable cavaliers an amiable and loquacious gentleman; Monro ate at his table, and even on one occasion, when they were quartered on Laaland, had the honour of a visit from the King which lasted until 3 o'clock in the morning; upon which Monro's only comment is that the King departed without saying farewell — a piece of absent-mindedness which is not perhaps entirely incapable of explanation, in view of the hour and His Danish Majesty's prowess with the bottle. Monro, it is clear, never had better quarters than those he enjoyed in Denmark — at least until the march through the Rhineland in the autumn of 1631. Minor clashes with their Danish hosts and with other regiments did indeed occur from time to time, but they appeared almost as an agreeable break in an existence which might otherwise have declined into torpid luxuriousness. Upon his return from Holstein, Monro (he had just got his majority) was sent with a portion of the regiment to Assens, on the island of Fyn, where he found another Major with some squadrons of the Rhinegrave's cavalry. The question as to which of them had the right to command the garrison soon produced a coolness between the two Majors, a coolness which communicated itself to their devoted troops; so that the ensuing street-fights soon showed a daily casualty-return of from four to five killed per regiment. Major-General Slammersdorff was forced to quit his headquarters at Odense, to hold a court-martial, and to pronounce a verdict in Monro's favour, before this civil war could be brought to a conclusion. When next these two regiments encountered one another — both were by that time in Swedish service — these little irritations seem to have been forgotten; or perhaps Gustavus Adolphus and his order-loving Field-Marshal Horn had effective prophylactics against private diversions of this sort.

When from time to time Danish burghers and peasants grew exasperated at the Scots billetted upon them, they had at first recourse to the obvious remedy of thrashing such of them as they encountered alone; but when this proved in the long run not to be a very paying proposition, they hit upon a better method, and brought accusations of rape. In one case Monro lost three men at a stroke, on account of a single peasant girl; the court-martial in Copenhagen, which had called in Monro as assessor, allowed itself to be persuaded to defer sentence on grounds of insufficient evidence. However, when this had been agreed on, and Monro had left Copenhagen, the court nevertheless caused the accused to be summarily hanged. Monro shook his head at this way of doing business, partly because he considered the accusations to be false, but mainly because he felt that the court-martial had acted in an ungentlemanly fashion towards him by arranging for the hanging privily and in his absence.

Monro in this connection is concerned to point out that the machinery for the administration of justice was by no means lacking in such a regiment as his; and his account of how it was organized is of its kind a good picture of his age:

To conclude this observation, there are lawes and justice observed as well among souldiers, as in other governments, and the strictest justice that is, with least partiality: our lawes are the Kings Articles, we are sworne to obey our President or Iudge, he amongst us present having the command, to whom his Majesty joynes, as assessor to the Iudge, an Auditor for doing of justice, our Assisers or Iury we have not to seeke (*viz.*) a competent number or thirteene of our owne Regiment, Officers, Captaines, Lievetenants, Antients, Sergeants and Corporalls, till our number be full: our Proforce or Gavilliger brings in the complaints, and desires justice, in his Majesties name, to the party offended, and to his Master the Kings Majesty or Generall, that fuers or leads the warre; and every Regiment is bound to have an executioner of their owne, which if the Regiment wants, the Colonell is obliged to hire another to doe the execution for paiment, and sometimes as the crime and the person is respected, that is to suffer, he is honoured to be shot by his camerades, or beheaded, not suffering an executioner to come neare him. Other slight punishments we enjoyne for slight faults, put in execution by their Camerades; as the *Loupegarthe*, when a Souldier is stripped naked above the waste, and is made to runne a furlong betwixt two hundred Souldiers, ranged alike opposite to others, leaving a space in the midst for the Souldier to runne through, where his Camerades whip him with small rods, ordained and cut for the purpose by the *Gavilliger*, and all to keepe good order and discipline; for other lesser faults, there is ordained slighter punishments, as Irons, standing at a poast, his hands bound up above his head; likewise sitting on a *Treen* or woodden Mare, in some publicke place, to make him ashamed of his fault: As also sometimes to stand six or seaven houres longer than ordinary at the centrie posture; as I was once made to stand in my younger yeares at the *Louver gate* in *Paris*, being then in the Kings Regiment of the Guards, passing my prenticeship, for sleeping in the morning, when I ought to have beene at my excercise, for punishment I was made stand from eleven before noone, to eight of the Clocke in the night Centry, Armed with Corslet, Head-piece, Bracelets, being Iron to the teeth, in a hot summers day, till I was weary of my life, which ever after made me the more strict in punishing those under my Command.

In May 1628 the regiment received orders to march with all speed to Elsinore, whence it was shipped to serve as garrison in Stralsund, which at that time was menaced by the attacks of Wallenstein, and had been taken under the protection of Christian IV. Here Monro and his men were to experience their severest trials in the Danish service. Wallenstein, who had sworn to take the town "were it grappled to Heaven with iron chains", pushed the siege with great fury. Three attempts at storm were made upon the positions held by Monro; outworks were taken and retaken in desperate nocturnal encounters with pike, club and partisan; the regiment in a few weeks lost more than half its strength. But Scottish blood did not flow in vain: the town was held, despite Wallenstein's efforts, and the Imperialists, as Monro points out with satisfaction, lost in their attacks at least thrice as many men as he. When the crisis was at its worst, he was cheered by the arrival of a famous fellow-countryman, Alexander Leslie, Major-General in the Swedish service, who had been sent with sufficient aid by Gustavus Adolphus; and Monro in reporting this unexpected deliverance compares Stralsund with Sara the wife of Abraham, who was made fruitful when she least expected it. The Danish troops were now withdrawn; and with such of his men as survived — and, for his own part, with a musket-ball in one knee — Monro returned to Copenhagen. Here Lord Reay now appeared with a large number of new levies which he had raised on a recruiting tour in Scotland, and the regiment was again brought up to its full strength of twelve companies. In the winter of 1628–1629 Monro lay in quarters in "Malline [Malmö] in Skonland", with a couple of companies in "Alzenburg" [Hälsingborg] and one in "London" [Lund] in the same kingdom. Malmö makes a favourable impression on the observant Lieutenant-Colonel: the food in burgher homes he finds excellent without being extravagant; silver articles were plentiful and servants numerous; while the better class of people made laudable efforts to imitate the King, as far as possible, in dress, manners and appearance.

In June 1629, when peace with the Emperor was imminent, the regiment was paid off from the Danish Service; since the Colonel was as usual absent on a visit to England Monro on his own initiative sent an envoy to enquire into the possibilities of employment with the King of Sweden. Gustavus Adolphus sent by return an affirmative answer, journey-money, and orders; and thereupon half the regiment sailed to East Prussia and was installed as garrison in Braunsberg, while the other half was sent to Stockholm, whither Monro followed it soon after in company with his Colonel, who had by this time returned. Here His Majesty showed off his infantry, and demonstrated for their benefit

his new order of Discipline of *Briggades,* then first brought in use, at which time his Majesty having showen unto my Colonell and his Officers, the Order of his Majesties discipline, in which Order, his Majesty commanded to put my Colonels Regiment, which was presently obeyed, insomuch, that his Majesty was so well pleased with the capacity of my Colonels Souldiers going so orderly and readily to their Duties, that his Majestie did wish in open presence of the Army, that all his Foot were so well disciplined as my Colonels Regiment: for which, his Majesty would bee content to be indebted of a huge great summe of money, and having caused the Regiment march by towards their Quarters his Maiesty did mightily and much praise the Regiment for their good Order; saying, hee hoped one day, to get good service of those men for his monies...

The King went over to Germany soon after; Lord Reay accompanied him with the available half of the regiment; Monro was sent to East Prussia to take over the independent command of his six companies there, with orders to rejoin the King with them as soon as possible. He presented himself to the "Rex-Chancellor", who was installed as Governor of that province, and a few months after the opening of the campaign was ready to embark his men at Pillau, whence they steered for Wolgast in Pomerania.

He reached the Pomeranian coast in a heavy storm, which caused the ship to spring a leak, and finally piled it up on a sandbank, whence Monro with great difficulty made his way ashore; his arms and men were indeed retrieved, but all his baggage and ammunition was lost, and in this condition he found himself isolated on the coast, twenty German miles east of Stettin (where the King was) and with enemies ensconced everywhere in the surrounding country. He succeeded, nevertheless, in extricating himself adroitly from his precarious position, and made contact with the main army; and despite the crossness of fate he essays on this occasion a short lyrical flight:

Having thus by the providence of God happily landed againe on the faire, fertill, and spacious Continent of *Dutchland,* with a hand-full of old experimented Soldiers, able to endure all misery, toile, or travell, being valourous to undertake any perill or danger, they were to be commanded upon, being led by such a Generall as GUSTA-

VUS the *Invincible,* their new Master was: (under whose command and conduct, as their supreame Leader, and me, as his Majesties and my Colonels inferiour Officer, they marched from the Coast of *Pomerne,* out of *Rougenvalde,* through *Dutchland,* unto the foot of the Alpes in *Schwabland*)...

Alas!, he sighs upon a later occasion, had but our master not been taken from us, "the King of Captaines and the Captain of Kings", we should have crossed the Alps at that time, and paid Rome a visit.

From the moment when Monro enters upon his long march through Germany in company with the King's army — to which he and his regiment continued to be attached almost until the battle of Lützen — his tone is pitched higher than before, and his attitude to the trade of war undergoes a certain transformation. During the Danish campaigns it is his regiment, its weal or woe, its battle honours, which is all in all to him: the army as a whole scarcely exists for him, so little does he feel himself to be a part of it; and in enterprises common to them all he takes but little interest. When he writes "we", he invariably means simply "the regiment". But under Gustavus Adolphus he at once sees the operations as a whole, feels a strong *esprit de corps:* when now he writes "we", he means the whole army. Naturally he continues to use every suitable opportunity to vent his purely Scottish sentiments; but they do not now stand in the way of his corporate loyalty: the King may certainly be proud to possess such a regiment as Monro's, but on the other hand Monro takes unbounded pride in serving such a King — *of never dying memory ... Illustrissimus among Generalls ... the Phoenix of his time.* The exploits of the Scots of course claim the greater part of his space, for he narrates only what he personally has witnessed; but he freely admits that others than the Scots can distinguish themselves: the German foot, particularly those of the blue and yellow brigade, are not the men to be daunted by bagatelles; the Swedes too bear themselves worthily in the open field and in attacks on fortified positions; and the Finns, whom he calls *Haggapells*, are useful men on horseback, valuable in dangerous enterprises, and well able to meet the cuirassiers of Holck and Monte-cucculi on level terms.

Within his own branch of the military art Monro has very definite views on the differing value of musketeers and pike-men, which together composed, in almost equal proportions, the infantry of that age. Musketeers, he considers, are no doubt serviceable in many ways, especially to send forward ahead of the army as skirmishers; the new Swedish system of inter-spersing the cavalry with musketeer platoons is also highly to be recommended. But when there is really serious work to be done, the musketeers reveal their limitations: in large-scale fron-tal attacks on fortified towns, in particular, they show a lack of sense of duty and a certain insecurity in morale, which some-times it is impossible wholly to counteract; they have an in-grained tendency to scatter in search of plunder as soon as they have got inside the ramparts, leaving standards and officers to take care of themselves; while pikemen have better self-control. And in general Monro holds the view that the pike is a far nobler weapon than the musket:

Pike-men being resolute men, shall be ever my choyce in going on execution, as also in retiring honourably with disadvantage from an enemy, especially against horsemen: and we see offtimes, ... that when musketiers doe disbandon, of greedinesse to make booty, the worthy pike-men remaine standing firme with their Officers, guard-ing them and their Colours, as being worthy the glorious name of brave Souldiers, preferring vertue before the love of gold, that va-nisheth while vertue remaineth... The Pike [is] the most honour-able of all weapons, and my choise in day of battell, and leaping a storme or entering a breach with a light brest-plate and a good head-piece, being seconded with good fellows, I would choose a good halfe-Pike to enter with.

In mid-winter the King broke up from Stettin with a portion of his army, and moved forward in snow-storms and severe cold to Neu-Brandenburg, which was easily taken. According to

Monro, the officers and men who composed its garrison were, in a military point of view, the most wretched collection he had ever set eyes on; but (he adds) that was no more than was to be expected, since they consisted exclusively of poor simple Italians, who could hardly be expected to have much idea of warfare. Nevertheless the garrison duties of this battered troop had left ample leisure for plundering the surrounding country; and hence the leading elements of the King's troops came upon considerable quantities of money and gold chains. Despite the feeble resistance Monro had been profoundly impressed by the whole operation, and here breaks into a long dithyramb on the King's unique endowments as a commander. "Such a Master would I gladlie serve; but such a Master," he adds sadly, "I shall hardly see againe." Knyphausen was now put in command of the place; he was in Monro's view a man well experienced in the science of war, and in his company a cavalier with his wits about him could pick up many a useful lesson, for all that he did not love Scots. It was Knyphausen who formulated the dictum that in war an ounce of luck is worth a pound of calculation; but he was himself invariably unlucky, and not least at Neu-Brandenburg. That half of Lord Reay's regiment which had come over from Sweden was installed as garrison, after which the King turned his attention elsewhere. Shortly afterwards Tilly appeared before the town and took steps to make himself master of it; Knyphausen delayed too long in treating, and in the final storm almost the entire garrison was put to the sword: only the commandant himself and a number of officers were spared. This was a hard blow for Monro, who here lost many old comrades-in-arms; but he had not long to wait before taking his share in the great revenge at Frankfurt.

The storming of Frankfurt on the Oder, on 3 April 1631, is the most successful piece of narrative in the whole book: it was an event in which Monro personally played an important part. His regiment, or half-regiment, formed — now that the King had finally settled the composition of his tactical unit — together with three other regiments, "the Scotch Brigade", under the command of John Hepburn, a chivalrous and valiant gentleman, and a boyhood friend of Monro. Besides the Scotch Brigade, there were present in this action the Blue and Yellow Brigades; and with the cavalry the King had 10 000 men outside the walls; while inside them Field-Marshal Tiefenbach with 9 000 men awaited the onslaught with the utmost composure. Monro here inserts a long strategical discussion on the extreme daring of the enterprise, with Tilly encamped at no great distance, strong in numbers and no less so in the terror inspired by his success at Neu-Brandenburg; and expatiates on the extraordinary nicety of the King's calculations and general dispositions. Since there was no time for a regular siege, either Tiefenbach must be lured into the open, or the town must be stormed without delay; but neither of these possibilities appeared immediately practicable. After the advancing Swedish army had approached within one German mile of the town, it was drawn up in battle-order by the King in person, and then in all its splendour — the memory of which seems to have been particularly vivid when Monro wrote his book — advanced to offer battle with martial pomp and ceremony. But Tiefenbach was not to be drawn, and the infantry was therefore sent forward to take up suitable positions for a storm. The Scotch Brigade was to attack one of the main gates of the town. It was required to cross a moat, climb an earth rampart furnished with palisades, traverse the space between this and the town wall, and then, if all went well, force its way into the town itself on the heels of the retreating foe. The operation was under the command of Banér. When after a day or two all preparations were complete, the artillery gave the signal for the assault by firing a general salvo, and the Brigades, veiled in smoke, began to advance upon their objectives. The Blue and Yellow Brigade, "being esteemed of all the Army both resolute and couragious in all their exploits", came up against Walter

Butler's Irish, and were twice beaten back with great fury and severe losses; it was not until the greater part of Butler's men had been hewn down and he himself taken prisoner, with a pike wound through the body, that they succeeded in mastering the resistance of these energetic sons of Erin; "and truely," declares Monro, "had all the rest stood so well to it, as the *Irish* did, we had returned with great losse, and without victory." On his own section of the front they made shorter work of a less heroic resistance, and the Scots quickly found themselves immediately before the gates; but here the enemy resolutely barred the way, supported by a couple of small cannon placed there, and by "a flake of small shot, that shot a dozen of shot at once" — clearly some sort of contemporary machine-gun or multiple-barrelled weapon. Monro was the first to enter this somewhat uninviting thoroughfare:

...the valorous *Hepburne,* leading on the battaile of pikes, of his owne *Briggad,* being advanced within halfe a pikes length to the doore, at the entry he was shot above the knee, that he was lame of before, which dazling his senses with great paine forced him to retire, who said to me, bully *Monro,* I am shot, whereat I was wondrous sorry, his Major then, a resolute Cavalier, advancing to enter was shot dead before the doore, whereupon the Pikes falling backe and standing still, Generall *Banier* being by, and exhorting all Cavaliers to enter, Colonell *Lumsdell* and I, being both alike on the head of our owne Colours, he having a Partizan in his hand, and I a halfe Pike, with a head-piece, that covered my head, commanding our Pikes to advance we lead on shoulder to shoulder, Colonell *Lumsdell* and I fortunately without hurt, enter the Port, where at our entry some I know received their rest, and the enemy forced to retire in confusion, being astonished at our entry, they had neither wit nor courage, as to let downe the Portecullis of the great Port behinde them, so that we entering the streets at their heeles, we made a stand till the body of our Pikes were drawne up orderly, and flancked with Musketiers, and then wee advanced our Pikes charged, and our Musketiers giving fire on the flancks, till the enemy was put in disorder. After us entered Generall *Banier,* with a fresh body of Musketiers, he followed the enemy in one street, and *Lumsdell* and I in another, having rancountred the enemy againe, they being well beaten, our Officers tooke nine colours of theirs, which were to be presented to his Majestie, and the most part of the Souldiers were cut off, in revenge of their crueltie used at *New Brandenburg,* but some of their Officers got quarters, such as they had given to ours.

However, even this glorious day proved no unmixed pleasure for Monro; for the streets were choked, not only with corpses, but with the baggage of the Imperialists — lines of carts and supply-waggons, where a man might pick up "silver services, jewels, gold, money and clothing". It was too much for the soldiery to resist, especially as they had had the King's own word for it that a good time was coming. The ranks around Monro quickly thinned, as men slipped off upon their own private concerns; officers were no longer obeyed; by way of increasing the festive spirit, or in order to obtain more light for ransacking the darker recesses, the excited troops set the town alight in various places; some of their own standards were lost in the confusion, and could not be found until next morning, and in some regiments not a man remained with the colours — all of which is gravely deplored by Monro, who frankly admits that on that evening his men were utterly out of hand.

When towards evening the King rode into the town with the Rhinegrave's cavalry, he appears to have felt no more than modified rapture at what he saw there; he issued a number of stringent orders, but since there were relatively few men within earshot, it took some time before they produced any perceptible effect. A few days later, after the taking of Landsberg, which had proceeded in a more orderly fashion, he had recovered his good humour, and

on the Sabbath day in the afternoone suffered the principall Officers of his Armie (such as Generall *Banier,* and Lievetenant Generall *Bawtis,* and divers others) to make merry, though his Majestie did drinke none himselfe; for his custome was never to drinke much, but very seldome, and upon very rare considerations, where he had some other plot to effectuate, that concerned his advancement, and the weale of his State.

It is of course no accident that Banér and Baudissin are mentioned in connection with this carouse: they were both mighty men with the bottle. The Scots too had famous performers in this way: Major-General Patrick Ruthwen, called Pater Rotwein, who in spite of the sternest competition quickly secured for himself an acknowledged pre-eminence as a tippler: he had a head of iron, and could take incredible quantities. He and Baudissin (who was pretty near on the same level) often drank together; but after the King's death Baudissin took his discharge and entered the Saxon service, presumably attracted by the reputation of the electoral cellars. The two boon-companions were to meet once again: during one of Banér's earlier campaigns, when each was in command of an independent corps, (though now on opposite sides), they met early one morning in a very odd battle near Dömitz; and here Ruthwen, being a shade the soberer of the two, seized the opportunity to add one last brilliant victory — though this time of a rather different sort — to his earlier triumphs over Baudissin. Monro, for his part, lingers with pleasure over the companionable carouses he enjoyed when he lay quartered next to Axel Lillie, at Treptow in the Mark of Brandenburg:

a Towne ... renowned of old, for brewing of good beere, which during our residence there with the *Swedes,* we did merrily try, till that we had both quarrelling and swaggering amongst our selves, who before our departure againe were made good friends, reserving our enmity, till we saw our common enemy.

Axel Lillie's friendship with Monro seems to have stood the test; for six months later, before Mainz, he was sitting in Monro's redoubt — he had dropped in for a pipe and a chat — when a cannon-ball came and took off his leg.

Immediately after the capture of Frankfurt Monro was given a taste of the King's hot temper, when he was detailed to put in order a redoubt outside Landsberg, and despite unremitting labour throughout the night did not succeed in having it ready for the King's early morning inspection. The King took him

severely to task, and would hear of no explanations or excuses;
but when later on he understood all the circumstances, he was
sorry for his hard words. Monro shows no resentment; on the
contrary, he thinks all the better of the King for his impatience,
which, he says, always caused him to press on the work on
field-fortifications to the utmost of his power. And at the same
time he concedes that in the matter of digging the German soldiers are handier than the Scots: this is the only instance in
which he concedes a superiority to any other nation. And indeed it is one of the King's most notable qualities as a commander, that he can induce his men — even the mercenaries —
to wield the spade without wages:

> Likewise his Majestie was to be commended for his diligence by
> night and by day, in setting forwards his workes; for he was ever
> out of patience, till once they were done, that he might see his
> Souldiers secured and guarded from their enemies; for when he
> was weakest, he digged most in the ground; for in one yeare what
> at *Swede, Francford, Landsberg, Brandenburg, Verbum, Tanner-
> monde, Wittenberg,* and *Wirtzburg,* he caused his Souldiers to worke
> more for nothing, than the States of *Holland* could get wrought in
> three yeares, though they should bestow every yeare a Tunne of
> gold: and this he did not onely to secure his Souldiers from the
> enemy, but also to keepe them from idlenesse.

After sundry less colourful episodes from the campaign in
Brandenburg and the march to Berlin, Monro's simple epic
winds deviously on to the camp at Werben — a camp of a type
which was invented by Gustavus Adolphus, and was considered
by contemporaries as a miracle of field-fortification. Werben
not only confirmed Monro in his enthusiasm for the King's
military genius, but afforded him a proof of his singular good
fortune in everything he undertook, so that he might indeed
fitly be called *Mars his Minion and Fortunes Favourite.* For in
Brandenburg the plague had raged so hot, that Monro lost
thirty men of his regiment in a single week; while in Werben,
only six days' march away, every trace of it vanished at once
from the whole army, which could not be considered other-

wise than as a miracle from God. Tilly showed himself before the camp, with a view to trying an assault; but he was much harassed by anxiety for his food-supply, since the King's cavalry had swept the country clear beforehand, and after considering the matter for a day or two he sullenly retired. The Swedes soon broke camp to follow him; and passing the Elbe at Wittenberg, there made their junction with the army of the Elector of Saxony. The Saxon army, when they first met it drawn up in parade-order, looked brand-new, and glittered amazingly, while the King's men looked worn and tattered; "nevertheless," says Monro, "we thought not the worse of our selves." And now at last they were ready, as he puts it, to advance *"conjunctis viribus"* against the champion of the House of Austria and the Catholic League; and the united armies set themselves in motion towards Breitenfeld.

"As the Larke begunne to peepe, the seventh of September 1631" the drums of the Swedish army beat to arms; and after the men had fortified their bodies with victuals, and their souls with meditation and the confession of their sins, they covered — not without some difficulty — the last piece of the way to Tilly's positions. By noon the armies were ranged front to front, and the exchange of cannonading could begin; this was sufficiently trying for the foot, who during a wait of some hours had nothing to do but to stand still and fill the gaps in their ranks; "the sound of such musick being scarce worth the hearing, though martiall I confesse, yet, if you can have so much patience, with farre lesse danger, to reade this dutie to an end, you shall finde the musicke well paide; but with such Coyne, that the players would not stay for a world to receive the last of it, being over-joyed in their flying."

The Scotch Brigade was placed in the second line, but after the armies came to grips had the good luck to get a better chance to distinguish itself than the Brigades further forward, which were never engaged at all. For when Tilly, after crushing the Saxons, sent the mass of his infantry crashing into

Horn's wing, it was the Scots, among others, whom the King himself sent forward to check them. And Monro has succeeded in capturing a sort of smoke-swept impression of the obscurity and confusion of a seventeenth-century battlefield, in his description of the moment when his men came to grips with Tilly's *tercios:*

> The enemies Battaile standing firme, looking on us at a neere distance, and seeing the other Briggads and ours wheeleing about, making front unto them, they were prepared with a firme resolution to receive us with a salve of Cannon and Muskets; but our small Ordinance being twice discharged amongst them, and before we stirred, we charged them with a salve of muskets, which was repaied, and incontinent our Briggad advancing unto them with push of pike, putting one of their battailes in disorder, fell on the execution, so that they were put to the route.
>
> I having commanded the right wing of our musketiers, being my Lord of *Rhees* and *Lumsdells,* we advanced on the other body of the enemies, which defended their Cannon, and beating them from their Cannon, we were masters of their Cannon, and consequently of the field, but the smoake being great, the dust being raised, we were as in a darke cloude, not seeing the halfe of our actions, much lesse discerning, either the way of our enemies, or yet the rest of our Briggads: whereupon, having a drummer by me, I caused him beate the *Scots* march, till it cleered up, which recollected our friends unto us, and dispersed our enemies being overcome; so that the Briggad coming together, such as were alive missed their dead and hurt Camerades.

According to Monro the King attributed the victory (under God) to the Swedish and Finnish cavalry; but among the foot it was the Scotch Brigade which earned most thanks and commendation. In his general discussion of the battle Monro enumerates a long list of reasons for the victory, mixing impartially the religious with the military and technical; but the principal cause in his view is still the King himself, who in his own person was worth more than twenty thousand men:

> O would to GOD I had once such a Leader againe to fight such an other day in this old quarrel! And though I died standing, I should be perswaded, I died well; ... he that would labour an Army as *Gus-*

tavus did, he will finde fruite, yea even the best that groweth under the Empire, good Rhenish and Necker wine, not onely for himselfe, but for the meanest Souldier, and that unto excesse, which hath made me sometimes complaine more of the plenty our Souldiers had after this victory, through the abuse of it, then ever I did before for any penury.

The long triumphal progress after the victory, through Thuringia, the Rhineland and Bavaria, brought Monro many experiences, often worth pursuing through his clotted text, but hardly on the same plane as Frankfurt and Breitenfeld. He commanded the palace-guard in Munich, when the King held his court there in company with the Winter King of Bohemia; and he was still with the royal army at Nuremberg. But he was not present at Lützen: it was the first major action in which the King had not had Scots to rely upon, as Monro points out in his explanation of why the battle turned out as it did. He was at that time in South Germany, serving under Horn, and among other places was plaguing the diocese of Dunklespiel on the Upper Rhine — the same diocese in which Ritt-master Dugald Dalgetty had so enjoyed himself with the episcopal property. After the King's death a shadow began to creep across an existence which hitherto had been uniformly sunny; and after Nördlingen the survivors of Monro's regiment numbered less than a company — a twelfth of the strength with which it had entered the Swedish service. If the King had lived, he must have conceded that the hope he had expressed when he mustered them in Stockholm had been abundantly fulfilled: from this regiment he had gotten good service for his money.

Translated by Michael Roberts

SERGEANT BOURGOGNE

*T*HE story of Napoleon's Russian campaign, and of how the Grand Army went down to destruction, has been written by two men who took part in it: one was Philippe de Ségur, a Count and a Staff Officer, in his *Histoire de Napoléon et de la Grande Armée pendant l'année 1812;* and the other was Adrien François Bourgogne, sergeant of grenadiers in the Guard, in Memoirs which for long remained forgotten in manuscript, and were not published until the 1890's. Ségur treats the campaign in broad perspective, and aspires to write history in the grand manner. He divides his work into twelve books, like a properly-proportioned epic, takes his motto from Vergil, and adorns his account of the more important discussions with passages in *oratio recta,* after the antique manner. His presentation is conscientious and at times brilliant; he has a clear head and a sound judgment, and is himself deeply stirred by his subject; but he is also a trifle theatrical, and in his loftier passages — his apostrophes to his comrades-in-arms, and his ejaculatory sentences about heroism and undying honour — there sounds sometimes an echo of the rhetoric which flourished in Imperial bulletins and proclamations: a rhetoric which moved on pseudo classical stilts, and was adapted to the more primitive types of subaltern psychology.

His book is, as a whole, interesting reading; but it cannot compete with the chronicle of the Sergeant of the Guard. Bourgogne makes no attempt to rival Ségur as the historian of the campaign: he is concerned exclusively with his own experiences; but despite his lack of learning he stands as an author on a higher plane than the literary Count. He possesses to a high degree the ability to produce a strong impression by simple means: every scene he dwells on becomes sharp and clear to the eye of the reader. Among his merits are a sober matter-of-factness, an unadorned style, a sparing seasoning of picturesque Guards-slang, and, here and there, an undertone of phlegmatic humour; not to mention a capacity for reflection by no means despicable, and a notable memory for detail. A historian is naturally at a disadvantage in relation to a writer of Memoirs in the matter of communicating a sense of vivid reality to the reader; for the historian is as a rule the more abstract of the two. Ségur relates each fact to the whole, gives us general surveys, broad movements, summary accounts of battles, a generalized view of the miseries of the retreat. Bourgogne translates us to a world where broad aspects are things distant and mythical, and where every interest is concentrated on tangible personal details: each day's measure of hunger and cold and dead comrades; problems of packing and clothing; difficulties about transporting booty from Moscow; frost-bite, exhaustion, lice and colic; he tells of lives preserved by bivouac fires or dead horses; of *cantinières* whom no hardships can kill; of Lithuanian Jews profiteering on quarters; of the Emperor afoot in the snow; of what happens when a man loses the way; of desperate skirmishes; and of life-giving draughts from some captured Cossack brandy-flask. Bourgogne has a sensational subject; but there is no striving after sensation in the manner of his narration: in his concreteness, his freedom from every trace of declamation or theatricality, he shows himself to be in the highest sense of the word the more classical author of the two.

Very striking in this Napoleonic soldier is his respect for truth, even to the smallest detail. He seems to have possessed complete assurance, in small things as in great, that what really happened is interesting in itself, without the aid of any doubtful embellishments: a very remarkable attitude in a time and milieu such as his, when the powerful example of the Emperor himself — whose respect for truth was virtually non-existent, and whose efforts as a war-correspondent gave rise to the expression "to lie like a bulletin" — must have constituted a considerable temptation to imitation for every loyal narrator of the exploits of the Grand Army. A somewhat embroidered anecdote about the Guard, reproduced by Ségur, is corrected by Bourgogne, though there must have been a strong temptation to let it stand uncontradicted. Ségur narrates — undoubtedly in all good faith — that during the retreat, the remnants of the army, after breaking up from Smolensk, found at one place near Krasnoje that the heights on either side of the road were strongly held by Russians, who opened fire on a number of unattached persons in the centre of the column and produced much alarm. At this the Old Guard, which was immediately to the rear, at once formed itself into a hollow square around the Emperor, and so continued its march through the cross-fire, as unconcernedly as if there had not been an enemy in sight, while its band, no doubt with the idea of inspiriting the Emperor and emphasizing the point that he might feel himself secure among his Guard, broke in with

Où peut-on être mieux qu'au sein de sa famille?

The Emperor, whose taste for musical witticisms was not at that moment very pronounced, at once ordered them to cease playing that air, and the band was bidden instead to oblige with

Veillons au salut de l'Empire!

This anecdote, which so greatly redounds to the honour of the Guard, and sheds so favourable a light on its ability to keep up its spirits in trying circumstances, is rejected by Bourgogne. "I have often," he says, "heard this story told, and have even seen it in print" (his final revision of his manuscript dates from the 1830's, after he had read Ségur); "but it is incorrect: all that about the band is a mistake. For at that time even the

Guard had no band; and if there had in fact been a band, how could the poor devils have blown their instruments or fingered the keys in such a temperature, quite apart from the fact that their fingers were frostbitten already? No: the incident of the band took place in Smolensk, the day before the evacuation of the town, when the Emperor had lingered four days, and the army wanted to be off. Berthier on that occasion collected a few bandsmen and made them play

Où peut-on être mieux qu'au sein de sa famille?;

but the Emperor came out at once and ordered them to play the other air instead; it was quite possible for them to blow at Smolensk, for there were fires there at which they could thaw their instruments and their fingers."

Although Bourgogne was only twenty-seven at the time of the Russian campaign, he had already seen so much service that he could be reckoned among the genuine *vieux grognards*. At the age of twenty he had been accepted for the Guard; and since then had seen something of most parts of Europe in the Emperor's company. He had been present at Jena, Heilsberg, Eylau and Friedland, had received a ball in the knee at Aspern, and had twice been in Spain; a couple of years before 1812 he had been promoted Sergeant. His own narrative begins at Almeida in Portugal: it was here that in March 1812 his regiment received an Imperial order to make their way homeward forthwith. Masséna's Portuguese campaigns had made heavy demands on them; and after a march of some 700 miles the old grenadiers approached Paris with some slight hope that after years of exertion they might be vouchsafed an interval of repose — a chance to smoke their shag quietly for a little in their barracks at Courbevoie, to make merry on a hunk of sausage and a pennyworth of Suresnes wine between reveillé and breakfast, parade *en grande tenue* once a week before the Emperor, and dance with their sweethearts on the Barrière de Roule. But when they arrived the Emperor cast his eye over

them, found them in tolerable condition, and after allowing
them forty-eight hours' rest packed them into a park of
waggons collected for the purpose, and before they knew
where they were, they were on the road to Germany. Through
Westphalia, Saxony and Poland they went, awheel or afoot,
and on midsummer morning they passed the Russian frontier.
Six months later they passed that frontier once again, in the
reverse direction: Bourgogne's regiment, which was among the
better-preserved, then counted some sixty men in the ranks —
all that remained of two thousand.

Apart from a severe thunderstorm during the first few days
of the campaign, which caused great disorganization in the
army, and was considered a bad omen, there was not much to
report of the march to Moscow. The Guard, which marched
with the Emperor, were rather better off for provisions than
the troops of the Line, and suffered no serious casualties; and
at Borodino they formed the reserve, and were not engaged.
Even in the Guard, however, the conditions were not exactly
luxurious: a few days after Borodino, when Bourgogne was on
guard with a small party outside the Emperor's quarters, he
and his patrol secured an extra meal by dining off a worn-out
baggage-horse which had been left lying close at hand.
"Patience!" said the Emperor, smiling as he passed by, "things
will soon be better; in four days we shall be in Moscow." On
14 September, in beautiful summer weather, they breasted a
height "called Mont-de-Salut"; and thence the men of the
Guard had their first view of Moscow, with its gilded cupolas
and pinnacles, and agreed that it appeared to be a fine city, —
a city in which, perhaps, they might recover their wind for a
day or two after having been incessantly on the move since
quitting Portugal. The Guard made a ceremonial entry, with a
band; but the Emperor was out of temper, because no mayor
and city council had come out to surrender the keys of the
city; and all that appeared, in answer to his summons, was an
exiguous collection of riff-raff, whom Murat had succeeded in

beating up in the empty streets, and had persuaded to masquerade as the deputation which the Emperor desired. Bourgogne does not mention whether on this occasion the Guard donned the celebrated white trousers which every grenadier carried in his knapsack, for use exclusively on entries into captured capitals; but he records that when they left the town a month later he threw away this part of his wardrobe, since he wanted room for his Moscow souvenirs: he had a feeling, perhaps, that he should not be needing these trousers in the immediate future.

The Emperor had issued strict orders against looting, but in this matter the *Grande Armée* always interpreted its orders with the utmost latitude, the more so since the supply services were largely based on the assumption that the troops would fend for themselves. The grenadiers of the Guard, who bivouacked in a large square surrounded by empty palaces of the nobility, began looting for their own immediate needs the very evening they arrived: meat, preserved fruit, liqueurs, brandy and other delicacies were soon available in superabundance, and the only complaint was the difficulty of obtaining bread. Then came the burning of Moscow, which gave them a freer hand. Bourgogne was sent out on various occasions to aid in extinguishing the flames and to capture and execute Rostopschin's incendiaries; but in reality his main preoccupation was to snatch as many chestnuts as possible out of the fire. The more experienced soldiers made long-term arrangements in Moscow, and contemplated with equanimity the prospect of wintering there; with next year a march to Mongolia, maybe, or — who could tell? — perchance to India. They were not unduly perturbed by the destruction caused by the fire: the whole army could have lived very comfortably in cellars, says Bourgogne. They stocked up with food and brewed beer; a couple of captured tailors were set to work in Bourgogne's company; he himself succeeded in getting hold of a brace of peasant women, who were installed with the N. C. O.'s

to make themselves useful with the washing and other odd
jobs. They even arranged a splendid fancy-dress ball, at which
the two laundresses appeared dressed as rococo marchionesses,
blissfully drunk; but unfortunately after a day or two an officer
came and borrowed them from Bourgogne, and forgot to return
them.

The pleasures of Moscow came to an end on 17 October,
when the Emperor at last grew tired of sulking in the Kremlin
in expectation of a peace-offer from Alexander. The army
moved off to the South, through the Kaluga Gate, cluttered
with innumerable baggage-waggons, and presenting, with its
remarkable assortment of bundles and boyars' furs, the appearance of a crowd returning home from market-day. Mortier
with the Young Guard remained to the last; and after the army
had marched a couple of days they heard a dull vibration in
the air — it was Mortier, blowing up the fortress of the Tsars
at his departure. Soon the baggage-waggons began to break
down, as their teams or their axles — despite much swearing
in all the languages of Europe — gave up the struggle; and
even the packs of the infantry frequently began to feel un-
comfortably heavy. At this point Bourgogne took an inventory
of his knapsack, and he gives us a detailed list of its contents.
He found there a couple of pounds of sugar and rice, some
crusts of loaves and half a bottle of liqueur; a woman's dress
of Chinese silk; several small objects of silver and gold, among
them a piece of the great cross of St Ivan which the Emperor
had caused to be dismantled, that he might take it home with
him; his parade uniform; a woman's riding-cape edged with
green velvet; two silver platters, a foot long and eight inches
broad, with scenes in relief — one representing the beauty-
contest on Mount Ida, the other Neptune in his car drawn
by sea-horses; and lastly various medallions and a spittoon set
with brilliants which had belonged to a Russian prince. Next
to his shirt he wore a quilted vest of yellow silk, which he had
himself made out of a woman's skirt, and outside his uniform

a long cloak with ermine facings; from his belt dangled on a
silver cord a purse containing sundry small articles, including
a Jesus in silver and gold, and a little Chinese porcelain bowl
— the only two things which he eventually brought home to
France. Finally he had sixty cartridges and his musket — a
musket which he had had for six years, and with which he
had become so familiar that he could identify it in the dark
among a pile of arms, and recognize it by the rattle of its fall
to the ground. "Add to this," concludes his inventory, "good
health and spirits, with the hope and inclination to pay my
respects to the ladies of China and India, and you have an
idea of a sergeant of *vélites* of the Imperial Guard."

It soon became clear, even to the man in the ranks, that
any calls upon the ladies of China and India would have to be
postponed for the present; for after the bloody fight at Malo-
jaroslavetz, where Kutuzov and the Viceroy of Italy exchanged
savage punishment, the Emperor abandoned his plan of retreating by a southerly route, and headed for home by a more northerly course: impressed by the strength of Russian resistance,
he reluctantly reconciled himself to the only resource which
seemed to remain to him — to return along the same road by
which he had come. But simultaneously Kutuzov, equally impressed on his side by the desperate valour of the Viceroy's
assault, had also ordered the evacuation of his positions, so that
the southern route was left open. Of this, however, Napoleon
knew nothing when he took his fatal decision: his star was
that day shining dimly indeed.

The retreat of the Grand Army now lay through country
which had already been swept completely bare during the
advance. On one of the last days of October they traversed the
battlefield of Borodino, which presented no very encouraging
appearance, and about the same time the first snow fell. It was
now that the private stores of food which the soldiers had
brought with them from Moscow began to give out, and with
that their real sufferings began. All bonds of discipline and

human ties were quickly loosened. Convalescents from Borodino, who had lain in field hospitals in the neighbourhood of
the battlefield, were now by order of the Emperor to be taken
home on the baggage- and provision-waggons; but from these
waggons, crammed with the loot of Moscow, they were tossed
by the drivers at the first opportunity, and left to die undisturbed by the roadside. The flesh of worn-out or stolen horses
soon formed the only food of the army; and the men learned
swiftly to bleed the horses on the march, whenever they fell in
with a squadron, and thus to improvise a simple pudding —
or even, if time pressed, to lap up the blood raw. Bourgogne
noticed — as a proof of how the Emperor to the last tried to
take care of his Guard — that usually the regiment was assigned a bivouac for the night in some place where cavalry had
lain the night before, and where in consequence there were
dead horses available. But soon even this resource ran out:
King Joachim's proud cavalry ceased to exist; melancholy droves
of mane-helmed centaurs stumbled forward on foot at the rear
of the imperial column, in high riding boots which were ill
adapted to extended promenades.

'To the snow and the hunger was now added bitter cold;
and every night the three worked in concert to wipe out and
entomb *la Grande Armée*. In the narrative of his experiences
after the fall of darkness on 8 November, when the temperature reached its lowest point, Bourgogne succeeds in conveying
something of the actuality of the horrors of that night. In the
evening he witnessed a fire, which had broken out in a gigantic
barn belonging to the Russian post-office: about 800 men,
mostly officers, had packed themselves into the barn for the
night, and barricaded the doors from inside; some seven badly
injured persons were dragged out, thanks to a plank that had
broken loose, but for the rest there was nothing to be done but
watch from a distance a sea of fire which heaved and quivered
with the death agonies of the imprisoned multitude. Soldiers
passing by stopped to warm themselves, or to roast a bit of

horseflesh on a bayonet, while they commented with quiet satisfaction on the "beautiful fire". Later that night Bourgogne was on guard by Mortier's quarters, and sat with his men in a shack by the side of a fire, while the Marshal bore them company as he supped on a bit of horseflesh, a crust, and a swig of brandy; and they heard how the air was filled with a muffled, desolate sound: it was the sound of the approaching snowstorm. In the morning Bourgogne saw a large detachment of the Guards' artillery still bivouacked around their guns: every man of them had died during the night. Prince Emil of Hessen-Cassel, a youth of twenty, who accompanied the army with his own contingent, was saved that night in a curious way: when the storm fell murderously upon his open bivouac, all that remained of his dragoons, about 150 men, ranged themselves in close concentric circles around him, wrapped in their white cloaks, and so stood throughout the entire night: in the morning only about a quarter of them remained alive.

A few days later the army entered Smolensk, where it was hoped they would find provisions and quarters: at the sight of that host of skeletons the French garrison of the town was seized with terror; and at first refused to open the gates. They found little to assuage their hunger and misery in Smolensk, where scarcely anything was to be had: the Guard was issued with a ration of one handful of flour. One night Bourgogne wandered about the town in search of a comrade, and met with all sorts of adventures — stumbled over corpses, fell headlong into snow-filled cellars, pitched on his head into a den occupied by an organized band of thieves, composed of deserters who now concentrated on plundering their comrades in quarters, and who moved on with the army in order to establish themselves in good time at the next halting-place. Bourgogne, who was especially suspect as belonging to the Guard, was lucky to escape from their hiding-place with his life. Throughout these nocturnal adventures he was vexed and bewildered by an incessant accompaniment of distant organ-music, and after some time began to entertain serious apprehensions that his mind was giving way. At last he groped his way to a cathedral, around whose walls were stacked a large number of frozen corpses, and found inside a party of exhilarated comrades, some of whom were performing on the organ. In the enjoyment of good company, music, brandy, a little boiled rice and some pieces of a horse which they had succeeded in stealing from a dead-cart outside the church, he spent the latter part of his eventful night in Smolensk in unexpectedly agreeable fashion.

In Smolensk he saw an old Chasseur, who could march no further, and was being helped into the town by some of the garrison; and of him he draws a vivid portrait:

The old Chasseur had nearly all his toes frozen, and had wrapped them up in a sheepskin. His beard, whiskers, and moustache were filled with icicles. They led him near a fire, where he sat down, and then he began to curse Alexander, the Emperor of Russia, the country, and the God of Russia. Then he asked me if brandy had been given out.

I said, "No, not yet; there does not seem much chance of it."

"Then," he said, "I had better die."

The young German officer, on seeing the veteran suffer so terribly, could resist no longer, and, drawing a bottle of brandy from his pocket, he gave some to him.

"Thanks," he said, "you have saved my life. If I ever have an opportunity of saving your life at the cost of my own, you may be sure I shall not hesitate a moment. Remember Roland, Chasseur of the Old Guard, now on foot, or, to be exact, on no feet just at present. I had to leave my horse three days ago, and blew out his brains to put an end to his sufferings. I cut a piece off his leg afterwards, and I am going to eat a little now."

Saying this, he unfastened the portmanteau he carried on his back, and, taking out some horseflesh, he offered some first to the officer and then to me. The officer gave him the bottle of brandy, and begged him to keep it. The old Chasseur was grateful beyond all words. He again asked the officer not to forget him either in garrison or in the field, and finally said:

"The right sort never die." But directly afterwards he reminded himself what a foolish speech he had made. "For," he said, "there were many as good as me among the thousands who have died these last three days. I have been in Egypt, and, by God!, it was no comparison to this. I hope to goodness we are at the end of our troubles; they say we are to take up our quarters here and wait for the spring, when we can take our revenge."

He did not know, adds Bourgogne, that our troubles, far from being over, had in reality but just begun. After Smolensk things got worse and worse; and after the desperate battle at Krasnoje, where the Guard suffered heavy casualties and was at last forced to retreat leaving its wounded in the snow, signs of dissolution began to appear even in its steadiest and best regiments. "Up to Krasnoje I had kept up my spirits," he says, "but when I saw our wounded comrades crawling after us in the snow, vainly calling for help, I was seized with deep depression and despair." It was immediately after Krasnoje, too, that he lost his knapsack with all its exotic contents; and the worst of it was that it also contained a little bag of flour, which he had managed to get hold of in Smolensk. Hitherto Bourgogne has always kept his place in the ranks; but while he is searching for his knapsack — which had disappeared with one of his comrades who had taken turns with him in carrying it — he loses sight of his regiment, and for some days becomes a straggler and marauder, wandering by himself along other roads than that taken by the Imperial column, until at last he strikes it again at the Beresina. One night, when he has lost his way and is nearly dying of cold and exhaustion, he tumbles down a steep slope and lands in a ravine where one of the Guards' pack-waggons had stuck fast. A Cossack attack on it had been beaten off, but the waggon had been abandoned, and subsequently plundered by French stragglers. Here he decides to establish himself for the night, and sets about collecting bits of wood for a fire, distracted only by a momentary interruption from a wounded Cossack who is threshing about in the wreckage; but when at last he decides to make himself really comfortable by setting fire to the entire waggon, the canvas of the tent is drawn aside, and a gigantic erect figure makes its ap-

pearance, swathed from head to foot in a white cloak, and
carrying a drawn sabre. Bourgogne, in terror and amazement,
asks if it is a Frenchman, and is answered that he must be
a stupid devil to come with a question of that sort. There
follows a scene of delighted recognition, and Bourgogne's
spirits rise again under the influence of his new-found comrade. This proves to be one Picart from Picardy, an indomitable
spirit, and one of the real veterans of the Grenadiers. He, it
seems, had been detailed to escort a convoy which left Moscow
ahead of the army, and had been left on the scene of action
after the Cossack attack to guard the pack-waggon until horses
could be sent to rescue it; and he is still ignorant of the disasters
which have overtaken the army. When at dawn the two comrades imagine they hear trumpets in the distance, Picart guesses that it must be the *diane* being blown for some cavalry-
regiment, and is of opinion that it sounds most like the reveillé
for the horse-grenadiers of the Guard:

> Fillettes, auprès des amoureux
> Tenez bien votre sérieux...

When Bourgogne enlightens him that it is now a fortnight
since either *diane* or reveillé has been blown in the *Grande
Armée,* and that there is hardly any cavalry left, Picart listens
with amazement and suspicion; but at last the truth sinks in;
and as he crawls, half smothered and profoundly dispirited,
out of a deep snowdrift into which he has suddenly disappeared
in the course of their nocturnal march, he gives free rein to
his tongue:

He stood up without speaking, and I helped him out with his
musket; but as soon as he was safe he began swearing against the God
of Russia and the Emperor Napoleon, whom he called a *conscrit.* "He
is a regular fool of a *conscrit* to have waited so long in Moscow. A
fortnight was long enough to eat and drink everything we found there;
but to stay there thirty-four days simply waiting for winter to come
on...! I call that folly. If he were here, I would tell him to his face
that that isn't the way to lead men."

But when a few days later in the course of their wanderings
they hear a Russian rumour that the Emperor and the entire
army are prisoners, Picart forgets his momentary indignation;
he keeps on repeating to himself that the rumour is a lie,
that — *nom d'une pipe!* — the Emperor and the Guard *cannot*
be prisoners — they would die first! — but he is oppressed with
anxiety and consumed with longing to get back to his regiment as soon as possible. In the end, after many adventures
and divers skirmishings with Cossacks, they get hold of a Jew,
who undertakes in return for fair payment to lead them to
the army's line of march. Despite their guide they miss their
way and trudge on at haphazard, when suddenly Picart throws
himself at full length on the snow-covered ground, and roars
to them to be quiet. Bourgogne thinks that his companion
has lost his senses; but he rises to his feet with shining eyes:
"The guns! Now we are saved! *Vive l'Empereur!*" Their march
has now a definite objective, and soon Picart is in such soaring
spirits that he strikes up his favourite melody, an air which
was all the rage in the army in 1805, when they broke up from
the camp at Boulogne to march against the Austrians:

> Les Autrichiens disaient tout bas:
> "Les Français vont vite en besogne;
> Prenons, tandis qu'ils n'y sont pas,
> L'Alsace et la Bourgogne!"
>   Ah! tu te souviendras, la-ri-ra,
>   Du départ de Boulogne!

Soon afterwards they reach the great highroad; they smarten
themselves up as best they can; and the two grenadiers stand
by the roadside, leaning on their muskets, and watch the imperial column approach:

Those in advance seemed to be Generals, a few on horseback, but
the greater part on foot. There was also a great number of other
officers, the remnant of the Doomed Squadron and Battalion formed on
the 22nd, and barely existing at the end of three days. Those on foot
dragged themselves painfully along, almost all of them having their

feet frozen and wrapped in rags or in bits of sheepskin, and all nearly dying of hunger. Afterwards came the small remains of the Cavalry of the Guard. The Emperor came next, on foot, and carrying a baton. He wore a large cloak lined with fur, a dark-red velvet cap with black fox fur on his head. Murat walked on foot at his right, and on his left Prince Eugene, the Viceroy of Italy. Next came the Marshals, Berthier, Mortier, Ney, Lefebvre and other Marshals and Generals whose corps had been nearly annihilated.

The Emperor mounted a horse as soon as he passed: so did a few of those with him, the greater part of them having no more horses to ride. Seven or eight hundred officers and non-commissioned officers followed, walking in order and perfect silence, and carrying the eagles of their different regiments, which so often had led them to victory. It was all that remained of 60 000 men.

After them came the Imperial Guard on foot, marching also in order. The first were the Chasseurs. Poor Picart, who had not seen the army for a month, gazed in silence; but it was easy to see from his convulsive movements how much he was feeling. He struck the ground many times with the butt of his musket, and then his breast and forehead with his clenched fist. Great tears fell from his eyes, rolled down his cheeks, and froze in his moustache. Then, turning to me, he said:

"I don't know, *mon pays,* if I am awake or dreaming. It breaks my heart to see the Emperor on foot, with a baton in his hand. He, so great, who made us all so proud of him!"

Of the horrors of the passage of the Beresina Bourgogne has much to tell, though he was not a witness of the culminating scenes. Here he lost a bearskin, which he had carried with him almost from Moscow, and which had saved his life on some of the worst nights; and from this time his sufferings became even greater. He now falls back among the rabble, and is more than once near to falling asleep for ever by a burnt-out fire; with superhuman efforts he keeps going and regains his regiment at Vilna. Every time he rejoins his company it has markedly diminished since last he saw it; but certain steady men are always there, always in their places in the column, and always ready, as far as they can, to help those that come back: Adjutant-Major Roustan, Lieutenant Césarisse, Sergeant Grangier — the last of these Bourgogne's best friend, and a man who, he says, was "physically not strong, but of an indomitable spirit". Another spirit of the same sort flits occasionally across the scene during the last stages of the retreat: Marshal Ney of the rearguard — the one commander (except Gouvion St-Cyr) who was to return from Russia with enhanced reputation. All the way from Smolensk Ney led an existence which in the eyes of the army made him a mysterious and ever more astonishing figure: at times he would disappear from sight for several days — cut off, surrounded by enemies, and already given over for lost; but sooner or later he would always turn up again, emerging from a cloud of Cossacks with a remnant of his men around him, carrying a musket like a simple soldier, always ready to halt and face about in order to give the disorganized procession ahead of him time to get clear. Rearguard after rearguard melted away around him; but he himself came through it all unscathed, as though sustained upon the wings of inspiration, and always succeeded in once again scraping together sufficient men to keep up a brisk rattle of musket-fire — a rock of defence for the whole army, to the very last.

As Bourgogne roams about Vilna by night, hunting for something to eat, he again comes across Picart for a moment; and Picart takes him to some Jews, whose sympathy he obtains by giving out that he is an adherent of the Mosaic faith: the result is a bottle of brandy, after which Picart has to go off on duty, and shortly afterwards Bourgogne is offered poisoned coffee by certain other Jews, who hope thus to get a chance to rob him. For some time after this he is more dead than alive, and suffers from terrible pains in his stomach. The regiment again gets ahead of him, but he continues to drag himself on as best he can, with the rearguard in action only a short way behind him. Just outside Vilna the army's pay-chest has to be abandoned; the soldiers rummage unchecked in waggons loaded with coin; but most of them have by this time had their bellyful of carrying a heavy pack, and bags of five-franc pieces are exchanged at enormous discount for a mere trifle of minted gold.

Here Bourgogne came upon an old sergeant of his regiment by the name of Daubenton, who was marching on in a curiously bowed posture. Above his knapsack, and secured to it by a rope, he carried a large dog; and Bourgogne wondered if it were a dog he was intending to eat. The old sergeant indignantly repudiated the suggestion, remarked that he would sooner eat Cossacks, and expressed surprise that Bourgogne had not recognized the dog. When Bourgogne looked more closely, it revealed itself as Mouton, the regimental mascot. Mouton had joined the regiment in Spain in 1808, and had since accompanied it on all its campaigns; had been present at Aspern and Wagram, and subsequently once again in Spain and Portugal. At the time of the invasion of Russia he had been lost in a village in Saxony, and it was supposed that he had been stolen; but a week after the entry into Moscow he had turned up again, to the great surprise and delight of the regiment. A detachment of the regiment which had left Paris later than the main body had passed through the same Saxon village, and Mouton had recognized the uniform and rejoined his old friends. But now his forepaws were frost-bitten; and though the old sergeant fully realized that ultimately there was no chance of saving him, he had not been able to bring himself to leave him behind. A swarm of fugitives and charging Cossacks separated Bourgogne from Daubenton at a moment when the old sergeant had knocked one Cossack on the head and Mouton was attempting to fly at the throat of another: the subsequent fate of both has therefore remained unknown.

A sort of pendant to the story of Sergeant Daubenton and the regimental dog is provided by the story of Mellé the dragoon and his horse. In the course of the retreat Bourgogne repeatedly came across his friend Mellé, who was in the Dragoon Guards — "one of the best dragoons in the army," he calls him. He saw him marching alone, leading his horse by the bridle when the animal was too tired, or the snow too deep, for riding; and once he saw him working for a long time with a little hand-axe, in order to break the thick ice to get at drinking-water for the horse. Another time Mellé returned at night from a Russian encampment in the neighbourhood, driving a prisoner before him, and with a truss of hay at his saddle-bow: he had entered the Russian lines alone, wrapped in a Cossack cloak, to get fodder — a plan to which he more than once resorted with success. He had ridden the same horse since the campaign of Jena in 1806, and it had taken part with him in every one of the Emperor's campaigns since that date. He got home from Russia with his horse still in his possession, took part in the Saxon campaign of 1813 and in that of France in the following year, still with the same horse; until at last the animal was shot at Waterloo, after a record of service including twelve major battles and thirty minor actions. Mellé himself, on the other hand, was still alive, and a member of the Legion of Honour, when Bourgogne finally revised his memoirs in the 1830's.

At Kovno Bourgogne once again succeeded in joining his regiment; and since he had by now so far recovered as to be able to bear arms — he had only one foot and one hand frostbitten — he took part in the fighting there; on 14 December the regiment crossed the Niemen, after their Colonel had made a short speech complimenting the sixty survivors on the fortitude with which they had borne privations in that land which, at long last, they were now to leave behind them. Once on Prussian soil all discipline broke down, and the troops roamed in bands about the countryside hunting for good quarters. But they were not yet out of the wood: apart from the cold, there was the Prussian population, which showed itself predatory and ill-disposed; and the Cossacks still clung obstinately to their heels. In Wirballen, which was cram-full of the wrecks of the army, and had quarters only for officers,

Bourgogne met Picart again: he found him comfortably installed, and engaged in sewing a pair of Colonel's epaulettes to his greatcoat, that he might enjoy his lodgings undisturbed. At last, on the day before Christmas Eve, Bourgogne reached Elbing, the appointed rendezvous for the remnants of the Guard, and was billetted on a young and vivacious grass-widow named Mme Gentil. After he had eaten and slept his fill, bathed and shaved himself, and — by way of supplementing the deficiencies of his wardrobe — bartered from an old-clothes man an extraordinarily handsome pair of scarlet breeches (originally the property of one of Murat's adjutants, to judge by the ornamentation), he quickly recovered his zest for life. After an acquaintance of three days he calls his hostess the loveliest woman he ever saw, and finds her not unsusceptible to appreciation of this sort. Other grounds for rejoicing are not lacking: vanished comrades, long since given up for dead, gradually turn up in by no means contemptible numbers; there are good supplies of drinkable wine, and the population of Elbing is friendly; Bourgogne and Picart blossom out in company as guests at an imposing petty-bourgeois wedding. But one fine day the three surviving drummers of the Guard sound *la grenadière*, and the time has come for departure. Bourgogne, touched and grateful, takes leave of Mme Gentil and starts on his homeward march to France; and with that the brave sergeant's story of his Russian adventures comes to an end.

Next year he was captured after the battle of Dresden, and it was as a prisoner of war that he wrote down his first memoranda, while his experiences were still fresh in his memory. When the Napoleonic wars were over, and after his appointment as *adjutant de place* in Valenciennes some years later, he worked up his Memoirs from this material, aided by conversations with various comrades-in-arms, whom he details at the end of his book in his list of "witnesses". Sometimes, when he read through what he had written, it all seemed to him to be but a dream, or the wild imaginings of delirium; but his Russian memories so haunted him, that he felt impelled to put them down in writing, in the hope that by doing so he might rid his mind of them for ever. Let us hope that he succeeded, and that the dreams of his old age were not made nightmares by terrible visions from Smolensk or the Beresina: it is at all events incontestable that in his attempt to disburden his memory of the horrors that lay upon it he produced a work in which many of the episodes are invested with an almost visionary splendour.

He died in 1867; without doubt one of the very last of those who took part in the retreat of the *Grande Armée*.

Translated by Michael Roberts

*I*T was the summer of the year 585, and good King Guntchramn of Orleans — son to King Chlothachar, and grandson
to that great King Chlodovech who first conquered Gaul for
his people and his dynasty — was journeying northward from
his capital in the direction of Paris, accompanied by a large
retinue, and complaining now and then of the heat and the
hard times. As head of his family he had been summoned to
Paris for a royal christening by his sister-in-law Queen Fredegunda, now widowed and living at Soissons, her capital; and
this was an occasion of great importance for the future of the
Merovingian line. In the previous year Queen Fredegunda had
presented her spouse, Guntchramn's brother, King Chilperik
of Neustria — called the Nero and Herod of his age — with
a baby boy, the only son now remaining to her; but this event
had occurred shortly after Chilperik, dismounting in the dusk
after a hunt at Chelles, had received from an unknown hand
a sword-thrust through armpit and belly, whereof he straightway fell to the ground and gave up the ghost, and much black
blood gushed from his mouth. Many said that it was Queen
Fredegunda that caused him to be murdered; but King Guntchramn, who was old and full of solicitude for the future of
the dynasty, was disinclined to believe this of her, though
indeed she had earlier perpetrated misdeeds of a like nature:
as he sat at meat in Orleans he had imparted to his assembled
court and clergy (among whom was Bishop Gregory of Tours,
the historian of these times) his opinion that the murder had
rather been instigated by Bishop Theodore of Marseilles, upon
whom he thought presently to take vengeance. But as to

Fredegunda's son all were agreed that its paternity was highly uncertain, now that Chilperik had departed this life without having had an opportunity to offer his opinion on the point. When King Guntchramn upon arrival in Paris found that the child was not yet come, and that Fredegunda kept herself still in her capital, his ill-humour increased, and he proclaimed aloud that henceforth he should not account her son as of the blood-royal, but consider him rather as begotten of some courtier or bailiff. Whereupon Queen Fredegunda with all speed caused to be collected in her kingdom three bishops and three hundred laymen of good birth, who presented themselves at Paris and made oath that King Chilperik was indeed the father of the child; and therewith Guntchramn allowed himself to be contented. On a later occasion he himself lifted the infant from the font, and gave it the name of Chlothachar after its grandfather, and in the fulness of time this child came to be father to good King Dagobert, and ancestor to the later Merovingians. But as King Guntchramn sat now in Paris, after his exchanges with Fredegunda, waiting for cooler weather for his return journey, he found that his melancholy still hung about him. He began to lament before all the people that there was now a great lack of kings in the land — only himself, and Childebert the Young (son to Queen Brunhilda, and but recently declared of age and raised on the shield by Austrasians and Burgundians) and this son of Fredegunda, of whose legitimacy it might still be possible to entertain some doubt, despite the three hundred and three oathhelpers. Times had been better in his youth: four or five grown rulers with new queens every other year, and the royal manors full of young princes, to say nothing of the bastards. But sword and pestilence and step-mothers had dealt hardly with the family since then; he himself had lost all his four sons, and was now too old to think of more; and what vexed him more than all was that the last surviving adult sons of his brother Chilperik — Merovech and Chlodovech — who

had been killed a few years previously by their step-mother
Fredegunda, had never been given any burial, but had been
suffered to rot on the ground, or had been tossed into some
unknown swamp or ditch, as though they had been ordinary
subjects, instead of kings.

When King Guntchramn had proceeded thus far in his lamentation, a man stepped forth before him, and announced
himself as a fisherman on the River Marne. One morning a
few years before he had found a corpse in his net, and had
thought to cast it adrift again, as was usual with such finds in
that river, whose waters took their rise in Chilperik's and Fredegunda's domains. But suddenly he had realized that this was
no ordinary catch, no official victim of the royal anger, no
deacon, oriental jeweller or court-doctor; for the long hair,
which wound itself into the meshes of the net, bore witness
to the fact that the dead man was of the race of the Merovings. He had therefore brought the corpse to land, buried
it and covered it over with smooth turf, and the place he
could point out still; and, since the dates seemed to tally, he
believed that the man whom he had found and buried was
Chlodovech, Chilperik's son. King Guntchramn was glad at
these tidings, and at once sallied forth — "with retinue as great
as if it had been to the chase" — to the place which the fisherman indicated; and there, when the corpse had been dug
up, they found the long hair still visible as witness (save at
the nape of the neck, where it had loosened from the skull
and fallen off, as careful Bishop Gregory tells us); and thus
King Guntchramn had the satisfaction of seeing his nephew
decently interred in the church of St Victor in Paris.

This is a little vignette of everyday family life among the
Merovingians in the dynasty's better days, remarkable only because of the long hair, which here, as in a number of other
places in Gregory's chronicle, appears as the *Leitmotiv* in an
anecdote. Gregory, Bishop of Tours, author of *Historia Francorum* or *The Cronicle of the Franks*, is no word-painter, and

unluckily had no illustrator of his work to help him out. He
was an honourable man and a good hand at a story; a man, no
doubt, of "marvellous simplicity" — *mirae simplicitatis* — as a
critic named Hilduin is said to have observed even as early as
the tenth century; with a touching faith in all the miracles that
crowd his pages, moving among wonders as though they were
the most natural thing in the world, unshakably convinced
that dust swept from the gravestone of St Martin in Tours
Cathedral, stirred in water, and poured down the throats of
deaf-mutes and paralytics, will immediately cause them to
arise and dance and praise St Martin in a loud voice; but
none the less a man who honestly and straightforwardly narrates what he believes to be true, things which he really has
seen and heard, and an author who has succeeded in making
his artless chronicle of a barbarous age one of the more entertaining of the great history-books in the literature of the
world. He is capable of lively descriptions, and can tell anecdotes without end from his own experience — edifying anecdotes of bishops and hermits (though even the most pious in
sixth-century France were only good in parts, and he makes
no effort to conceal this), and anecdotes far from edifying
of Merovingians and Frankish magnates — and to a limited
extent he is also able to depict character; but the outward
aspect of the persons of his drama interests him not at all,
or at least he tells us nothing about it. All his life he consorted
with these long-haired Merovingians — with some of them
upon a footing of intimacy — but he gives us no hint of what
they looked like. For many years he had much to do with
good King Guntchramn, who was for some periods his immediate lord. Merovech, Chilperik's son, he received into
the sanctuary of his church, when he was pursued by his
parents after he had married his uncle Sigibert's widow,
Queen Brunhilda, and had thereby incurred their displeasure.
He knew Queen Brunhilda too, and her son Childebert the
Young likewise. He had dealings with pious queens who took

to nunneries, and with others who were put in them against
their will, and found it not to their liking. He was a member of
the episcopal commission which was appointed to clear up the
complicated business of the royal nun Chlodechilda of Poictiers, — Chlodechilda, daughter of King Charibert, who, having
been thrust into the convent of the saintly Queen Radegunda,
quickly wearied of the cloistered life, raised a rebellion, and,
taking with her some thirty-odd nuns whom she had incited
to revolt, collected around her a numerous band of "robbers,
man-killers, fornicators and other miscreants" and began to
busy herself with deeds of violence and plunder like a true
princess of the blood-royal. He had more than once met Queen
Fredegunda — on one occasion had even suffered some small
anxiety concerning a rumour that she had assassins out after
him. Fredegunda's daughter Rigunth, who was sent to Spain
to be married, with sixty waggon-loads of trousseau, but returned home and subsequently displayed great valour and resource in hand-to-hand encounters with her mother — Rigunth
was his particular friend: on one occasion she tried to help
him to success in certain ecclesiastical affairs by devoting herself, in company with her women, to prayer and fasting. And
he has detailed accounts of a number of meetings with perhaps the most fantastic of all the Merovingians, King Chilperik, who from time to time included Tours in his dominions.
On one occasion they were sitting together in conversation
on the royal manor of Nogent, when the King in an access of
good humour seized his Jewish jeweller Priscus, who con-
veniently happened to be present, lifted him by the scruff
of his neck, and presented him to the bishop with a command to convert the Jew to Christianity — an attempt which
made no inpression upon that obdurate jeweller-soul, despite
the king's firm grip and the salvos of theological arguments
which Gregory forthwith began to discharge at him. On another occasion they had a private discussion concerning the
king's circular letter to his bishops about a new view of the

doctrine of the Trinity, to which Chilperik (who had evolved it himself) wished them to conform; and in the course of the debate Gregory was compelled to listen while the royal theologian delivered a furious onslaught, not only against Gregory himself, but also against the Blessed Fathers Eusebius and Hilarius, who (it appeared) entertained ideas of the Trinity which did not accord with his own. And once, rather earlier, when Chilperik had summoned a synod to Paris to get Bishop Praetextatus of Rouen expelled from the church, and if possible condemned to death by his colleagues (Praetextatus had performed the marriage of Merovech and Brunhilda, and, by Chilperik's account, stolen money too; but to kill a bishop without further ceremony appeared something of a risk even for a king like Chilperik, a bishop being a superior kind of warlock) — Gregory, who had spoken in favour of the accused, was summoned to a garden in the neighbourhood where the king was eating his breakfast, and received a lengthy reprimand for his pig-headedness (together with a cordial invitation to partake of a couple of dishes, which he found it wiser to decline); whereupon the king, irritated by this corporate solidarity in his bishops, bitterly remarked that "one crow does not peck out the eyes of another".

To a modern man, given Gregory's opportunities among all these various Merovingians — even if he happened to be a writer of correspondingly simple and mediocre type — it would have seemed self-evident that he should attempt to give some sort of indication of how these persons looked. With more or less of concision and brilliance he would have noted their physiognomy, their beards, complexions, figures, costumes, and so forth; and even if he had achieved no more than cheap *clichés*, the imagination of the reader would have had something to take hold of. But Gregory discloses nothing, save the solitary detail of the long hair; and of all these characters, with whom the reader of the *Chronicle* gradually becomes tolerably well acquainted, the image remains perfectly indefinite. Did they conform to the ideal Germanic type — tall, blue-eyed, ruddy-blonde — or were they of more varied physique? Did they appear in the lightly-trimmed primitive-Germanic beard; or were they clean-shaven, with long pendent moustaches, as was certainly the case a little later, in the period just before Charlemagne? No contemporary art exists, which could give us any enlightenment on these points. We may guess that physically they must have been a very well-equipped race; for they lived at high pressure for generation after generation, and long retained their vigour: it was not until about a century after Gregory that a great weariness overtook them, and they came to content themselves with sitting at home as *rois fainéants* among their cupbearers and their womenfolk, and allowed the business of government to be managed by Mayors of the Palace (we should call them prime ministers with a dash of the dictator) such as Pipin of Heristal and Pipin of Landen. And it may be conjectured of such a person as Fredegunda that she must have been extraordinarily beautiful: not necessarily beautiful according to the porcelain artificiality of modern ideals, nor even with the orthodox and statuesque beauty of a goddess in classical draperies, but beautiful with the fearful beauty of a wild beast, elemental, devouring, daemonic, a beauty which was compelling and enduring even for men who in general regarded women as mere utilities. She was able to rule a man like Chilperik, and for that no ordinary qualifications were required — one of them being precisely beauty of this order: for Chilperik was the Nero of his age in this also, that he was a man with marked aesthetic leanings; being, as far as we know, unique in this respect among the members of the long-haired dynasty. But it would be difficult to find in Gregory anything more than the most general indications upon which to base our guesses as to the physical appearance of the royal house.

Such as they were, all the same, these long-haired Merovingians were truly royal, superior to ordinary mankind as the aurochs and the wolf are superior to the cow and the mongrel; and they wore their long hair as the sign of this deeply-rooted royalty or sanctity, as though they had been some wild and terrifying variety of Nazirite. Like the aurochs and the wolf, their brethren from the earliest times in the Germanic forests, they consented only with the greatest reluctance to be tamed: they were too true-bred for that, too innately imperious, and of a mentality too inaccessible. Their line went back to the primaeval forest, to a mythical ancestry, probably to forgotten gods; for them it was the clearest of truths that lordship inhered in the long-haired dynasty, for so it had been as long as the people of the Franks could remember. When they stepped out of the woods and the old tribal existence, when in their harryings of the plains of Gaul they grew from tribal chiefs to monarchs, and came to settle themselves in the spear-won land, planted out their warriors here and there, and with their help began to rule over the tax-paying Gallo-Roman peasants and citizens — then for their own part they stepped into a great void, into a moral sphere of limitless space, into the realm of absolute liberty. The old bonds had fallen from them, the old customs that bound the chief had been left behind, and it accorded little with the natural endowments of the Merovings to allow themselves to be caught in those new and artful snares with which the representatives of Christianity sought to encompass them. "Bow thy neck in humility, Sigambriant!," said St Remigius to the conqueror Chlodovech, when he came at the head of his warrior-band to the font in the church at Rheims to be baptized: "Worship that thou hast burned, and burn that thou hast worshipped!" For this St Remigius was a very learned man, and felicitous in the use of words, as Gregory points out with pride; he contrived both to use the distinguished old appellation "Sigambrian", and at the same time to lay appropriate emphasis upon the significance of conversion, in one sonorous and dignified sentence. It is probable that Chlodo-vech did indeed bow the neck — how far he also succeeded in bowing it in humility is a matter of some doubt; and it is also probable that it did not appear to him to be difficult to comply with the later half of the holy man's exhortation, for he had certainly never believed in any of the heathen gods, nor himself offered sacrifices to them. But as far as Chlodovech was concerned, the matter went no further than that. He never gave himself up to the worship of any new gods, nor showed himself affected by any new moral principles; after immer-sion, as before it, he believed in a simple, well-tried trinity which was for him sufficient: his sagacity, the strength of his arm, and the amiable persuasiveness of his double-edged *francisca*. Water had been poured on an aurochs, that was all: the hair dried soon enough; and the next time the aurochs bowed his neck, it was that he might use his horns, as he had always used them.

The theological radiance which ennimbuses Chlodovech in the *Chronicle* is derived exclusively from the fact that he was not an Arian. Arius was the arch-heretic, the perverter of the nations, the rival of Antichrist; the Devil himself seems for the orthodox Catholics of that age to have been almost an estimable character in comparison with him; and it is with a cry of holy joy that Gregory informs us that this apostle of abomina-tions ended his life in a privy, where his bowels dropped out of him. If only one did not perjure one's self to Arius, the battle was already more than half won; compared with this point, all else was trivial; and Chlodevech, who through his baptism into orthodoxy saved a whole people from wandering in the darkness of error, could hardly avoid appearing — in contradistinction to all other similar German princes — as a man of God, and almost as a sort of lay saint, however little he may have troubled his head about rising to such exalted heights. His religion was severely practical: as an orthodox Catholic King at war with Arian Visigoths he was able to enlist the support of all sorts of native Gallo-Romans, who would have given but a surly and constrained adhesion to a heathen or an Arian. Gratitude to God for timely aid he could indeed manifest as was meet. After his victory in the battle at Campus Vocladum, at the tenth Roman milestone from Poictiers, where the Goths had been scattered like chaff and he himself had laid low their King, Alaric, he hurled his *francisca* before him in a Merovingian hammer-throw: the distance of the flight of his battle-axe should be the length of the nave of a church to the glory of God, and in witness of a great king's gratitude for all those fruitful lands stretching down to the Garonne which had been the prize of victory.

After the conquests were completed, he paid a visit to his old homelands, and for the stablishing of his power undertook there a bloody peregrination among his numerous family and relations — petty kinglets of the Salian and Ripuarian Franks who had stayed at home in the old tribal haunts, while Chlodovech had been leading the more mobile elements to the South. Chlodovech had already half passed into legend at the time when Gregory was writing; two generations had gone by, and the tales of the great king's cunning, his strength of purpose, his rough apophthegms, and his unerring hand, had circulated so long upon the lips of the Franks that even in Gregory the account of him has something of the character of a dynastic myth. He enticed the son of Sigibert the Lame of Cologne to murder his father, and thereupon slew him as a patricide, and took his land. Next he laid hands on the Salian King Chararik and his son, caused their long hair to be shaved, and had them ordained priests; and when they murmured comfortingly to one another that their hair would grow again, he had them slain. He defeated in battle King Ragnachar of Cambrai, who with his brother Ricchar was led bound into his presence. "Thou hast dishonoured our race by allowing thyself to be bound," said he to Ragnachar; "it had been better thou hadst died!", and he clave his skull with his battle-axe. Then turning to

Ricchar: "Hadst thou stood by thy brother, he had not been bound!", and struck him dead like the other.

After this he began to feel himself old and weary; and as lord of all the Frankish, and almost all the Gallic lands, he held his last host-meet (or *champ de mars*) with his Franks. Then he spoke to his people and said: "Woe is me, for I am as a solitary traveller in a strange land. There is not one of my race to give me aid, if the evil day should come upon me." But this, adds Gregory, who knew his Merovingians, this he said from guile, that he might see if any unknown relative might be lured into disclosing his presence, and thus give Chlodovech a chance to kill him. But Professor J. P. Jacobsen, the learned Danish translator and commentator of the *Chronicle,* puts forward another, and most attractive explanation, which lends a gleam of high tragedy to the terrible founder of the Frankish state. Chlodovech was old when he spoke these words, and it was to the Franks that he spoke them; for a moment a memory of the old traditions may have overmastered him, and he may have felt that his now completed life-work had been purchased at too dear a price. For as he sat there on his throne before his Franks he was in truth a lonely man, excluded from human commerce by another barrier than that of royalty, branded to every honest German eye by a law from which there was no escape, a law which bore its own punishment, and which neither magic spells nor mysteries nor the power of holy water availed to modify: the ancient law of blood which laid it down that he who killed within his own family was an outcast beyond all aid. He was a very great king, at that moment, the strongest living Germanic prince after his brother-in-law Theoderic in Italy; but for an instant, it may be, he felt the curse that lay upon him as something stronger than he.

This is but a theory; perhaps a sentimental and euphemistic one, perhaps also with a real grain of truth in it: if so, this is the only indication that has been preserved to us that any male member of the long-haired dynasty was capable of experiencing something like the pangs of conscience.

The phenomenon was not repeated in his successors. Four sons inherited the kingdom, three born in wedlock with the Burgundian princess Chlodechilde, the fourth a son by a concubine. Concerning the succession, as in all other matters, there was no pedantry about the Merovingians. If a man were on his father's side one of the long-haired race, that was sufficient: whether he were the son of a queen or a cook-maid, whether priests had mumbled over his beginnings or no — these things had no importance at all. The kingdom was divided according to the number of sons available — divided at random, till the map looked at times like a patchwork quilt — with supreme indifference to "the idea of unity", "historic mission", "organic development", and other such high matters, which later historians adumbrate sadly when dealing with this period. For the land was the Merovingians' land, to be treated as it pleased them; and the Merovingians had no historico-philosophical axe to grind, turned no speculative gaze upon the future, pondered not at all upon the right advancement of poor humanity, knew nothing of historic mission, but carried on their own affairs with artless simplicity, following their own notions, dealing with each case as it arose, hastily, violently, and without unnecessary subtleties. It is true that they zealously sought each other's lives, and thereby did what lay in their power to diminish the number of separate kingdoms; but they did this with no idea of a historic mission, but rather because each one of them desired as fat a portion as possible to enjoy for himself and afterwards to partition among his sons. They and their state formed the basis, and gave the impulse, for the later history of Europe; but they were personally no layers of foundations; they were content to be long-haired Merovingians, with thought and action concentrated upon a sufficiently eventful present.

The normal course of the life of a Merovingian king during

the generations immediately after Chlodovech — the generations which Gregory describes — ran something after the
following fashion. A motley litter of long-haired progeny would
grow up in the nursery of some royal manor, in Metz, Soissons,
Paris, Orleans, or elsewhere, brought up or dragged up by a
swarm of mothers, step-mothers, servants, apothecaries, cham-
berlains, and so forth. The young princesses were picked out
from time to time, put in a convent or married off; the young
princes were thinned out by step-mothers and apothecaries,
some few of the more fortunate surviving. Education and training took in the main the form of practical, home-made object-
lessons; and as the Merovingians were in general a gifted race,
they one and all made all speed to learn every kind of evil,
and occasionally a little Latin too — though it would have been
rash for any wretched preceptor to correct their declensions, or
reject their rendering of Martianus Capella (that universal
educator) once they were big enough to swing a weapon. At
thirteen they were combed, as promising young men; at fourteen they took concubines from among the weaving-women and
chambermaids; at fifteen they were grown-up and ready to be
raised on the shield. In the meantime their royal father had
usually perished — killed in battle, poisoned by his women,
or run through the body with spear and scramasax in the course
of some parley with his brothers; for in this family, as one
historian remarks, they were in a hurry to step from the cradle
to the throne, and from the throne to the grave. Some sort of
regency was kept going by queens and their favourites; in-
trigues were woven, ambitious magnates began seriously to
dream of the power and the glory; but suddenly the doors of
the nursery were flung wide, a swarm of new kings rushed
out, split the skulls of a number of dukes and court officials,
and thus gave to the survivors a hint that the time was still not
ripe for any ducal thistles to blossom unchallenged among the
king-cups.

Thereupon they settled themselves to reign, each one in his

own town: Chlodovech's four sons — Theodorik, Chlodomer, Childebert and Chlothachar; or Chlothachar's sons, likewise four (after the fifth, Chramn, was burnt alive for rebellion against his father) — Charibert, Guntchramn, Sigibert and Chilperik; or the son and grandson of Theodorik, in an Austrasian line which died out with them — Theodobert and Theodovald, powerful princes in their day; or Childebert the Young, son of Sigibert and Brunhilda; or, finally, that Childebert's two sons, who came after Gregory's time.

Once firmly seated on their thrones, they surveyed the state of affairs with a wary eye, and found much that was in need of their attention. Their private affairs they regulated after their own taste and fancy, and strictly speaking almost everything was reckoned by them as their private affairs. They rioted in every form of vice, they committed every form of crime, as though it were the most natural thing in the world. To the exhortations tentatively offered by bishops and wise women they listened angrily and abstractedly, their heads being full of more important matters. They had at their command a superfluity of energy, a raging vitality, and they felt in their bones that life was short. They were absolutely innocent of all ethics, and in the most literal sense they did whatever seemed right in their own eyes. Some, like Chlothachar and Chilperik, were worse than the average, by reason of greater intelligence, longer life, and more favourable opportunities; others were a hair's-breadth better; but even the most acceptable of them all, good King Guntchramn, much beloved of Gregory, and in course of time regarded as a regular saint by the Catholic church, would have been esteemed by any moralist or sociologist, however modest his standards, a person of extraordinarily dubious character.

The distractions of private life did not afford adequate scope for the restless energy of the earlier generations, and an extremely strenuous way of life did not notably impair their physical resources. They kept a sharp eye open in all directions, and conducted a notably vigorous foreign policy to every point of the compass. They waged war against everything and everybody with whom they could by any means come into contact: they fought the Burgundians, the Visigoths, the Alemans, the Ostrogoths, the Thuringians, the Lombards, the Saxons, the Avars, the Frisians, the Basques, the Bretons, the Bavarians and the Byzantines. They were invariably the aggressors, except in the cases of the Avars, and of the famous King Chochilaicus of Götaland (the Hygelac of *Beowulf*) who as the first known Viking made a great expedition to the coast of Frisia, and there fell in battle against King Theodobert. They conquered kingdoms, subjected tribes, divided spoils, drank royally in celebration of victory, and suffered Venantius Fortunatus to manufacture classical lays about the power and glory of the Merovings. Now and then some trifling accident would befall them: the Burgundians thrust King Chlodomer through the body, and set his head upon a spear; the Avars did many unpleasant things to Sigibert; the crafty eunuch Narses, commanding the armies of East Rome, crushed a great Frankish host which had thought to conquer Italy, and had indeed reached the Volturnus; other armies melted away from dysentery, plague, and immoderate consumption of new wine; the Visigoths put up a valiant resistance against good King Guntchramn in Septimania; Childebert the Young's warriors returned as beggars from an unsuccessful enterprise against the Lombards. But such things did not for one moment damp the ardour or destroy the appetite of these Merovingian rulers: new armies could always be collected, fresh dukes be found to do their errands, and such a thing as public opinion had not then been invented. Occasionally some incautious ruler would enter into an alliance with them, and very remarkable allies he found them. Sacks of gold coin arrived from the Emperor at Byzantium, with proposals for a joint attack upon the Ostrogoths or the Lombards in Italy. The sacks of gold were accepted; a Frankish army was fitted out, burst into Italy, beat everything within sight in pitched battles, and penetrated the country, plundering as it went. Suddenly, maybe, there came into view a Byzantine army, which burst into a festive trumpeting and waved pleasedly at its approaching allies. Without a moment's hesitation the Franks hurled themselves upon it also, annihilated it despite its astonished protest, collected everything that was worth carrying away, and returned again to their own country. In the fulness of time there would then appear before the appropriate Merovingian monarch a Byzantine embassy, which would deeply deplore this unfortunate mishap, and ask for its money back; and it requires no great effort to imagine the splendid outburst of diplomatic eloquence which, in more normal circumstances, both parties would have deployed over an affair of this nature. But the Merovingians were indifferent to things of this sort; they cared not a whit for diplomatic phraseology, were not in the habit of speaking of "a regrettable misunderstanding", did not call to witness the acknowledged spotlessness of their reputation, troubled not to put the blame on the vexatious blunders of their younger commanders, promised no amendment, swore no unshakable fraternity for the future. They flung the embassy out, and passed to the next item on the agenda; and with that the episode was, as far as they were concerned, closed; and anyone else who desired the aid of the Frankish spears might come along with his sacks of gold as soon as he liked. Their hand was against every man, and every man's hand was against them, and it does not appear that this state of affairs gave them undue concern.

It was to each other, however, that they devoted their greatest efforts. Few things in history more truly deserve the name of nightmare than the gigantic family quarrel which fills almost the entire Merovingian epoch. Brother seeks the life of brother, father is against son and son against father, with determined queens at fisticuffs all round them by way of completing the picture. Against the foreigner they succeeded on the whole in presenting a united front: they were capable of forming alli-

ances against Burgundians, Thuringians, and others; but as
soon as such an incident was over they returned to their normal
avocations: dastardly plots were devised, treacherous meetings
arranged, bands of assassins and counter-assassins traversed the
country on the king's errands. In 531 Theodorik of Austrasia
and his brother Chlothachar set off on a joint campaign against
the Thuringians, defeated them utterly, subjected them, and
won (among other booty) the Thuringian princess Radegunda,
who was made Chlothachar's queen. (Later, after a period of
concubine-ridden matrimony, she wearied of the world, entered
a nunnery, and became St Radegunda.) As soon as the victory
was won, it occurred to Theodorik that this was an excellent
opportunity to get rid of his brother, now that they were buried
in the depths of the Thuringian forest. He therefore hung a
curtain in a hall, posted armed men behind it, and invited
Chlothachar to a conversation. But the curtain was a shade too
short; someone happened to take a look into the hall and saw
feet sticking out below it; and Chlothachar made his appearance
with a strong force of well-armed men. Theodorik mustered
the newcomers with a calculating eye, spoke abstractedly of
this and that, declared at last that he had summoned his brother
that he might bestow upon him a precious gift, and thereupon
handed over to him a large silver dish. Chlothachar took the dish
and departed; Theodorik sat plunged in gloom, and broke out
into lamentations that he had lost his best dish to no purpose.
At last he turned to his son Theodobert and said: "Go to thine
uncle and ask him to give thee the gift I gave him." Theodobert succeeded in getting it, by some means which Gregory is
not fully able to explain, and with that the episode closed. "In
devices of this kind Theodorik was very skilful," adds Gregory
simply, leaving the reader much less shocked by the attempted
murder (Chlothachar was a man whom we would cheerfully
see murdered, and the sooner the better) than over this incredible business of the dish.

Perhaps the most appalling villainy which the pages of the

Chronicle contain was committed somewhat later by this same Chlothachar, who in this instance, alas, came off scot-free. His elder brother, Chlodomer, who had fallen in battle against the Burgundians, had left behind him three sons of tender years, who now lived in Paris under the guardianship of their grandmother, the pious Queen Chlodechilde (the Burgundian widow of King Chlodovech) who was greatly attached to them, and tried to keep them out of the way of their uncles. Chlothachar was now invited by his third brother, Childebert the Elder, to a meeting in Paris to discuss the future of these princes. After the two kings had met and finished their conversation, they seized on Theodovald and Gunthachar, the two eldest nephews, and sent to Queen Chlodechilde a pair of scissors and a sword, with a summons to her to decide which implement should be used. Despite the old queen's piety and her love for the young princes, her pride of race overmastered her in the first moment of emotion, and her answer to her terrible sons was "Rather let them die than be shorn!" With that, they had obtained the sanction of the oldest member of the family, and Chlothachar at once struck down the two princes with his own hand, despite a feeble attempt by the less hardened Childebert to rescue one of them. Chlodovald, the third and youngest of the princes, Chlodechilde was successful in saving, in return for a promise that the scissors should be used on him: he was shorn and put in a monastery, and became one of the family's two male saints: his memory still lives in the name St Cloud.

When Chlothachar had grown old and was beginning to feel himself infirm (he was by this time ruler over all the Frankish realm, the sole survivor of Chlodovech's sons) he came to Tours to the church of St Martin, and gave a major exhibition of royal piety. "He went in to St Martin's tomb, and there he reckoned all the evil deeds which by heedlessness he had been betrayed into committing, and with many sighs prayed that the holy confessor would obtain for him God's grace for his offences, and by His aid wash him clean from all the sins of which he had so thoughtlessly allowed himself to be guilty." After which he betook himself to his manor of Compiègne to hunt, contracted a fever, and was laid in his bed to die. His last words were more in the Merovingian manner than the visit to St Martin: as the end approached he was heard to mutter testily: "He that is above must be uncommonly powerful, to be able to take the lives of such great kings." His four sons bore him with all pomp to Soissons, and buried him in the church of St Medard; and thereupon began, without further loss of time, to fight each other for the inheritance.

Gregory makes no comment on Chlothachar's character or prospects of salvation, and one gets the impression that this king, who for the reader appears decidedly the most repulsive of all the figures in the *Chronicle,* did not to him seem to vary much from the normal. But this may depend on the fact that Gregory was only twenty-two when Chlothachar died, an insignificant young deacon as yet unused to the society of kings; while on the other hand he was personally acquainted with Chilperik, the leading scoundrel of the next generation. And he does in fact succeed in pronouncing a number of reasonably adequate judgments upon Chilperik, for in this case his eye for the defects of royal character was sharpened by a lively personal hatred, which had been wanting where Chlothachar was concerned. Besides, Chlothachar had, immediately before his demise, caused a new lead roof to be set upon St Martin's church in Tours, and this undoubtedly spoke in his favour. But in general it may be said that not much is to be expected of Gregory in the way of moral judgments on Merovingians; for him they were by no means isolated phenomena in that age, and a bishop had so much to do with every kind of crime and barbarism in the ordinary course of business that even quite notable Merovingian exploits ran the risk of appearing comparatively inoffensive. These long-haired kings of whom his chronicle treats were no doubt to a high degree given over to the empire of the world, the flesh and the devil; but all

around, wherever Gregory directed his gaze, that empire was
so universal, so flourishing, and so extraordinarily pervasive
— even to the most sacred quarters — that a poor bishop, far
from having time to lament over bagatelles, must be glad at
the smallest whiff of anything that could be called virtue or
humanity, at all events in the world which lay outside the very
narrow limits of the Church's discipline. It was well, no doubt,
that there were commandments which said that a man should
not kill, nor steal, nor commit adultery, and from a purely
theoretical point of view a servant of the Church must naturally
realize that all these things must in all circumstances be straitly
reprehended; but in this world such commandments were
hardly more than a theory, misty and remote, and for Gregory
much was gained if he could restrain his subordinates and his
flock — not from stealing, but from stealing relics and com-
munion-cups; not from killing, but from killing within the
sanctuary of the church, so that the blood splashed on to the
altar and the tomb of the saint; not from fornication, but from
too flagrant fornication by monks, nuns, hermits or priests. The
contact between the Franks and the Gallo-Romans had led to
a reciprocal education in iniquity, which proceeded throughout
this century with the greatest enthusiasm; the Gallo-Romans
learned brutality from the Franks, and the Franks greedily
swallowed all that the Gallo-Romans had to offer in the way
of Roman vices. Even the higher clergy, the last refuge of
culture and morality, was quickly barbarized; and nothing
perhaps throws a clearer light on the world in which Gregory
lived, and the strange weeds which flourished in it, than his
simple notices of the careers of sundry of his clerical contemporaries. Cautinus, bishop of Clermont, was so given over to
drunkenness that it required four men to drag him from the
dinner-table. Eunius, bishop of Vannes, being in the highest
degree intoxicated, emitted "a neighing sound" while officiating
at Mass in Paris, and fell prone on the floor. Badegisil, bishop
of Le Mans, was accustomed to travel round the countryside

with a cudgel, roaring "Though I have given myself to the Church, shall I therefore be prevented from avenging my injuries?" Abbot Dagulf, who in his leisure moments busied himself with highway-robbery and murder, and "had no limits to his concupiscence", went to visit a woman whose husband was from home, and got drunk in her company; after which they both retired to bed — "the *same* bed", as Gregory severely remarks — and remained there until the husband came home and killed them both with an axe — a circumstance which Gregory hoped might serve as a useful warning for clerics. But the most notable item in Gregory's gallery of curious colleagues is undoubtedly his picture of the two bishops Salonius and Sagittarius — an episcopal pair whose like the world has presumably seen but seldom, and who flourished in the period immediately after Chlothachar's death — *i. e.* in the 560's and 570's — in good King Guntchramn's realm.

These two men of the spirit were brothers, and they seem to have maintained harmonious fraternal relations, for they are constantly appearing together. They had enjoyed an education at the hands of St Nicetus of Lyon, a relation of Gregory's, but they can hardly be reckoned among the Saint's more creditable pupils. What store of piety, learning and clerical zeal they may in the beginning have possessed is now beyond our knowledge; but by one means or another they became bishops — Salonius in Gap *(Vappensis Urbs)* and Sagittarius in Embrun *(Ebredunensis Urbs)*. Here they immediately forgot all that the Saint had taught them: "they were transported with joy that now they might do what they would, and gave themselves over to the extremest delirium of wickedness, to robbery, murder, fornication and every other kind of crime". Among other things they put themselves at the head of a band of highway-robbers, and sallied forth to pay a call upon a colleague, Bishop Victor of *Tricastinorum Urbs,* who was engaged in celebrating his birthday — possibly by way of indicating their dissatisfaction at not having been invited to the festivities. They broke into the house with sword and spear, came shouting a battle-cry into the bishop's dining-room as he sat at meat, slew several of his servants, tore his clothes from his back, took away his plate and other accessories of the feast, and left the bishop wounded and half naked. King Guntchramn now gave them a sharp reproof, and deprived them of their episcopal offices, but Salonius and Sagittarius were equal to this emergency. They went as pilgrims to Rome, complained to the Pope, brought home with them a letter which set everything right, and resumed their offices. After a time they took a vacation and followed Duke Mummolus on a campaign against the Lombards, "where they fought like laymen, and with their own hands killed many foes". On their return home they quarrelled with a number of citizens, whom they belaboured with cudgels; and their drunken arrogance went so far, that Sagittarius broke out into evil words against the king, asserting that his children were of base birth, and could not therefore inherit the kingdom — an assertion which evinced great ignorance, remarks Gregory, since all the children of a king are royal, whether born in wedlock or not. King Guntchramn, now much enraged, caused them to be taken captive, deprived them of all their possessions, and immured them in two monasteries far removed from one another, where they were to be kept completely cut off from the outer world. But after a time one of Guntchramn's sons fell sick, and several courtiers pointed out to the king that the two bishops had perhaps been unjustly punished, so that God was now afflicting the king's son with sickness, by reason of the sin which had been committed. "Let them out at once," commanded Guntchramn, "and tell them to pray for my son." They returned to their dioceses and fell into one another's arms for joy, after so long a separation. For some time after this they were patterns of piety, read the psalms of David every day, and sang hymns zealously by night; but in a little while the voice of the spirit died within them, and their old habits reasserted themselves. "No word of God was now heard upon their lips, and they no longer remembered the Order of Service. Not till daybreak did they arise from the festal board; and then they clad themselves in soft raiment and slept until the day was far advanced, being drunk with much wine; nor were women lacking, with whom they might defile themselves. When they had arisen and taken a bath, they fell to meat again, and continued until the eventime; and thereupon were they soon ready for their evening meal, which once again outlasted the night. And so they continued, until at last the wrath of God slew them..." At a synod in Chalon, where they were accused of lasciviousness, godlessness, several murders, lèse-majesté and high treason, they were finally and definitively declared to have forfeited their episcopal dignity, and became wanderers about the countryside. Of Salonius we hear no more: perhaps he grew weary, or in some way met his end at the hand of a member of his flock who owed him a grudge; or perhaps he wandered to foreign lands to carve out a new career for himself. Sagittarius, however, we are permitted to follow to the end. He attached himself with enthusiasm to a considerable revolt, which was raised in the southern parts of the country by a pretender to the throne of the name of Gundovald (who gave out that he was Chlothachar's son) and was seen, clad in helm and breastplate, perambulating around the walls of the fortress of Convenaes (where Gundovald was besieged) casting stones upon the heads of the besiegers below. When the fortress was surrendered, and Gundovald and his leading supporters had been taken and done to death, Sagittarius wound a shawl about his head and attempted to flee to the woods; but he ran too close to an inquisitive individual with a drawn sword, and a quick sweep lifted the bishop's head, shawl and all, from its shoulders.

Such were the characters of men who lived in the most law-abiding class of society; the layman's world was much worse, and reached a climax of barbarism in the higher Frankish officials — all those dukes and counts whose escapades occupy so much of the *Chronicle*. These magnates are, almost without exception, of such a nature that in more than one way they succeed in transforming the Merovingians into characters for whom the reader can feel a certain sympathy and respect. For one thing, their crimes are on the average more bestial than those which the kings commit; for another it is the kings who represent justice, so that even the worst of the Merovingians frequently afford both Gregory and the modern reader the most lively satisfaction by causing them to die an evil and speedy death. The mills of Merovingian justice often grind extremely slowly as regards these magnates; or rather, for long periods they do not grind at all, since the royal millers have other things to think of; but when for one reason or another they jerk into gear, they grind with frightful thoroughness. The many dukes and counts of whom Gregory gives a more or less circumstantial account — Rauching, Eberulf, Leudast, Beppolen, Guntchramn Boso, and a multitude of others — sit in their various towns all over the country as royal lords-lieutenants, strongly armed, with numerous retinues, indifferent to all law human or divine, always drunk, always greedy for money and gorgeous clothes and goldsmiths'-work and women, always up to some barbarous villainy, and ready for bestial brutalities at the slightest pretext. They rob, rape and slaughter, force an entry into churches with drunken howls, abuse the bishops, mishandle the clergy, plunder the widow and orphan, and enjoy themselves generally. No one disturbs them; complaints die away unheard; the kings are far away, busy with high matters of family politics among themselves. Duke Rauching causes persons who displease him to be buried alive, and is accustomed when in festive mood to fasten burning candles to the legs of his slaves; Beppolen, created duke of Angers, begins his tenure of office by plundering the whole neighbourhood, and is a man who "never waited for the keys when he wished to enter a house"; Leudast, a man of low birth who rose from the kitchen at King Charibert's court by petticoat influence, and

was made Count of Tours, conducts himself there with such
bloated arrogance and effrontery that even the patient Gregory
becomes quite desperate, and is depicted by him with unusual
particularity as an unmitigated monster. To cut short this
dallying on the primrose path, or in any way to modify their
behaviour without being constrained to do so — this is a thing
which never occurs to your genuine duke or count: despite
their veneer of refined vices and their possible command of
Gallo-Roman jargon they are really still simple barbarians from
the Iron Age in every respect — not only in their actions, but
also in the limited range of their cunning and their foresight;
they live from day to day, utilize every situation as it presents
itself, and rarely trouble themselves with superfluous anxieties.
But in the majority of cases something happens to them in the
end which takes them by surprise, after they have perpetrated
some deed which for them does not appear to differ greatly
from any other, but from which nevertheless it would have
been wiser to abstain. They steal something which they would
have done well not to steal; they involve themselves in some
treachery which draws attention to them; they have the ill-
luck to murder a person who is acquainted with a queen; they
ally themselves to a rebellious prince; they bluster indiscreetly
at a drinking-bout: — and one fine day some king somewhere
takes note of all these things, his interest is excited, and the
millstones of Merovingian justice come suddenly into action.
A message arrives which sends a cold shiver down the spine of
the duke or count in question, and the bumper falls from his
hand. He scrapes together an armful of weapons and treasures,
rallies his bodyguard and favourite women about him, and flees
in terror to the sanctuary of the nearest church, where he casts
himself at the feet of the same bishop whose beard he was
pulling only yesterday; for fate is following hard upon him —
the bloodhounds of justice and the wrath of the Merovingians.
A famous church, such as St Martin's in Tours, guarded by
some mighty saint who happens to be buried there — this is

the only chance for him now, its sanctuary the only hope he can cling to; he must now live night and day, he must eat and sleep, inside the church's walls, and preferably for safety upon the saint's very gravestone, after the sick and the beggars have been swept off it to make room for a wretched hunted duke. Outside, death is certain; but here there is perhaps some possibility of escaping with a whole skin. For the hallowed space about the grave of a famous saint has a certain significance even for an infuriated Merovingian.

It is sometimes said that the Merovingians were completely emancipated from all religious and ethical scruples; but an exception should be made in regard to such places of sanctuary: here was a spiritual power which they did to some extent recognize, a barrier which sometimes caused them a good deal of difficulty. To slay without further ado in the chapel of a great saint was something from which even they recoiled, and theoretically a criminal who reached such refuge was in safety. But the Merovingians, who believed that difficulties were created in order to be overcome, did not lose heart; they wrestled with this problem, and succeeded in evolving a variety of techniques which satisfied them, and which they considered ought not to cause serious annoyance to any broadminded saint. Some of the magnates they were pursuing never reached sanctuary at all, and then the procedure was much simpler. With Leudast, the thorn in Gregory's flesh, no less a person than Fredegunda had a bone to pick; and since he was, for all his experience in wickedness, a very simple character, he allowed himself to be lured to Paris, where he was seized by the queen, and subsequently suffered a complicated death which Gregory reports with lively gratitude. Duke Rauching — he who buried men alive — attracted the attention of King Childebert by his complicity in a grand plan (supported by Queen Fredegunda) to murder that young monarch. He was invited to pay a call at the palace, where he and the king had a private conversation in an inner room on the first floor — a conversation of which it would have been satisfactory to have a detailed report. When it was ended Rauching made as though to depart; but outside the door of the room were men stationed on either hand ready primed with instructions, who looked enquiringly at the king over the duke's shoulders as he emerged. Childebert nodded; a spear-shaft playfully thrust between the duke's legs brought him to the ground, a hack from a sword found its mark on his neck, and the corpse was thrown out through a window. It fell in the courtyard among Rauching's men who were waiting below, and surprised them so much that they easily suffered themselves to be disarmed. But such cases were isolated and more favourable instances: much more elaborate arrangements were required for dealing with such as succeeded in reaching sanctuary.

Among those who took part in the same conspiracy as Rauching were two dukes named Berthefred and Ursio. After Rauching's death they barricaded themselves in a country church, where they were beleaguered by Childebert's men. The church in question was of minor importance — probably it did not even have a saint's grave — and was set alight; Ursio came out of the fire, fought long and valiantly, and was at last hewn down; but in the meantime Berthefred had succeeded in fleeing unobserved and made good his escape to Bishop Agerik's church in Verdun, a building of very much greater prestige. There he was surrounded; and since Childebert was anxious to settle the matter without delay his men clambered up on to the roof, wrenched loose the stones and timbers, and dropped them down on the man in sanctuary until he was crushed beneath them. Bishop Agerik might deplore the incident as much as he pleased, but Childebert was undoubtedly in a position to adduce weighty arguments in his defence. To promenade on the church roof and pick away at the slating was no sin; that some odd bits should have fallen inside during the process was no more than natural; and if a person who ran around inside the church should happen to be hit by them, he could hardly blame anyone but himself. Not even the most exacting of saints was entitled to feel himself aggrieved on that account, especially if a liberal contribution were made to the repair of the roof.

On another occasion the wrath of good King Guntchramn was kindled against Duke Eberulf, and he swore an oath to extirpate him and all his kindred to the ninth degree, for he suspected him of having been involved in the murder of his brother King Chilperik. King Guntchramn was a man who was much attached to his relations, and he wished, says Gregory, to "wean folk from the evil habit of murdering kings", since in his view this was a prerogative of the royal family. Eberulf may possibly have been innocent in this particular case, though his catalogue of crimes was already so long as to make this neither here nor there; however that may be, he fled at once with his men to St Martin's church, where he abode for some considerable time, and caused Gregory grave concern. For when he had as it were found his feet on the saint's gravestone, he began to celebrate drinking orgies there with his men, to the sensible distraction of the arrangements for Mass, and he even brought women into the church for his godless amusement. Gregory had an anxious time, torn between his zeal for the inviolability of sanctuary and his lively desire to be quit as soon as possible of the turbulent Eberulf, especially after that individual had one day promised to kill, first Gregory himself, and afterwards all the priests he could lay his hands on, if the king's men should enter the church to carry him off; "for then," declared Eberulf, who was clearly a full-blooded Germanic type, "I should not feel it an ignominy to yield to death, when I had first been revenged upon the saint and his clerks." Guntchramn now commissioned a man named Claudius (who despite his name appears also to have been of Frankish birth) to try to have Eberulf killed by guile, or removed without infringing the peace of the sanctuary; and Claudius arrived with a large band at the church, swore brotherhood and fidelity to Eberulf, and began to carouse with him. One night, when all Eberulf's men had been sent out into the town in search of more wine, the two new friends strolled out to the church porch, and there at a given signal Eberulf was seized from behind by a strong man and held fast "with his chest dilated". Claudius now drew his sword, and with a gesture in St Martin's direction and a prayer for the saint's indulgence, ran Eberulf through, but at the same time received from him a knife-thrust in the side. The whole affair now degenerated into a full-blown horror-story, and scenes were enacted such as St Martin probably was not to see again until some centuries later, when Ragnar Lodbrok's sons came to Tours. Claudius, grievously wounded, was dragged by his men through the church into the "abbot's cell" (apparently some sort of annexe to the church), where an abbot and a number of priests were sleeping. They had hardly succeeded in bolting the door behind them, when Eberulf's men returned, saw their lord lying dead, hastily set down the wine they had brought, battered in vain at the door of the abbot's cell, broke open the shutters, hurled in spears, and pinned Claudius fast to the wall. The priests skipped about sleepily between the beds, dodging the flying spears; a few of them succeeded in dragging out their abbot; as they opened the door Eberulf's men came in, and a general fight ensued. At the same time "some of the church's almoners, and others of the poor, enraged at the violence that had been offered, tried to tear the roof off the cell; and a number of beggars and men who were possessed came rushing in with stones and cudgels, incensed that things had been done which had never even been attempted in that place". All Claudius' men were killed — as they deserved to be, says Gregory, since it was they who were primarily responsible for the sacrilege — and Eberulf's men plundered and stripped them, and fled in the night with their booty. What happened to the valiant beggars and their lunatic friends Gregory omits to mention; he was himself by great good luck away from home, and thus escaped hurt. King Guntchramn "was at first greatly enraged at what had happened; but when he learnt the whole story his wrath abated and he consented to be pacified". The main point, even for so relatively pious a man as Guntchramn, was that Eberulf had been called to account, and that a satisfactory demonstration had been provided that "the evil habit of murdering kings" was one which did no good to those who practised it; though it was no doubt true that in this case the demonstration had taken a slightly more violent course than the king had originally intended.

King Guntchramn, who has to do duty for the idyllic element in a work which has not otherwise much of the idyll about it, recalls in more than one way — in character, in behaviour — the traditional patriarchal monarch of folk-lore. At the period when Gregory has most to tell us about him he was already well advanced in years — itself a rare phenomenon in a family where the average expectation of life for males seems to have lain between twenty-five and thirty. This lends him an aura of dignity and wisdom; he has that care for the future of the race which is peculiar to the old and reflective; he is a sort of benevolent uncle to the whole family, the sagacious supervisor of nephews of tender years, and of their unruly mammas. He is a man of comfortable temper, affable in his ordinary intercourse, merry and talkative at table; he is zealous for religion, as long as it does not involve him in serious difficulties, and on good terms with his bishops. By his people he is regarded with devotion and reverence; he is the good king, in contradistinction to all the others, he is even in some degree holy and supernatural, as a really good king should be: when on one occasion he is walking in the streets of Marseilles, a woman plucks a piece of the fringe of his mantle to make a decoction which shall cure her son of the ague. At the same time he is obstinate, extremely careful of his dignity, and very slow to forget an injury. The Visigoths in Spain are somewhat remiss in their treatment of

a Merovingian princess — Ingunde, married to Hermen-
child — and in Guntchramn's view are directly responsible for
his unfortunate niece's death, since they sent her to Constantinople; and accordingly he persists until his extreme old age
in sending armies against them to requite this injury, long
after everyone else has forgotten the whole story in the general confusion of the period. His temper is hot, and his outbursts of rage are in truth royal; in his gusts of anger he
behaves precisely as a king of folk-lore ought to behave, without any inhibiting presentiment that he is one day to figure
in the calendar of saints as St Guntchramn. On one occasion,
when he is out hunting in the Vosges, he sees signs that an
aurochs has been killed in his own forests; the thought of so
painful a loss — for the aurochs was beginning to grow rare,
and was carefully preserved by Guntchramn — puts him in
a passion, and after a fruitless enquiry he commands that the
local game-warden and a chamberlain named Chundo (clearly
a sort of Master of the Buckhounds) shall forthwith engage
in Trial by Battle with spear and short-sword, so that all may
see where the guilt lies. The chamberlain excuses himself
on grounds of age and being out of practice, and is permitted
to put forward a nephew in his place; the game-warden and
the nephew fight valiantly before the king, and kill one
another; at the sight of this (which shows that both parties
are guilty) the chamberlain takes to his heels in the direction
of St Marcellus' church hard by, but the king roars that he
is to be seized before he reaches the threshold. This is successfully accomplished; the chamberlain is bound to a stake
and stoned, and the poached aurochs is avenged; "but afterwards the king bitterly regretted that for so small a matter
he had lost so good a servant, since it was troublesome to be
without him."

There were moments when Childebert the Young could
show himself courteous and complaisant towards his uncle
Guntchramn, since it was understood that he was to inherit

Guntchramn's kingdom — as indeed he did. On one occasion Childebert seized a certain Duke Guntchramn Boso, whom he had long wished to get into his clutches; for Boso had been involved in gross treasons and rebellions during Childebert's minority, and had in particular offended his mother, Queen Brunhilda. The duke was led bound before Childebert, but an influential bishop pleaded earnestly for him, and Childebert accordingly decided that the duke should accompany him under guard to a meeting with King Guntchramn which was to take place shortly, and that there King Guntchramn should pronounce upon his fate. The two kings met (it was to arrange the great settlement in regard to the succession which goes in history under the name of the "Treaty of Andelot", 587) and Childebert raised the question of the captive duke. King Guntchramn, who at once recollected numerous villainies committed by the duke, decided with no long delay that he should immediately be put to death. The good king's indignation was audible over a wide area, and as the duke sat waiting at no great distance, information of what was coming to him reached him well in advance. With some few companions he ran into a house in the neighbourhood, within which was Bishop Magnerik of Trier — a man highly esteemed by the king — with a number of his clerks. He laid hold of the bishop, held a sword over his head, explained his delicate situation, and ended by saying persuasively: "Holy bishop, we are foredoomed to the same fate. Contrive my liberty; otherwise I kill you here before I go out myself to meet my death." The unfortunate bishop despatched a clerk, who reported how matters stood and earnestly implored the king to grant the duke a pardon; another messenger followed shortly after with further explanations and entreaties. But King Guntchramn, who was in no humour to be stopped by trifles, "cried with a loud voice: 'Set fire to the house! The bishop must burn if he cannot get out'." This particular story has a happy ending: when the house was in flames a number of courageous priests rushed forward and succeeded in hauling the bishop out of a window, and the subsequent course of events ran in accordance with the normal rules of old-Germanic legal procedure: Guntchramn Boso "and the few men who were with him" came out through the fire and fell at the door "for many spears". And it may be presumed that King Guntchramn afterwards administered friendly consolation to Bishop Magnerik for the risks to which his impetuosity had subjected him.

The privilege of dying in one's bed, at all events for laymen, is not very usual in the *Chronicle;* hardly more so than in another great work of similar type, Sturla Thordsson's *Sturlunga Saga,* where likewise an eye-witness depicts the decay of a heroic age and the collapse of society into violence and darkness, — though in Gregory the thread is double, inasmuch as he describes two distinct dissolutions, one of the heroic age of the Franks, the other of the last survivals of Roman culture. After both comes the absolute dark: after Gregory the seventh century; Europe's blackest century, the midnight silence of the abyss; after Sturla the fall of the independent Icelandic state and the end of Icelandic literature; and the same eruptions of blood, fire and evil lend a predominant colour to what in both cases is in truth (to use Macbeth's famous definition) "a tale, full of sound and fury, signifying nothing". But the assertion may perhaps be ventured that on the average the Merovingians emerge as a shade less repellent than the Sturlunga chiefs (though certainly these last had the benefit of being described by a historian who is immeasurably superior to Gregory in literary talent and mental calibre); for one thing, the Merovingians do not chop off the feet of such opponents as they are prepared to refrain from killing, as was the general custom in Sturla's chronicle; and if on the other hand the Merovingians used torture in forms which Sturla's chieftains never thought of, it should be noted that this is a habit confined almost exclusively to Queen-Mothers — for instance, Brunhilda, and above all of course Fredegunda —; and they resort to it partly against each other's minions and by way of compensation for woman's weakness in the ordinary dealings with intractable nobles; partly — in Fredegunda's case, — when the lioness has lost some of her cubs, and in blind savagery seeks to assuage her sorrow by making a funeral sacrifice of medical attendants, court-functionaries and anybody else she can lay hands on. But the long-haired kings themselves do not as a rule indulge in such practices; they kill, and that is sufficient. And if it should happen that good King Guntchramn, attending Mass early one winter morning, should find a gigantic footpad-like figure (personally unknown to him) snoring in a dark corner near the royal pew, with a broad-bladed spear leaning against the wall, it is understandable that he should have this hulking sleeper awakened, and not remarkable that he should wish to have him racked a little; for he is anxious to get it quite clear as to what all this is about. Is it merely a private enterprise in regicide; or is it possibly some new caprice of his restless sister-in-law Fredegunda, whose ill-will to King Guntchramn is no secret, and whose methods are wellknown? — a conjecture which indeed turns out to be perfectly correct. But such things in no way cloud our impression of King Guntchramn as being really at bottom a very benevolent and genial old saga-king.

Thanks to good luck and a sharp eye for slumbering footpads King Guntchramn succeeded in living through the whole *Chronicle*; and it is comforting to learn that he was one of the few who were privileged to end their lives, full of years, in their bed — an end which admirably accorded with his whole temper and habits of life. The *Chronicle* stops with the year 591; Guntchramn died some years later, and was followed to the grave soon afterwards by Bishop Gregory, worn out by many cares which did not permit him to write a narrative of the last three years of his life. Fredegunda survived them; and for that reason we have, unfortunately, no such general obituary notice of her as Gregory devoted to her husband Chilperik upon the occasion of his demise. Venantius Fortunatus, a friend of Gregory's, and poet laureate to all the Merovingians, has lauded her in his copious classical style, and especially celebrated her virtue — which was undoubtedly the wisest line for a poet who had to declaim his *opus* to her face in the hope of a handful of gold; but it is hardly probable that Gregory, despite the respect which he entertained for the views of his learned and poetic friend, would have permitted himself to be seduced into anything of that sort. He was no pedant in his demands upon his fellow-men, provided only that they kept themselves clear of Arianism; but just as he calls Chilperik "the Nero and Herod of his age", so in one place he terms Fredegunda "the enemy of God and man"; and it is likely that his final judgment upon her would have pronounced her to be an evil and accursed woman, and assumed as a matter of course that Hell was her destination. The firm belief in a decent Hell must indeed have had great importance, must have been in the nature of a ray of comfort, for all who contemplated Fredegunda and her career; for on earth she had unvarying success and suffered no punishment. She too died peacefully in her bed, in the year 597, with the victories of Droisi and Latifao newly won, with her mortal enemy Brunhilda humiliated, and with the surviving spawn of her basilisk's den raised one after the other to the throne of Neustria (which was a great solace to her maternal bosom) — and was buried in the resting-place of the Merovings in Paris, under a tombstone which is still to be seen in St Denis.

The great vendetta between her and Brunhilda — one of the really titanic duels of history of a strictly personal character — began in the 560's, and had its origin in King Chilperik's bedchamber, where conditions of notable disorganisation were more or less endemic. Chilperik had been first married to a queen named Audofleda, of whom nothing further is known; when she had borne him three sons, Fredegunda, who was one of her serving-women at the time, began to think (and presumably Chilperik began to think also) that she had been queen long enough. She therefore lured the poor simple queen, who had borne a daughter while the king was away on campaign, into lifting the child from the font herself, and thus into becoming her own daughter's godmother; as a result of which her marriage with Chilperik, according to the ecclesiastical law of the age, became incestuous. Audofleda could now be shelved with complete propriety and put in a convent (where she was presently murdered by her thoughtful exservant), and Fredegunda was promoted to be the official sharer of the royal couch. So far so good; but suddenly young Fredegunda's felicity was disturbed in the most alarming manner by the enterprise of Chilperik's brother Sigibert, King of Austrasia. Sigibert had wearied of the practice, so general among these brothers, of making servant-girls queens, and had sent to Spain for a wife of royal blood — Brunhilda, daughter of Athanagild, king of the Visigoths. This brilliant match caused Chilperik great concern; he was the youngest of the brothers, but he had a particularly good conceit of himself, and wished in every respect to stand out as their superior, and he began now to contemplate Fredegunda with a pensive eye. One fine day he sent emissaries to Spain to seek Princess Galswintha, Brunhilda's elder sister; presented her with five fine cities in the south of France as bridal portion; and could now feel himself every bit as good as Sigibert. Fredegunda, who once again had been forced to content herself with a place in the background, was highly indignant, especially as the king for some time seemed to find his new wife really attractive — "for she had brought great treasure with her". But in a little while Galswintha was found one morning dead in her bed, and Fredegunda resumed her former position. Brunhilda had no doubt (and Gregory had no doubt either) that the queen had been murdered by Fredegunda; and indeed the only possibility for anyone else to doubt it lay in the idea that possibly Chilperik had done it himself; but in view of the fact that Fredegunda was usually the quicker thinker of the two there need be little hesitation in placing the deed to her account.

Thus Brunhilda acquired a blood-feud with Fredegunda, while Fredegunda on her side quivered with anger against the arrogant Visigoth, whose very existence brought her into shame and contempt; and so began in real earnest the great duel which was to last for three generations of Austrasian kings. The two husbands, incited by their wives — and with these kings no great incitement over and above their normal inclinations was required — at once went to war; and after various encounters and irritating machinations from Chilperik's side, Sigibert's temper became so exacerbated that he decided to thrash the matter out with his brother in true Frankish style, and to that end brought over men of the heathen tribes from the country east of the Rhine, and launched a large-scale invasion of Chilperik's kingdom. All resistance collapsed before it, and Sigibert penetrated as far as Soissons. Here he was by way of being hailed as king and lifted upon the shield in the place of his fugitive brother, when Fredegunda — "drawing upon her past experience," says Gregory — once more intervened in the manner of which she was so notable an exponent. Two unknown men drew near to Sigibert when he was being borne round on the shield; and as he leant towards them to hear what they had to say, each ran a scramasax through his body, so that he sank back dead immediately. And thus Brunhilda found herself suddenly a widow, with one more murder to avenge, and a five-year-old son to look after in a most troublous world. She was of pretty near as tough a constitution as Fredegunda, and she succeeded in preserving the kingdom for her son, despite every difficulty with insubordinate nobles, and all the violent proceedings of Chilperik and Fredegunda, who now that Sigibert had been successfully murdered flourished like the green bay-tree. At first she had a very difficult time of it: she was forced to flee from her country, took refuge in Rouen, and there (presumably in desperation) further complicated her affairs by contracting a remarkable marriage with Chilperik's grown-up son Merovech, who was in flight from his step-mother. The newly-married couple were forced to fly in different directions; Bishop Praetextatus, who married them, was in the end stabbed to death before his own altar at Frede-gunda's command; after sojourns in various sanctuaries Mero-vech committed suicide rather than fall into his step-mother's hands; but Brunhilda herself succeeded at last in getting back to her country and resuming the regency for her son. One comfort in her misfortunes was afforded her by Fredegunda's invariable ill-luck with her family. For Fredegunda could indeed kill her step-sons at pleasure to secure the succession, but she saw all four of her own sons die in childhood, one after the other — not excepting him to whom (presumably in des-peration, and in violation of all Merovingian traditions) she had given the name *Samson,* by way of laying encouraging emphasis upon his physical strength.

King Chilperik, who seems to have been little interested in his offspring, allowed Fredegunda to deal with them as she pleased, and in the meantime devoted himself (provided no major villainy demanded his cooperation) to theoretical and artistic interests which for a Merovingian monarch were re-markably extensive. He achieved, as we have seen already, a draft of a new doctrine of the Trinity (sufficiently original to make the pious Gregory's hair stand on end all round his tonsure), but met with vexatious obstacles to its acceptance as dogma. He also wrote a book of verse, in accordance with his own idea of classical Latin; but, says Gregory with satisfaction, "since he was incapable of distinguishing between long and short syllables, none of his lines would scan". If he was thus an unconscious pioneer in the field of free verse, he was on the other hand a fully conscious one in the matter of spelling reform; and with something of that donnish itch to reform which is still prevalent among our modern pedagogues he devis-ed three new symbols (as the learned Emperor Claudius had done before him) which should simplify the writing of certain recurrent combinations of letters, and sent instructions round his kingdom that books in libraries should be gone through with pumice-stone, so that the royal letters might be brought into use without delay. For some reason this order seems never to have been carried out, an omission which does not however appear to have involved any perceptible inconvenience, the supply of well-meaning experts anxious to rush to the assistance of humanity having subsequently proved fully equal to the demand. Chilperik was in his way undoubtedly a really gifted and talented man, with more extensive intellectual equipment than his Merovingian contemporaries, though they were by no means lacking in brains; a literary amateur among the earlier Merovings, even if his verses did halt a little, was certainly (as O. M. Dalton, the excellent English translator of Gregory, points out) an extremely remarkable phenomenon. He possessed a certain unruffled, supercilious impudence, reminiscent of Caligula's, so that at times the reader, forgetting for a moment all his bottomless rascality, cannot help but laugh at him. On one occasion he received a message from Guntchramn and young Childebert (Brunhilda's son, who was now growing up) with the information that these two kings, who hitherto had been bickering pertinaciously, to Chilperik's great advantage, had now banded together against him; they summoned him to return immediately all the lands he had stolen, or otherwise to prepare for war; and in the latter case he was invited — perhaps in accordance with some honourable old Frankish custom — to appoint in advance the place of battle. But Chilperik, says Gregory, "listened to this with contempt, and turning his attention to the Circuses in Soissons and Paris, caused spectacles to be given there for the benefit of the people". An effective and eloquent gesture, undoubtedly.

However, there came at last that day in 584 when Chilperik on returning from the chase at Chelles received from an unknown man a sword-thrust through his body, and falling to the ground set free a soul which even by Merovingian standards was exceptionally murky. Who it was that arranged the murder has never been made clear. There is a strong initial presumption that Brunhilda here at last got her chance to pay off her old score with Fredegunda: Sigibert had been stabbed to death in very similar circumstances. Moreover, Brunhilda's son was now of age, and already half-adopted by Guntchramn, who had no son of his own; Chilperik had for the moment no male heir, and if he were removed before be obtained a new one, Childebert would become the nearest inheritor of his kingdom also, and thus unite under his sceptre all the land of the Franks. It was, no doubt, a nuisance that Fredegunda was once more pregnant, but there was always the hope that the child would be a girl, or that, if it were a boy, it would die like the others. Brunhilda might well, therefore, have had ample motive for sweeping Chilperik from her path; but on the other hand there is no evidence to suggest that this nicely brought-up Visigoth had yet been sufficiently barbarized to start dabbling in assassination. Contemporaries seem to have been very uncertain as to who really was behind the deed. The continuator of Gregory, the so-called Fredegar, who is hostile to Brunhilda and paints the gathering gloom of her declining years in lurid colours, says that one of her agents named Falco was the murderer; good King Guntchramn, on the other hand, for some reason or other adhered obstinately to the idea that Bishop Theodore of Marseilles was the real instigator — he and our old friend Eberulf whose kindred was to be rooted out to the ninth degree, and who was also, incidentally, vehemently accused by Fredegunda. One strong argument in favour of Brunhilda's innocence is that Fredegunda did not bring any accusation against her.

But a general report, which has been preserved in *Gesta Francorum*, alleged that in reality it was Fredegunda who had engineered this murder also. According to this version Fredegunda had taken her *major domus* Landerik for her lover, which

Chilperik, who in this as in all other matters was inclined to be sensitive, had unexpectedly discovered. One day, in fact, the king had returned unexpectedly early from the day's hunt and gone in to the queen's chamber, to find Fredegunda leaning against the window-frame. Without saying anything Chilperik proceeded to give her a friendly slap upon the most readily available portion of her person, and Fredegunda, under the impression that it was Landerik, uttered compromising words. The king at once retired, somewhat pensive, and it was not until he had closed the door behind him that Fredegunda became aware of who it was that had slapped her. She realized that it was now a matter of her life or his, and with her usual decision made up her mind on the spot. Landerik seems to have been generally reputed to be the father of her son Chlothachar, who was born some time afterwards — despite all her efforts with the three hundred oath-helpers and so forth to establish his irreproachable paternity; it was not until Guntchramn was finally induced to give him an extremely hesitant recognition that this, the most vigorous of her progeny, obtained official status as Chilperik's son — a position which he succeeded in retaining despite the persistent protests of Brunhilda, and the military measures with which she was in the habit of underlining them.

The period after Chilperik's death was for Fredegunda as difficult as the period after Sigibert's death had been for Brunhilda. She was pressed back to a handful of towns in the northwest; Guntchramn, as guardian of her dubious son, administered the major portion of her country; and Childebert applied to Guntchramn to have her handed over to him, since he had the lives of five near relations to avenge upon her. Fredegunda's life hung upon a hair; but she was equal to the situation. The magnates in her kingdom, one might have thought, could scarcely feel themselves fired by any great loyalty to the widowed Fredegunda, a former serving-girl with a more than suspect son as her only asset when it came to claiming the privileges of royalty; but none the less the amazing fascination of her personality always sufficed to preserve the loyalty and devotion of a majority of those with whom she came into contact, and she was always a woman equal to quashing the recalcitrance of a minority by the prompt use of sword and battle-axe. She must at this period have been forty years old, if not more — a considerable age for a woman even down to quite modern times. Hard living, primitive conditions, hate and malignity, frequent confinements, fights with her heavy-handed daughter Rigunth — all these things and many others ought by this time to have set their mark upon her, and she might well have been a toothless, chap-fallen and slatternly old peasant, shrill and scolding, her face fixed in a malevolent grimace. Chilperik may indeed have been the Nero of his age, but he is hardly likely to have offered to his wife such a rejuvenating bath of ass's milk as the original Nero put at the disposal of the Empress Poppaea, and whatever other resources Fredegunda may have commanded in the way of cosmetics, her powers of attraction and her sway over men should by this time have passed their peak. But the indications are that this was by no means the case: an all-compelling physical quality, which can most easily be described as a beauty of a quite unusual type, must have persisted in her undimmed; for the fear of her cruelty was always exceeded by the willingness of men to subject themselves to the power of her charm. Many of those despatched on her errands went off unhesitatingly to a death which was virtually certain, after she had "fired and strengthened them", as Gregory says on one occasion; and even old King Guntchramn, who as regent was anxious to bring under his control large portions of her country, could not bring himself to think really badly of her, once her fascinating proximity had had time to take effect on him. He obstinately refused to comply with the demands of Childebert and Brunhilda that she should at last be punished for all the misdeeds she had committed; but later he admitted to Gregory that he had been mistaken about her character. For it was only for so long as Fredegunda had need of his help that she showed herself so seductive and appealed to his compassion as a poor hard-working and misunderstood woman; later, when her position had become stronger, and Guntchramn in the meanwhile had definitively bequeathed his kingdom to Brunhilda's son and not to hers, she altered her attitude and began to send out assassins to lie in wait for him in churches and other suitable places. Of her could good King Guntchramn in truth have said, as Antony says of Cleopatra in Shakespeare's play (though indeed with a different intonation and in another spirit)

> Age cannot wither her, nor custom stale
> Her infinite variety.

Guntchramn's death was followed shortly after by that of his heir, Childebert the Young, king of Austrasia and Burgundy, who died in 595, twenty-six years old, poisoned by his queen Faileuba. No adult male of the long-haired dynasty now survived: the two old rival queens alone dominated the scene, and could devote their attention to each other with less interruption than ever before. Brunhilda was again regent and guardian, now for her two grandsons, the elder of whom at his father's death was ten years old (by no means a contemptible age in the circumstances: Childebert, a father at sixteen, had in true Merovingian style made the most of his time); and Fredegunda had her eleven-year-old Chlothachar to look after. Hostilities at once broke out with great violence: strong Austrasian armies moved against the Neustrians; but Fredegunda herself took the field with her people and won victories at Droisi and Latifao. A tradition asserts that the first of these victories was in great measure due to her own wisdom and guile. Among the ten thousand odd theories about Shakespeare and his work there is one which attempts to prove that he had read *Gesta Francorum*, in which Fredegunda's proceedings at Droisi are described: in the misty dawn she caused her army to advance against the camp of the Austrasians, and ordered that the horses be provided with bells around their necks such as were used for untended cattle, and that the footmen should carry boughs before them; and Shakespeare, it is said, found here the idea for Birnam Wood in *Macbeth,* and also made some attempt to model Lady Macbeth on Fredegunda. It is to be hoped that this theory is correct, for it would then be possible to say that even Fredegunda served some useful purpose — a contention which it would otherwise be difficult to substantiate.

"The enemy of God and man" died at last and was laid to rest among kings; but the long vendetta did not end there. Brunhilda had her day of triumph on the field of Dormeille, in the year 600, when Chlothachar was overwhelmed and his kingdom shivered to atoms. But Fredegunda's son — like his mother and other pests — was not to be eradicated so easily, and dissensions among his opponents contributed to his salvation. Around Brunhilda — old, hardened by ambition, the sole survivor from her generation in a world where the forces of anarchy were increasingly getting the upper hand — the veils of darkness and crime fall thicker and ever thicker (in part, perhaps, because of the marked hostility of the Fredegar-chronicle to her), especially during her closing years, when among other things she egged on her grandsons against each other, and in the end it is Chlothachar who emerges victorious. After many confused horrors came the final scene — a scene over which broods the inspissated murk of the midnight of the world (though the first annunciatory glimmer of a new dawn was to flicker a few years later in the depths of Arabia about the head of a temperamental camel-driver named Mohammed) — when in 613, at Renève in Burgundy, not far from Dijon, Brunhilda, Athanagild's daughter, was by Fredegunda's son bound by her hair to the tail of an unbroken horse, and by it dragged to her death; and with that the vendetta which began in 568 at last reached its conclusion.

But by that time the pious Gregory had been sleeping for twenty years under his gravestone in the church at Tours, and was probably already a legend in his town and already, maybe, able to cure sick pilgrims almost as well as St Martin himself. On pilgrims who resort to him to-day — not to his grave, but to his chronicle — he can in some measure still exercise a beneficent influence; for without doubt it can be at times a great consolation and pleasure to contemplate for a little such an age as he has depicted; an age which decidedly, and in more than one respect, must be pronounced to have been worse than our own.

Translated by Michael Roberts

*T*HE photograph is probably still somewhere to be found. I came upon it some years ago, and remember it well as being in no way remarkable; a boy of about four or five, I should think, dressed up in his best clothes, is seen standing on the floor, his arm in a somewhat strained manner around the neck of a younger sister. She, in her turn, has been placed on a stool somewhat too high to suit the pose in question, and sits in placid contentment, playing with her fingers and obviously pleased with her pretty little frock. To the face of the boy, however, where no trace of either happiness or contentment can be seen, the photographer has not succeeded in cajoling any smile, although to the initiated his expression, apart from a certain wildness about the eyes, is surprisingly composed. No sign of inward turbulence in the form of swollen eyelids or noticeable wanness is apparent; but this may well have been obliterated by the process of touching up which is one of the secrets of photographic artistry.

Be that as it may; I can only record that the actual taking of this particular photograph represents the most terrifying moment of my whole experience. I should never have remembered the occasion, of course, had it not been for this unique sensation of horror; but as it is I remember the details vividly.

We, my parents, my sister and I, were on a visit to my grandmother, who lived at Kristianstad in a house which possessed a window mirror. This mirror was an unfailing source of delight, and I used to sit in front of it whenever I had the chance, watching the continuous procession of life in the East High Street approach and pass by. Going out into the street and meeting other boys whom I did not know was both unpleasant and humiliating, but to sit by the window mirror was sheer bliss. When one fine day it was announced, that my sister and I were to be dressed up and taken to the photographer's, the scheme of the universe was rudely interrupted. From the very start this proposition sounded an alarming one, and became even more so when I found out that our parents were not going to be photographed, but only we children. In my experience unpleasant things such as the taking of castor oil or going to bed early were invariably reserved for children — never for their parents. I had no clear idea of what was meant by being photographed, except that in some way one became a picture on a piece of paper, and that a great deal seemed to indicate that this came about under hideous circumstances. Old men who had ceased to be of any use were often photographed and hung up on the wall; we had some of the sort at home ourselves. I felt that the situation was serious, particularly as here at grandmother's I was like a plant uprooted from its mould and had neither scullerymaid nor stableboy to turn to in an emergency. Under normal conditions the truth of matters could nearly always be found out from them, as opposed to which the explanations given by one's parents were often unsatisfactory, and sometimes completely untrue, in particular when they attempted to comfort one in the face of some danger, warn one against something amusing, or forbid one something good to eat. The aura of respect which surrounded my father made it quite impossible for me to speak to him on important subjects, but for want of a better informant I asked my mother, while she was brushing and dressing me, whether it hurt very much to be photographed.

"Hurt, what nonsense," she said in her cheerful manner, "there is nothing that *can* hurt. The photographer has a big sort of contrivance that he takes photos with. You stand in front of it, and he stands behind it with his head underneath a cloth, and hey presto! it's all over."

Thus spoke my mother in her innocence; and at the sound of her words, the latent and deadly fear within me spread to undreamed of proportions. I began to scream with all my might, clinging to her and imploring to be let off. I promised that I would always be good and obedient if only I were spared this ordeal. I knew that I had often been naughty, but did I really deserve such a punishment? Surely a good whipping was sufficient. Whether I said, or sobbed, all this I do not know; in any case I remember thinking it. My mother was astounded, could not understand what I meant, and kept on repeating that it was all over in a moment, and did not hurt; I only howled the louder, until my father poked his head in at the door, and ordered me in tones of thunder to be quiet.

Nowadays I realize more clearly that parents do not always have an easy time of it with their children. It might be thought that my mother had said nothing which could make me hysterical, apart from which I ought to have been able to enquire more closely of her as to what was frightening me; but at the time, although I was not afraid of her, this seemed quite impossible. Why? one wonders. In all probability because one of the strongest instincts in child nature is the fear of making oneself ridiculous. Laugh at me, by all means, when I say something funny, or which I myself think is funny; but for Heaven's sake never laugh when I say something silly in earnest, because this is completely unendurable. Children — or at least, some children — feel this; and it is fortunate that the acute sensitiveness to one's own comical stupidities gradually becomes dulled as one grows up, thereby restraining many an otherwise obvious case of suicide.

Not only, therefore, did I refrain from asking any more questions, but I made no attempt to explain the reason for my howling, and this in itself suggests the existence of some shadow of doubt in my own mind with regard to the theory about being photographed; a doubt, however, in no way comparable to the degree of terror I felt. For as a result of my mother's fearful piece of information, the said theory became clear, logical, and from an abstract point of view entirely acceptable. Her words engraved themselves on my consciousness: "He has a big sort of contrivance that he takes photos with..." I happened to know what was meant by the word contrivance (this was before a subsequent acquaintanceship with the telephone and numerous other modern "contrivances") for in an attic at home, standing against one of the walls, was a large and elderly mangle, a curious object, the like of which I have never seen since, with several pairs of rollers one above the other. This mangle, which probably dated from the 18th century, refused on occasion to function satisfactorily, and I had recently heard my father refer to it with emphasis as "a useless contrivance, only fit for firewood". It was easy to understand, after thinking the matter over, that being photographed must entail, amongst other things, being pressed through some sort of a mangle. "He stands behind it with his head underneath a cloth..." The reason for this precaution became obvious — in order, of course, to avoid being spattered with blood.

The thought of my late grandfather, hanging in a state of photography on the wall at home, gave necessary confirmation to my theory that it must be a question of mangling. I remembered him before he was photographed as an exceptionally large, red, stout gentleman, once an artillery sergeant major in the town, who had spent an enviable life driving about and firing off a cannon. Since then, however, he had been photographed, and was now imprisoned behind glass, in a frame, completely flattened out. One could still see plainly that it was grandfather, although all the blood had apparently been squeezed out of him, shrivelling him up in some way that I could not altogether fathom. It was said that he "had a stroke", and one could well understand that drastic treatment of some sort had been necessary before drawing him through the mangle, so large and stout as he had been.

In this martyrdom of the imagination, it may seem shocking that I should have believed my parents capable of wishing to see me mangled and pasted onto cardboard. Admittedly, and as was usual at that time, I lived in modified terror of my father, but he was by no means a monster, merely somwhat heavy-handed when occasion demanded. In actual point of fact, the dreadful train of my thoughts probably originated from a well-developed ethical consciousness. I realized that I was a naughty and troublesome child, and that a punishment of this sort was reasonable enough in itself. It is possible — although my chronology may be at fault — that the crushing of my sister's finger with a stone during the course of a battle of wills between the two of us may have preceded the photography; while she, at the first opportunity, had taken her revenge by hitting me in the neck with a broken brass doorhandle, which laid me out bleeding and unconscious on the floor. These happenings, according to my conception of things at the time, may have been the reason why we were both considered eligible to be photographed, though in my sister's case matters were easier, she being too young and too stupid to realize what was in store.

Of the actual walk to the photographer's, in the company of both our parents, I remember nothing. Possibly I may have entertained hopes to the last that the whole thing was a threat, and that we should turn back at the door. The photographer lived two flights up; one went in through a doorway and then up some stairs to the left. On either side of the entrance were glass cases full of photographs, in particular one of an individual with a long moustache, standing beside a whiteclad female, who looked as though his teeth had been pressed forward through his mouth during the ordeal of photography, and at the sight of whom everything collapsed for me. I resisted desperately all the way up the stairs, probably to the accompaniment of loud yells; how I was transported up, whether by the scruff of my neck or otherwise I do not know, my memory being a blank until I actually stood before the dreaded "contrivance". The photographer was a thin, pale man who seemed to have a great deal of arranging to do, and who tried various methods of cheering me up, the point of which I could not understand at all; this sort of frantic and useless effort, made by all photographers, has always been, to me, one of the many mysteries of existence. He put his head under the cloth, and I knew that the moment had come. The head, however, popped most unexpectedly out again. "Keep quite still, please," he said, and I take it for granted that even my heart obeyed him and suspended action. He lifted a little lid from the contrivance, and after a moment put it on again. "There now," he said, "that's all."

I felt myself sink with shame. I was so thoroughly ashamed that, after returning to grandmother's not even the beloved window mirror was able, that day, to give me any pleasure; and although my mother often tried to find out the reason for my strange behaviour on this unique occasion, she was not allowed to know anything about it until at least twenty years later.

This is the story of my first visit to the photographer, and one of my clearest early recollections. In its way it may be quite an instructive story, not unsuitable for the unhappy parents of children who create hideous and inexplicable scenes of violent obstinacy, simply because they are the victims of an uncontrollable imagination, or have become involved with some vision of terror which it is impossible to explain to the grown-ups.

Translated by Elspeth Harley-Schubert

HOW I BECAME A WRITER

*I*T was at the age of twelve that I first lapsed into authorship. I was attacked one summer day by a feverish condition, and wandered about a remote corner of the garden, manufacturing a long poem which brought tears to my eyes. It concerned the sorrows of Satan, and was inspired less by Scriptural sources than by an authoress of the name of Marie Corelli — a woman of some celebrity who wrote books for twelve-year-olds. I declaimed my poem in grave and poignant accents to selected members of my family, and acquired thereby such prestige that they often had recourse to me afterwards for complimentary, Christmas, and other occasional verses. This, my first poem, had a metre of a sort, and even rhymes, all properly placed at the ends of the lines; and I long retained a strong impression of the feeling of awe which suffused me when I found myself all unexpectedly able to perform this particular variety of parlour trick.

This knack of putting verses together later served me well, when as a schoolboy I set up as a professional bard by way of increasing my meagre stock of pocket-money. The Students' Union at Kristianstad High School produced a paper, which came out about once a fortnight, and ran to eight manuscript columns. The Union was in a flourishing condition, and contributions were paid for in cash, at the rate of threepence a column for prose, and sixpence a column for verse; and I set myself zealously to fill every vacant column in the paper with verse — which was the easier since I wrote quickly and seldom felt the urge to alter or delete. Half-a-crown, indeed, was the maximum income I could reckon on from any one number,

since at least three columns of prose were always contributed
from other sources; I offered therefore, in return for an increase in the remuneration from sixpence to sevenpence, to
write in a smaller hand, which would on the average permit
an additional eight lines of verse per column; but after a
short debate this was rejected. It was the first time that I
learnt what it meant to be an unappreciated poet, compassed
about by stifling materialism and wooden indifference. "All
the same," I thought, "half-a-crown is something; and fortunately my poems are things that will live, long after I have
perished of French irregular verbs in the Upper Third."

After passing my Matriculation, I hastened to the University of Lund, or at all events to its immediate environs, and
in the course of my first academic year wrote in my spare
time a great quantity of verse — ballades, elegies and a species
of contemplative lyric. My poems of this period were of ample
proportions, preferably of some fifty stanzas or thereabouts,
and I was in the habit of reciting them to some chosen friends
who chanced to be reading History of Literature. I read my
poems with strong emotion, and always hoped to induce similar
feelings in my listeners; but they confined themselves to stirring their coffee, scraping their pipes, cleaning their fingernails,
and lapsing into a state of passivity, and recommended me
with ever-increasing warmth to look at a number of Danish im-
pressionist poets, whose productions seldom exceeded twelve
lines in length. This depressed me no little; and after reading
these Danes — especially one by the name of Hoffman — I
realized that I neither could nor would write as they wrote, and
that perhaps therefore my case was hopeless.

All this was of course only adolescent rhyming of the simplest sort, the quiverings of a youthful sensibility which had
no inkling of the high craft of poetry. So green, so undis-
criminating was I — and long remained — that I thought, for
example, that few metres could compare with four-footed
anapaests, and I must have written several kilometres of earnest

verse in this form, although it is a measure which really is hardly suited to any but comic subjects, save in the hand of a master such as Viktor Rydberg. But such things take time to learn, for as a rule every man must find them out for himself.

My greenness in such matters — in so far as I suspected its existence — and the coolness of my knowledgeable friends when confronted with my interminable productions, I continued to bear with relative equanimity; for I had at that time (it was when I was about twenty) other and more important things to occupy me: above all, chess. Throughout four academic years I devoted my entire attention to the game; and few who do not play it can form any idea of the rich diversity of its pleasures, and its frightful capacity for the total absorption of its practitioners. I hoped to the last that I should turn out to have a marked talent for the game, so that I might be able to dedicate my life to a pursuit which was at once fascinating, intellectual, and utterly devoid of practical utility. I have always had a certain weakness for the useless, for only the useless can have value in itself — as for instance a rainbow, or poetry, as to which not even the most advanced thinker can assert that their beauty is a function of their utility. Chess is by no means poor in aesthetic values; the thirty-two pieces on the sixty-four squares reveal, to him who has made any progress in their mysteries, a realm of inexhaustible beauties. But the beauty of chess is far from being something merely passive: it is also living drama of the most attractive sort, with all the elements of battle — the measuring of strength, dreams of victory, breathless triumph, and black catastrophe. And all this happens while the player, emancipated from life's vexations, sits quietly on his chair, without other bodily motion than is required to move a piece occasionally, or — if one's opponent is perceived to be sunk in gloomy meditation upon an unexpectedly threatening situation — now and then, with unruffled brow and profound satisfaction, to light a cigarette. I know but one other occupation which affords such thorough and perfect contentment as the playing of chess; and to that I shall come in a moment.

Yet when all is said and done it is conceivable that there may be some use in devoting time to chess, because of some of the lessons that are to be learned from it. A man cannot intrigue his way to a result in chess: bluff is seldom successful on the chess-board, if the players are serious, and it is impossible to win even a single game by running about corridors and keeping well in with influential people: you must play better than your opponent, and that is all. And it does not help much to try to explain away failures, false moves, and defeat: it is one's own fault; one has one's self to blame; one must try to play better next time. The beginner, indeed, may be visibly out of humour at a lost game, and may on occasion throw coffee-pot and control-clock at the head of the happy opponent who has so humiliatingly lured him into a trap; but the more experienced direct their displeasure and their criticism exclusively against themselves. And it may not be without a certain importance to acquire something of this attitude even to matters which have nothing to do with chess.

During these years of chess-playing I retained always a certain interest in literature and verse-making. From time to time I visited my University friends, who now began to present a respectably learned appearance, in order that I might listen to their latest views, and I was even in the habit of going once a term to a lecture on the apparently alluring subject of "History of Literature with Poetics". I hoped that sometime Poetics would be allowed to get a word in, and that I should hear discourse of important matters: of form, of style, of verse, of the art of writing, of the poetic element in poetry, or, at the very least, of amusing metrical patterns — in short, that I should hear something which had a real connection with the great mystery of

> Writing, whose words like armies
> Rank-wise stamp out their song.

But the only stamping there concerned other matters, of which I did not understand the point, and in which I could not feel any interest.

After four years at the University, during which I heard ten lectures, wrote a great deal of bad verse, and played three or four games of chess which were good enough to be published, I fell ill, and was taken home in a pretty miserable shape. A doctor intimated that if I dropped whisky and late hours and went on a diet of milk and white meat, I might live another six months. I accordingly quietly drank my milk and accustomed myself to the notion of my impending demise, and filled in my time by picking out on a map the course of the first World War, which was then in progress. While thus engaged I grew for some reason gradually better, at all events well enough to find it tedious to sit as an invalid and do nothing. Physical exertion had been forbidden me; but since I was to die anyway in the late autumn, I thought that this prohibition might safely be ignored, and I began in a small way to lend a hand on the estate where my father was the agent.

That long-suffering man had hitherto had very little joy of his first-born, whom he had gradually fallen into the habit of alluding to as "Sample; of no commercial value"; and he received with marked scepticism my offer to make myself useful with odd jobs of a practical nature. With dour incredulity he openly wondered how far my academic intellectual training could have equipped me to shovel a floor of rye, or bottle-feed a collection of new-born calves — even if provided with a diet-sheet by an expert hand. I held the view that my intellects, in spite of everything, were in sufficiently good preservation for me to be able to master things of this sort within a reasonable time, and perchance even harder things too; and after a time I was given a wage of 27/- a week as storekeeper and herdsman. This was good pay; and it is the only form of remuneration I have ever, in the bottom of my heart, felt that I really worked for. You can make more by putting words together on paper, but the feeling of honest earning is not really the same.

I soon became intensely interested in managing the cows, and quite forgot that strictly speaking I ought to have died in the preceding November. I rose at half-past six (except on the days for test-milking, when I crawled out with much difficulty at four), worked ten hours a day or more and had my head always full of vital problems about fodder-accounts, frozen turnips, mouldy hay, bad oilcake, fat-content, udder-inflammation, blind-teat, actino-mycosis, heifers which would not be served, calves which had to be hauled into the world with ropes, prolapsed uteri, unexpelled after-birth, and a hundred other things which have provided laborious herdsmen with food for thought ever since the Bronze Age. One of these days, when a suitable opportunity offers, I shall put together a simple narrative, to be entitled "A Herdsman's Memories", which will (I trust) be very beautiful, and also have such a whiff of the authentic aroma as would be more than sufficient to cause persons of urban sensibilities or municipally-hygienic leanings to recoil in alarm.

These occupations gave me such satisfaction that I began to like working, a thing which never happened to me before or since; and to crown all I became physically a much improved young man, broad in the shoulder and strong as an ogre. To the best of my knowledge there are few better forms of all-round exercise than that which is provided by leading out a sexually-excited heifer who has never before had a rope round her horns; shovelling seed for a couple of hours a day is also very good for the constitution, and still better is carrying sacks single-handed, for a ten-hour day, from the threshing-machine up a flight of steps, with the sacks coming at about four-minute intervals. I am now a man of the pen, lazy and soft and somewhat fat, and no doubt I should not now make much of a hand of carrying sacks or dealing with pirouetting heifers; which is a lamentable thing to think of.

18 †—500581.

And never again shall I have such a pet as Pelle. Pelle was
a black bull-calf which I had personally reared and trained;
he was very devoted to me, and even when he was full-
grown I could let him loose and take him for walks with me,
without a pole or a chain or anything, and he would follow
faithfully at my heels like some frightful poodle, and from
time to time would give me a friendly poke in the back with
his nose, to remind me that he wanted an extra bit of linseed-cake. For linseed-cake was what he dearly loved; still
more dearly than he loved me, I suspect.

It was in these circumstances that I came at last to be an
author, of a sort — at least, in so far as I have ever become
one. There is a good deal of the work on a farm which is done
alone, and which, once the routine has been acquired, leaves
plenty of time for meditation while the job is being done. Such,
for example, is shovelling seed, which takes up much time
during the winter, when there is a good deal of threshed grain
lying in the granaries. During this oft-recurring turning over of
rye and oats I found it an excellent pastime to think out verses,
and to try to knock together a couple of decent stanzas, which
could be written down in the evening. It was at this time that
I began to get some idea of what verse really was: I understood now that my earlier facile methods of composition were
as faulty as if a jeweller had set himself to cut precious
stones with the sugar-tongs. I still retained a certain weakness for long poems; but usually destroyed them as soon
as they were finished, and the sacrifice was not unduly
painful.

At the same time I did not forget my University friends
in Lund and the criticism they had been in the habit of
levelling at me: they had always been very ready to suggest
excisions and contractions, and their wounding recommen-
dations of Danish impressionists in eight-line format still
touched me on the raw. I now decided to safeguard myself
against such criticism from them by writing sonnets: they

could hardly say, even of an only moderately successful sonnet, that it would have been better if the second quatrain had been deleted. I knew that no rational man writes sonnets nowadays, since this form of poetry offers little scope for that spontaneity which according to all contemporary authorities ought to be the prime characteristic of all true poetry (a view which was probably invented by the biographers of poets, and which is indeed wholly mistaken, though that has not prevented its distorting the mind of many a young poet); but I could not help that. If I could but succeed in expressing clearly what I had to say; if the phrasing were melodious, the word-order uninverted, the tone masculine, the rhyme euphonious, yet neither forced nor false, and the whole sonnet visibly cast in one block, then I felt I could be satisfied even if there were a certain lack of spontaneity. I got hold of Théodore de Banville's *Petit Traité de Poésie française,* a book on poetics which I had somewhere seen mentioned as being a sensible work by an expert, and found my purpose strengthened by the graceful expositions of this master.

I now worked diligently to learn how to make sonnets, and found it a pretty troublesome business; but for the trouble I cared little, for I had plenty of time. Sometimes a sonnet took a whole week's turning and twisting, sometimes it could be done in a few hours; and I made the interesting observation that the time consumed in manufacture seemed to bear no definite relation to the quality of the product: a sonnet which had taken a week might be good, while another which had demanded only a few hours might be bad, but exactly the opposite could equally well be true; the main point was that they should not, when finished, show any trace of the effort that had gone to the making of them. At first, naturally, they were unsatisfactory, one and all.

Whenever one of the better cows was to calve, I always insisted on being woken up so that I might be there if any complications should occur: for some reason cows always prefer to calve at night, about midnight or later. The old cow-man who slept in the shippon would bang on my door, and I would put on my trousers and go down with a lantern to see how things were going. Sometimes, when it seemed that everything was progressing favourably, but that it would take some time, I would send the cowman back to bed, since he was an old man and had to be up at four, and would myself remain with the cow to lend a hand at the right moment. Often while I was waiting I had some sonnet, or a section of a longer poem, to chew upon, and sometimes at these times a great peace and content would come over me. For there lay the cow, having a middling hard time of it with her calving, and here sat I, labouring with a trouble in some sort comparable to hers, and as things were it looked like going well for both of us. And this — to sit alone in a shippon at night with a lantern, busy with a calving and a sonnet — is the occupation I alluded to just now as being still more perfectly satisfying than playing chess; but I doubt whether it has been tried by very many.

My poetic productions were not concerned with cows and calves, nor even with my own psychological experiences, valu-able as these no doubt were, but rather with Hannibal and Sweyn Forkbeard and La Reine Margot and persons of that sort, for the good reason that they were the kind of persons I like to write about. I was certainly fond of cows and calves and of myself too, but I had my bellyful of cows and calves and myself from morning till night, and had no great urge to ruminate on these things in verse. I had therefore later on the pleasure of reading that "here we have a younger poet of lamentably hyper-aesthetic cast, a person out of touch with reality, a learned young man who has obviously never come into contact with life, but has spent his time dreaming in beautiful libraries". I wondered, with much relish, how my realist critic would have got on if I could have transplanted him to the surroundings in which some of those poems had been written, and asked him to take off the umbilical cord with his thumb-nail and attend to the new-born calf.

On one occasion during this period I completed a longish poem on a historical subject, written in a verse-form which I had invented myself, and of which I thought highly. This was in 1919; I was then twenty-five and had thoughts of remaining a herdsman, since I liked the work so much. But I felt a need to stimulate my family by showing them that I could do other things than manage cows, and I was also anxious to convince myself that this was true. I decided therefore to try if I could not get it into print — a thing I had never attempted before; and my first idea was to send the poem to the local newspaper taken by my family. But then I reflected that if I were to be printed at all I might as well be printed as finely as possible — that is, in the periodical *Ord och Bild*. There remained, of course, the other possibility, if *Ord och Bild* should reject it, which I held to be very likely. However, I sent it to the Editor, Karl Wåhlin, in a beautiful fair copy accompanied by a stilted little note and threepence for the return postage, with a request that if, contrary to all expectation, he found the poem usable, he would send me the money as soon as possible. After which I waited for a reply, much depressed, and vainly attempted to laugh at myself for my naïveté in approaching *Ord och Bild*. A few days later came a registered letter with a beautifully-written address, containing thanks for the poem and the sum of £3.6.6. as honorarium. I felt half dazed with the happiness of being really a poet, and I went in to my father's office, and put the whole dossier before him — letter, notes, silver and all — and waited in sublime silence while he took in what all this was about.

"£ 3.6.6. for verse you wrote yourself," he said; "that's not bad pay at all. Can you do more of it?"

"As much as you like," I answered simply.

"Are you thinking of becoming an author?"

"I don't know; I might, of course."

"I won't advise you for or against," said my father, "but this I can say now, that you are a good hand with cows, and you would make a fine herdsman, if only you would get up the dietetics properly."

Of all the compliments I have had in my life, I count that among the best.

So there I stood at the parting of the ways; and sometimes, when life among paper appears empty and foolish, and I think how well I got on with the cows, I am not sure that I chose aright. But sonnets, and other mirages, were beckoning — and pretty women too; for I was now very strong and healthy and could have lifted an average literary critic with one hand; and now that I was a poet into the bargain I felt that I ought to have a fair chance with the other sex; though hitherto, handicapped by a prosaic exterior and my inexpertness as a dancer (which combined to induce great shyness) I had been much at a disadvantage in this regard.

I said farewell to the cows, therefore — a heartbreaking farewell: I could name them all half a mile off when they went to graze, and knew the temper and peculiarities of each one of them — and returned for a time to the society of the learned in Lund, with the simple plan of producing a collection of verse and a book of prose in alternate years. It did not work out quite like that; for when the number of bills falling due began to be oppressive prose got the upper hand, and in time became a sort of habit; and now, though the bills are paid off, I hardly know whether I should be equal to serious verse again.

Translated by Michael Roberts

*T*HE sun becomes indifferent and austere, drives no longer with four horses, takes short walks and still shorter, half turning his back against everything, grins wryly and goes early to bed. Business and the family are left to themselves. "I am cold," says the earth. "By all means," replies the sun, "please yourself. I am going to sleep." The earth tears its hair, becoming black and white in its misery; and the sky itself puts away the colours of life and becomes green between flakes of burnt out cloud where the sun has disappeared: so green, so cold and clear, so incomprehensibly desolate, that it is as though the very bitterest dregs of cold were oozing through the inadequate barriers against outer space. The earth resigns and sinks into silence. Susceptible life dies, or goes into hiding, the more hardened specimens huddle together and await with stoicism that which is to come. "Cold weather for beaks and whiskers," say the toughened creatures of the fields, "but we can endure." "Winter is here," say the people of the grey countryside, shutting themselves in: "let us be comfortable now in our warmth." And their retreats, amusing contraptions a while ago, playfully fashioned in fancy styles and colours, with cubbyholes and glass verandahs (or else plain huts of rustic simplicity) are taken over by the elements, swept by the winds and polished by the snows, their contours and gables remodelled by the fingers of a mighty builder, until they cease to be mere incidental trifles and are once again simple objects of nature, grown from and at one with the earth; oases and places of refuge, isolated habitations of the fields, with smoke curling upward as a sign that living things still breathe in winter's quiet kingdom.

These primitive processes take place a long way from the consciousness and understanding of the crafty and enterprising human being who has come upon the idea of congregating in cities, lighting furnaces, turning on electric switches, and allowing headlamps to spray light before him on his nocturnal journeys; and who, in this self-glorifying form of existence, is not much affected by winter as a natural power. He is master of the situation, and smiles at the elements, which, since he has built up so much between himself and them, have become mere curiosities and legends. This notwithstanding, and in common with the simple country people, townsfolk, too, often exclaim: "Winter is here", certain indications still giving them to understand that such is the case. They are rulers of darkness, scarcely realizing that it exists, but they notice that lights have to be switched on earlier than usual. They are rulers over cold, born amidst heat-regulating appliances which, as time goes on, seldom let them down, even though the temperature of a bedroom may occasionally sink owing to neglect, to 55° F, and thus give them a hint of the proximity of old-fashioned winter. Pillars of the state in fur-lined coats may sometimes, on their morning walks, come upon newly fallen snow which goes over the rims of their goloshes — or, even worse, snow from yesterday which has not yet been sanded — in which case they are mightily astonished, probably come a cropper, and feel themselves suddenly at close quarters with an untamed Nature who has forgotten to tidy up. Women put away their silken underclothes and reach sombrely for others, a hair's breadth thicker, irritated by the sensation of wool fibre against skins accustomed to silk, and by the thought that the symmetry of waists and ankles may be adversely affected, with all the consequences this can entail; doubtless, on such occasions, feeling themselves to be the victims and martyrs of brutal forces of nature. Now and again it may even occur that whole cities are made aware of the presence of primaeval powers in a manner almost approaching insult. Trains do not run to time, journey plans are upset, the breakfast milk does not turn up and the whole scheme of the universe goes awry; for the reason that somewhere or other winter has coughed carelessly on the thunderous crescendo of approaching express coaches, or may have spat upon the ingenious signalbox systems of aggrieved timetablemakers.

This, however, is only a secondary form of the real winter. More is to be found in the countryman's world, where winter is not hiding on the other side of a town boundary, beyond the radius of the farthest street lamp, but exists immediately outside the walls and corners of the house: winter, with its cold, its darkness, its power to isolate, and its habit, common to lodgers who cannot be refused admission, of causing many interruptions in the routine of everyday life. Winter is a difficult guest, a grim besieger, and an enemy in the face of whom wise preparation is not out of the way. The unfortunate countryman knows this from experience, and begins in good time to watch for signs from squirrels, jays and other reliable augurs, in order to take measures in accordance with their forewarnings, and arm himself with the philosophy of foresight. The accuracy of observations and interpretations is not, however, infallible; and squirrels and jays — who knows — may reason in the same way, and watch in their turn, so as to learn from the precautions of the wise countryman what sort of a winter to expect; while winter itself lies in ambush, letting them go on looking at each other in the manner of earnest soothsayers, and thereafter causing them great trouble and surprise by behaving in an entirely unexpected manner and inflicting long periods of black frost when all the portents have indicated snow.

The countryman is by nature a pessimist, the seasons of the year, and in particular winter, having made him so; the law of contrariness, or the natural devilish inwardness of all things, is for him a phenomenon so familiar, a truth so firmly implanted by Nature's strict teaching, that words and formulas need scarcely be wasted on it. He does not become hysterical when

confronted by its manifestations, nor does he bewail dashed
hopes with lyrical groans; even in the darkest situations his
oaths retain an undertone of mournful equanimity, supported
by a realization that the rules of the game are what they are, and
that catastrophe and set-backs are nothing for grown-up people
to make a fuss about. Enlivened by the expectation of an early
winter which has been foretold by general presentiment, calculations of probability, printed prophesies, jays and all, he sows his
winter seed early the one year, sees it come up to green strength,
and looks forward with composure to masses of frost and snow.
Frost comes, according to programme, but snow is substituted
by a long period of sunshine by day and frost by night; after
which the interesting phenomenon known as frost crack de-
velops, during which a thin crust of earth is lifted up and the
growing crops thereby torn off at the roots, a few melancholy
surviving plants being all that meets the gaze of the horrified
farmer in the spring. Again, he may decide to sow at a later
date, for the reason that winter this year will be late; and if
all goes favourably winter certainly is late and everything appears to be in order, until suddenly masses of snow fall on the
unfrozen ground, and in due course large black patches of
damp and mould appear on the fields. In numberless other cases,
the most unpropitious combination of events may arise, from
a supply which seems to be limitless.

The countryman, however, has a store of chastened wisdom,
and seldom allows himself to be taken by surprise. "I can endure," he says in his heart: "it is as much as I can stand, but
it can be done." Everything is against him; hard times, harvests,
taxes, prices, parliamentary sessions, disappointing farrows,
and the learned men who write in the papers. This is the way
of the world, once and for all; why, then, should things be any
different in the case of winter? At the same time he is strong,
by reason of his experience and his powers of apprehension:
and whatever may happen in the open fields, where little can
be done in the face of calamity, he is at least in a position to

emerge unscathed from any tussle on his own doorstep, albeit even there the exigencies of winter are very much beyond a joke; they are in deadly earnest, and necessitate continual watchfulness, in a struggle as old as the race itself, in which human beings who have survived and collected reserves know themselves to be, for the time being at least, in the position of conquerors.

Unpleasant things often happen, it is true. For some unknown reason potatoes freeze, usually those of the best quality; no human precaution, however, can prevent the risk of happenings such as these, and the only thing to do is to check the misfortune as rapidly as possible, sort out the frozen potatoes and make pigfood of them, thanking God the while that things were no worse. The yard pump freezes, on a night of severe frost for choice, despite the fact that one has wrapped it in hay and sacking; and this is particularly aggravating, as human beings and horses require water, in addition to which the women in the kitchen are quick to anger; and one has to lie for hours on end, poking amongst iron and rust and ice slush, frozen bits of leather, and screws which slip out of the grasp of stiff fingers and fall into the well, before it shows any inclination to function as usual. But even worse than this —

> Childhood memories, foregather still
> To the tones of the playful lute:
> Ah, like the dew upon burned roses,
> Ye refresh my soul —

is it when the water pipes of the byre freeze; for cows are sensitive creatures, and the even tenor of their days must not, under any circumstances, be disturbed. The repairing of such a calamity can only be exceeded in importance and urgency by the catastrophic necessity of fetching a midwife, and acquires its special atmosphere by usually having to be tackled in a semi-conscious, dismal, shivering and ill-humoured condition, probably somewhere between five and six on a Sunday morning of bitter cold and darkness, in which the attempts at illumination of a stable lantern confine themselves to a sullen red globe of light, about one foot in diameter. One certainly does not romanticize over the charm of winter on such occasions; cheerful conversation on the topics of the day holds no attraction, and one is totally unable to appreciate the old proverb in praise of early rising; one busies oneself instead with the matters in hand, while wishing fervently that one had been born in the Sahara — or in blazing purgatorial regions where, at least, pipes do not freeze — or, preferably, that one had never been born at all. One hammers industriously at the pipes wherever they are within reach, in the hope that something will ultimately give way; one lights bonfires of hay and paraffin around suspect joints; one boils up water, manipulating it as ingeniously as possible with the help of a funnel, and trying everything within reason which, according to the advice of experienced spectators and one's own semi-roused inspiration, may possibly be of help. One need not worry, however; nothing helps. Provisional arrangements have to be made for watering the cattle, and in the end one is forced to accept the inevitable and begin digging up a long stretch of frozen ground with a crowbar. "Aye, it's a cold winter, this, and the frost has gone deep," say the ancients of the farm, stroking their beards with the peaceful resignation of wise old prophets.

Mythological expositions regarding Midgård and Utgård, the world of humanity and that of outer darkness, can more easily be appreciated in their true meaning by countryfolk than by townspeople. For the fullblooded slave of centralheating this sort of thing is simply a remote myth from the Iron Age, which to him is entirely uninteresting, or, at the most, "interesting". For winterfolk, on the other hand, it is an intimate reality, of supreme importance, and one of those which gives substance and, in some degree, meaning to existence. The barrier between these two worlds is not badly illustrated by, for instance, the stable door early on a winter's morning, just as the ordinary routine of stablework has begun, and when, by reason of the cold, the door is kept shut as far as is possible, being only opened to admit manure barrows and for watering; those who enter shut the door after them in a grey whirl of frosty vapour. The dim glow of light from a few lanterns, hung in a row along the centre gangway; heat from the warm bodies of horses; the smell of ammonia, sweat, crushed oats, hay, and leather, together combined in what is one of the incomparable odours of existence; the quiet, accustomed sound of wheelbarrows rolling along wooden flooring, of shovels striking against the cobblestones; the impatient rattling of chains from some horse, sawing with its binder in anticipation of an approaching feed, and noisy snortings in the depths of a manger from another with chaff in its nostrils: the whole an embodiment of human effort and the age old essentials of life, of method and orderliness, of steady sensible tasks without trace of anxiety, flurry or enthusiasm, executed in silence, with the possible exception of an occasional bawled oath, which might well lead the uninitiated to believe that some horse and groom, impelled by deadly hatred, were on the point of murdering one another, but which is, in point of fact, no more than a passionless admonition to the animal not to turn awkward when grooming reaches groin and belly. This is Midgård, the world of human beings; human beings in their serenity, their vigilance and their strength, occupied with fundamental tasks, with their animals and their tools, things as old as humanity itself, and with the shelter of walls and roofs still felt as a valuable conquest of the powers of winter. To step into this oasis of a winter's morning is not like walking into a banqueting hall, a heated luxury automobile, an inviting bedroom, or any other warm and pleasant place that may be called to mind; all that kind of thing being, in comparison, extremely trivial, lazily or indifferently accepted as a convention, a lifelessness, a superficiality or an automatic situation without meaning. Rather is it like arriving (minus some of the romance) at a homemade variation of Peri

Banus' garden, Tannhäuser's mountain, or the Land of Youth: something complete and enduring, an enchantment and a happiness.

For outside is the other world, and only three steps from the door it is already all-prevailing, with driving snow in one's face, with chill, and wind, and darkness; the resounding crash of a shoed hoof's kicking against the bar of a loosebox; the lighted windows of the byre, the shadowy contours of a range of buildings; suddenly, through an opening in the clouds, Orion's Belt, like a cluster of precious stones above the dark, uneasy outline of a row of birches; a hasty meeting with a figure whose lantern has blown out; then nothing but the breath of the fields, majestic impassivity, and the infinite murmuring of aged firs. This is the other world, the older and the greater, just as it was in times gone by when mankind, as yet its unspoiled tenantry, shivered before its onslaught in his rags of fur; its severity only modified now in so far as that the lone wanderer need not find himself marked down as breakfast for a flock of hungry wolves, or a horde of his starving fellowmen. Enmity and hatred exist of old in this world, which is Nifelhem, the beginning, and Fimbulwinter, the end of all things; it contains fear and calamity, both tangible and impersonal, and the fundamental striving of humanity is to escape from it to light and warmth. There remains, nevertheless, something of sensual pleasure and enticement about this world of cold, which has the power of arousing a feeling (not altogether within the category of the articulate) that it would be sheer bliss to go out into the darkness, be swallowed up by the emptiness, disappear in the snow, or fall asleep in the place where the wind has its cradle; a feeling entirely unconnected with sorrow, weariness, or tiredness of life, but akin, perhaps, to the sensation some of us experience when looking down from a height or a tower. The elements will destroy us if we hand ourselves over to them, but in some way, notwithstanding, we belong to them. We are enemies during life, but cousins, mayhap, in eternity.

Despite these feelings (which are without doubt the luxurious sensations of the warmly clad) we continue to fly determinedly, as we have always done, from this latter world, for the reason that we are of a practical turn of mind, and because, all things considered, it is good to be alive. We have thought out the advantages of clothing, lighting methods and fuel, discovered the shelter afforded by roofs and walls, and the stimulation of morning coffee, besides a number of other congenial things; and the satellites of central heating have advanced further than winterfolk. Can it be that they have gone ahead too quickly, and is this the reason why the poor central heating slave so often complains of his rootlessness? Has he forgotten his beginning and is it because of this that he no longer has any instinctive scale of values, nor any clear understanding or appreciation of the many advantages he so thoughtlessly takes for granted? In one way his plight is, without doubt, a tragic one. Let us schematize a little here, and propound a theory. When the central heating does not give out sufficient warmth, there is only one thing for its satellites to do; they ring for the caretaker and complain, in the same way as when anything else goes wrong they ring for the caretaker again, the business of the latter being to receive complaints and render necessary assistance; and thus, gradually, the whole existence of these central heating slaves becomes a matter to be attended to at every opportunity by a caretaker of some sort, butler, telephone operator, or Cabinet Minister, the quickest results being obtained by the lodging of as many complaints as possible. The ideal existence, they maintain, can be achieved by means of complaint; and probably no other solution remains open to them, incapable as they are of themselves managing the various appliances and refinements of life with which they have become involved. Possibly this enforced attitude of mind will gradually develop to the point of depriving them altogether of the ability to be happy or disgusted, humorous or serious; leaving them only as their natural condition, a certain whining dissatisfaction with everything and everyone in the world about them. The circle closes: "the wheel," as Shakespeare says, "has come full circle"; and the child crying in its cradle will be equal with the slaves of central heating crying in their civilization.

Winterfolk, on the other hand, have continued to be their own caretakers with regard to everything of any importance; there is no one to whom they can complain, nor do they consider that they have anything to complain about. "When things go wrong," say winterfolk, "one has oneself to blame; and as, for the most part, things do go wrong in spite of all one's efforts, there is nothing much to be done about it. Such is life; and if, for once, something turns out well, there is real reason for rejoicing. One should be thankful, too, for everything that is pleasant and comfortable in the house; for in the world of winter, little imagination is necessary to appreciate such things to the full."

This may sound all right, argues the opposite camp, but there is no truth in it. Are farmers never out of temper? Were they not in the habit of dethroning kings in the old days? Does not the greater part of our history deal with the bravadoes of dissatisfied farmers? Did they not gladly shoot down bailiffs and sheriffs, and is not this instinct latent within them to the present day? These arguments may in themselves sound reasonable, but they are, in point of fact, the result of misunderstanding. Dissatisfaction of the sort described is not dissatisfaction with fundamentals, which always remain what they are. Dethroning kings, creating a rebellion, lying in wait with a crossbow in order to snipe the king's taxgatherers — all this had the character of holiday amusement, to which one could devote oneself with advantage when there was nothing more important on hand — and an occasional detail could, without doubt, be remedied by such means. The law of contrariness, however, covering frozen turnips, cattle disease, and failing crops, could never be influenced thereby; such things had to be accepted, and neither complaints nor crossbows were

of any avail. Much of the elementary wisdom of farmers is to
be found in Dr. Johnson's lines:

> How small — of all that human hearts endure —
> That part which kings or laws can cause or cure.

It is said of Confucius that he often philosophized beneath
fir trees — "happy on the ground, with his bent arm supporting
his head". Perhaps these sturdy, tranquil trees helped him in
his philosophy, which became concrete, lasting, and dispas-
sionate; for there are certainly worse places in which to philo-
sophize. "It is cold," murmur the firs, wintrily, "but we remain
green. It is stormy; but we stand — our time out."

Translated by Elspeth Harley-Schubert